Study Guide

for use with

Children
Ninth Edition

John W. Santrock
University of Texas at Dallas

Allen Keniston
University of Wisconsin, Eau Claire

Peden Blair
University of Wisconsin, Eau Claire

Prepared by

Anita Rosenfield
Yavapai College

Boston   Burr Ridge, IL   Dubuque, IA   Madison, WI   New York   San Francisco   St. Louis
Bangkok   Bogotá   Caracas   Kuala Lumpur   Lisbon   London   Madrid   Mexico City
Milan   Montreal   New Delhi   Santiago   Seoul   Singapore   Sydney   Taipei   Toronto

The McGraw·Hill Companies

McGraw-Hill Higher Education

Study Guide for use with
Children
John W. Santrock

Published by McGraw-Hill, an imprint of The McGraw-Hill Companies, Inc., 1221 Avenue of the Americas,
New York, NY 10020. Copyright © 2007, 2005 by The McGraw-Hill Companies, Inc. All rights reserved.
No part of this publication may be reproduced or distributed in any form or by any means, or stored in a
database or retrieval system, without the prior written consent of The McGraw-Hill Companies, Inc., including,
but not limited to, in any network or other electronic storage or transmission, or broadcast for distance learning.

1 2 3 4 5 6 7 8 9 0 QPD/QPD 0 9 8 7 6 5

ISBN-13: 978-0-07-310732-5
ISBN-10:   0-07-310732-8

www.mhhe.com

Contents

A Letter to You, the Student

Dear Student,

I am writing this letter to you to offer some thoughts on how you can use this Study Guide to help you learn the material contained in *Children*, Ninth Edition, by John W. Santrock. Although these ideas come from many years of being a student (**many years**) and a psychology professor, they are not particularly new, and you may already know many of them—but sometimes we need to be reminded about how helpful these tips can be. I hope you will find this Study Guide and my suggestions to be useful.

First and foremost, let me tell you that **the most effective way to use this material is to apply it to your life!** What my students tell me at the end of the semester are things like: "This course really helped me to understand the things I did as a teenager—now I have better insight about how to live a more productive life as an adult"; "By taking this class, I have come to terms with some things in my life. I am getting divorced and am now better able to prepare for this stage in my life. . . . I have also seen what went wrong in my marriage. . . . I can see where things went wrong and I can now try to work them out"; "Now, when I think about middle age and late adulthood, I feel I have something to look forward to rather than be afraid. I can go through these stages with open arms now"; "The most important thing I learned in this class is a better understanding of people of all ages. I understand my son's feisty temperament and deal with him much more effectively"; "I thought that some of the things my 2-year-old was doing were problem behaviors; now I see how they are typical of 2-year-olds and I can work with her more effectively. It's amazing how this has improved our relationship and **her** behavior."

This is just a sampling, but you can get the idea of how you, as a consumer of information, can use the information in the text and your class for your own life, whatever your major in college.

Now, let me tell you how the Study Guide is set up. The first section contains a **Chapter Outline** and **Reach Your Learning Goals**, which are intended to help you organize your thoughts and your reading and be able to anticipate what you will encounter in the corresponding chapter of the text, and to use the various sections of this Study Guide to be sure you have understood the material in each section of the chapter. This first section also contains **Learning Goals**, a set of anywhere from three to five statements of the ideas and material you should be able to understand after having read the chapter. You may wish to read the learning objectives **before** you read the chapter, so you can have an idea of what you're trying to learn as you read; then again, after having read the chapter, by going through the learning objectives you can see if you did, indeed, "get it all."

The second section is a series of **self-tests** to be sure you are understanding the material. First you will find a set of **Flashcards** containing 24 sets for each chapter. Throughout my undergraduate, graduate, and doctoral studies my friends and I made our own flashcards because we found them to be so helpful. All key terms, many concepts, and many of the important researchers and theorists from the chapters are contained on the flashcards. This self-test section also includes three relatively formal subsections for testing: multiple choice, matching, and essays. The **Multiple Choice** section contains a set of approximately 30 multiple-choice questions covering the material in each chapter so you can be sure you are not only memorizing terms (Heaven forbid!), but are actually understanding the concepts contained in the text. There are many "applied" questions that require you to think about how these ideas would work if you were looking at real people (well, okay, in this case they are hypothetical, but use your imagination). In the answer key, you will discover that each question is keyed to one of the learning objectives. This allows you to pinpoint particular concepts you may find difficult to understand. Next is a **Matching** set where you are asked to identify the perspective of important researchers. New to this edition of the Study Guide are **True/False** questions about basic concepts and information in the text, and a few questions that apply to the **On-line Quizzes** that you will be able to access at the Web site for the text (http://www.mhhe.com/santrockc9).

The **Essay Questions** are designed to help you crystallize the many concepts contained in the chapter so that you can explain and apply what you have learned. In two or three questions, I tried to tie the material from the entire chapter together so you can see how all of the research, ideas, facts, and theories fit together. My answers to these questions are merely skeletal; should you choose to answer them, you will have to expand on what is there by drawing on the material in the chapter. To be honest with you, when I give essay questions in my own classes, I want my students to be able to put together information from more than one chapter to answer the questions fully––so you may want to think about how you could do that.

In the next two sections, **Research Projects** and **Personal Applications,** you will find suggested activities that will require you to search out more information about the material in the chapter, either by reviewing the literature, or through your own empirical investigations (i.e., doing research), or by actively applying what you have learned to your own life. The best way to learn the course material of any class is to use it—to think about its application to your own life. These activities will force you to do just that. You may ask your professor if you may choose one of these as a class project, or for extra credit, or just do them for the fun of it to see how they work. Go through all of the activities, from Chapter 1 through Chapter 17, in the beginning of the term because you may see one in later chapters that you might have wanted to work on through the term, and if you wait until the last week or two you may not have enough time to get it done. As indicated at the end of this letter, I really do enjoy interacting with my students, so feel free to "Ask the Professor" (me) if you have questions–don't be shy about sending me questions via e-mail (arosenfield@esedona.net); alternatively, all the way through college I found that my professors appreciated students asking questions (it's a sign that you're actually reading the material and thinking about it!), and instructors tend to learn the names of the students who do ask questions, so unless you have that rare faculty member who doesn't encourage student interaction (and to be honest, I've never met a single one), do pose questions that come to mind. Also, use these questions to help you study, especially if you get together with other students and form a study group–you may even generate questions that wind up on your exams.

The final group of sections may be new to some of you and part of everyday life for others (or anything in between). These are the **Internet Projects.** Note that the introductory section refers you to the McGraw-Hill Web site for some great activities (http://www.mhhe.com/santrockc9). Also to be found on the Web site are a substantial amount of suggested journal articles, exercises from the text, and other **visual aids**. In addition to the Santrock Web site, I have included two projects for each chapter that ask you to go beyond what is covered in our text. Finally, the **Internet Section** concludes with a compilation of many relevant Web sites for each chapter. Please note that all Web site addresses in this Study Guide have been checked and are correct at the time of publication; however, Web sites may be discontinued or addresses may change so when you search a given site it may no longer be viable. If that occurs, I apologize for the inconvenience, and would appreciate you notifying me so I could make appropriate revisions in future editions of this Study Guide. We try to ensure that they are up-to-date, however, as technology and businesses are constantly changing, this is not always possible.

Okay, so that's the structure of the chapters in the Study Guide. Now, let's talk about effective ways to study. As I mentioned earlier, you may already know some of these ideas, but oftentimes they can bear repeating because you say to yourself, "Oh, yeah, I knew that. I tried it before and it worked, but then for some reason I stopped. I think I'll try it again." Other ideas may be new to you, so you may want to give them a try. Remember that we are all unique, so some strategies work better for some people than for others—try out a suggestion for a fair period of time (only you can decide what "fair" is), and if it works, great—if it doesn't, try something else.

BEING AN EXCELLENT STUDENT[0]

Most students who are in college want to be good students, and most students have some particular goal in mind, which is probably why they chose the particular college or university they are attending. As you chose your college or university—and perhaps even an area of major interest or concentration—you had certain goals in mind, which likely included doing well in school, earning good grades, and graduating. Unfortunately, many students do not do as well in college as they had hoped and expected. Let's examine some of the reasons for this disappointing outcome to see how to avoid it and to learn, instead, how to be a good student and guide your behavior to improve your chances of achieving your goals.

A common definition of education is that it is "how people learn stuff." For most of our history, educators have focused on the "stuff." Teachers were required to be masters of their respective academic fields. Even today, some states have requirements that mandate only the need to be qualified in the subject matter one teaches, not in the teaching methods themselves.

In the 1960s, we became more interested in the "people" part of the definition, which was evidenced by moving to strategies such as open classrooms and free universities. The idea was that, given the opportunity to do so, people naturally learn. Although these experiments were dismal failures, they taught us something.

The key to the definition of education is the word "how." Today, thanks to a wealth of research on the principles that guide the phenomenon of learning and on the nature of learning and memory, we know much more about *how* learning occurs and *how* we can make it better. By using these principles, we can become better students.

Formulating the Plan

Anything worth having is worth planning for. Whether you hope to learn to teach, to fly, to write for profit, or to change diapers correctly, you have in mind a goal. A common question from the first days in elementary school is, "What do you want to be when you grow up?" The answer to this question is one way of formulating a goal. Now that you are a college student, many people expect you to know what you want to do for a profession or career, yet you may not have the foggiest notion, or you might have an idea that is still unclear. That's okay. What is clear, however, is that you want to succeed in your college courses. This is a relatively long-range goal, and as such can keep you on track.

But our day-to-day behavior is often hard to connect to our long-range goals. We need short-term goals to keep us organized and to be sure that the flow of our activities is in the direction we want to be going. To accomplish our long-range goals, we need to focus on three types of short-term goals: (1) goals for the day, (2) goals for the week, and (3) goals for the semester or term. Let's look at each of these separately.

Goals for Today

---

[0]Much of the information on "Being an Excellent Student," including formulating the plan, attending classes, benefiting from lectures, reading for learning, taking tests, and parts of the section on dealing with test anxiety, have been adapted from the 6th edition of the Student Study Guide to accompany *Lifespan Development* by John Santrock, which was prepared by Blaine Peden, John W. Santrock, and Allen Keniston. I would like to thank them for sharing those ideas with me for incorporation into this Study Guide.

It is helpful to keep a daily checklist, diary, or schedule as a reminder of what must be done each day. Check off the things as you accomplish them. A pocket calendar is particularly helpful for this task. After you complete your list, use numbers, asterisks (*), or letters to prioritize each item on the list and be sure that you put most of your effort into completing those tasks that have highest priority.

Goals for the Week

Students who are successful in college also schedule their time weekly. Sometime during the course of registration, you made up a schedule showing your classes for the whole week. If you have a job, you must allow time for that, too. Also, many college or university students have family obligations that need to be considered as well. Finally, everyone needs some time for relaxing, eating, sleeping, and playing (even in graduate school we were advised that we needed to find some time to have fun in order to stay balanced). With all these things in mind, it is no wonder many students find little time to study.

But good students do all these things, too, yet they study. Do they have more time? No, we all have the same amount of time, but successful students schedule their time carefully. So, make up a weekly schedule and block off time for all these necessary events: classes, work, relaxation, eating, sleeping, playing, family, errands, and studying. Students who actually schedule their time and keep to their schedules are amazed at how much time they find they have! Be sure to leave some blocks (10 to 20 minutes) that are *unscheduled* just to maintain some flexibility—sometimes emergencies arise and you need some slack in your schedule "just in case."

As you make up your weekly schedule, you may find that your study time fits into a large block. If this is the case, remember to take short breaks every 20 to 30 minutes. This is called distributed practice and is far more efficient than studying for hours on end. After the first 20 or 30 minutes, most of us become much less efficient anyway. When you take that break, reward yourself somehow, then go back to your studying. I always tell my students never to try to read a whole chapter in one sitting. In fact, when I am preparing for a new class or have changed texts in a class I have been teaching, I take that advice myself!

Many of us feel uncomfortable using the word "no." When friends or family members ask for help, students often give up important study time to accommodate the friend or family member (or feel so guilty about *not* doing so that their guilt interferes with concentration as they try to study). When people ask for our help, they usually could either get help from someone else (or become independent and do it themselves) or work with you to accomplish the activity during one of your free periods. Of course, if it's really an emergency, such as someone who needs hospitalization, then by all means help; if it's not, you need to consider yourself and your education as high priorities. Some of us really need to feel we have "permission" to say "no"—so, I am giving you that permission!

Goals for the Semester

At the beginning of each semester, we find ourselves immersed in many new courses. You will often be confronted by several new professors with whom you have never worked before. Sorting out the expectations and demands of these several courses is difficult; however, it is important to organize the information that will be needed for completing all of the course requirements in order to be successful in the courses.

If you can, obtain a large wall calendar (available in any stationery store) and mark on it the dates of tests, exams, and term paper deadlines, being sure to indicate the course for which each date applies. Now, estimate how long it will take you to make final preparations for those exams, and mark those dates as warning or alert dates. Look over the dates on which papers are due and see if they are bunched together. If your college is typical, these dates will probably be close. You can help yourself to avoid the last-minute all-nighters if you simply determine a spread of due dates for yourself and mark those on the calendar, too. As you do this step, please be sure to avoid any days that have personal significance for you, such as birthdays, anniversaries, upcoming weddings you'll be attending, and so on. This calendar gives you an overview of major dates in your semester.

If you have followed this plan carefully, you now have a large semester calendar plastered on your wall; a weekly schedule of major life events, classes, and study times taped over your desk; and a daily checklist of must-do items in your pocket or purse. So, your scheduling is on its way. Let's look now at other important strategies.

Attending Classes

Many students believe that because they are in college, they can decide whether to go to class at all. This is true. Some students also believe that attendance in class is not important to their grades. This is not true! Some colleges or universities have attendance requirements, so that if students miss a given number of classes it will either lower their grade a full letter or the instructor may drop the student from the course; some instructors have in-class activities that count toward students' grades, so if students are not in class they do not get credit for participating. Even without such strategies, students who do not attend class sessions almost always do more poorly on the tests, quizzes, and exams. Perhaps they were absent when a crucial item was discussed or when the instructor lectured over the material a particular examination required.

Remember that more often than not, instructors include information in their lectures that is not in your textbook. This information (whether from class lecture, videos shown in class, guest lectures, and so on) is fair game for tests. Moreover, if you are not there, the instructor cannot get to know you, and therefore cannot give you the benefit of the doubt on your answers. Not surprisingly, the data from many research studies clearly show that students who attend class regularly receive the highest grades and actually learn more, too! So, the first rule of being an effective student is to attend classes. Besides, how else can you get your money's worth? Now that you've determined you will go to class, what else will you do?

Benefiting from Lectures

Students sometimes think that if they come to class and "pay attention," they will remember what the instructor talked about; they think that if they take notes, they will miss much of what the instructor says. But sitting and paying attention is difficult. For one thing, most people can think much faster than they can speak. While the instructor lectures at 80 words per minute, the student thinks at about 350 words per minute. If the student is using this extra "thinking capacity" to focus on what the instructor is saying, it is fine. This rarely lasts more than 5 minutes at a time, however. Most of the time, this extra "thinking capacity" is used in daydreaming.

Daydreaming can be helpful in resolving our emotional problems, planning the course of our lives, and avoiding work. In fact, daydreaming is often motivated by the desire to avoid work. For whatever motive, however, daydreaming is not compatible with attending a lecture. Human beings simply cannot attend to more than one stimulus at a time. And you have to admit that your daydreams can often be more interesting than your professor's lectures.

Benefiting from lectures is best achieved by taking notes. Use plenty of paper and leave blank lines at regular intervals, or leave wide side margins. You will use these spaces later. If the instructor permits it, be brave and interrupt with questions if you do not understand what is being said. One thing I try to stress to my students is that I may know what I am talking about, but it may be unclear to them—and if it's unclear to one student, it may well be unclear to other students. So, for the sake of the other students who didn't understand what I was talking about, each student should take on the responsibility of asking me to clarify what I said or to expand in a way that will help them understand. Remember that lectures have a way of progressing and building on earlier information. It is important to understand each point or later points will be lost. (But please, *do not* ask the person sitting next to you what the professor said—it disrupts the class, disturbs the professor, and you are likely NOT to get an accurate response!)

When you take notes, write out the major points and try to make simple notations for the supporting minor points. If you miss something and you cannot ask a question about it, approach the instructor immediately afterward when the topic is still likely to be fresh in both your minds. *Do not* try to write down every word, and *do* try to use abbreviations or symbols (the Greek symbols Ψ [Psi] and Φ [Phi] are a lot shorter to write than the words "psychology" and "physiology"; using typographic symbols, such as < and >, is much shorter than writing out "less than" and "greater than"); or, you could do what I did— learn shorthand (or make up your own).

My students often ask if they may tape my lectures. Personally, I have no objection to this practice, although some professors do. Having returned to college after a 16-year break, I taped my psychology classes (somehow German didn't seem conducive to being tape recorded). It was so tedious transcribing the tapes, though, that I didn't do it after that first quarter. Taping may be particularly helpful for students who have visual, auditory, or motor impairments; however, you should never tape record a lecture without first asking for and obtaining the professor's permission.

Within 1 or 2 hours after the lecture, on the same day, go back over your notes and do two things. First, fill in the rest of the minor points. This often amounts to completing the sentence or other element. Second, write brief summaries and any questions that you now have in the blank spaces (lines or margins) you left earlier. These few minutes spent reviewing and organizing your notes will pay off in greatly improved memory. The questions you have you can ask in class—or during the instructor's office hours—and reap two benefits. First, you will get the answers; second, you will demonstrate that you are a serious student, which will impress your instructor.

One other thing about going to class: Although this is not always true, I have found that my best students typically sit in front. And most students seem to have a need to have "their seat," while a few students have a need to move around, sitting in one seat one day and a different seat the next. It wasn't until my graduate school days that I realized why I needed "my seat." As students, we are constantly being overwhelmed with new information, which is a stressful experience; we need some structure we can count on to reduce that stress. So, if you are one of those students who likes to wander, be considerate of your classmates' needs for stress reduction.

By the way, to get the most out of the lectures, do complete the assigned reading *before* the class so you are familiar with the material. This will help you keep up with what the instructor is talking about, will reduce the amount of information you do not understand, and may also bring up important questions for you to ask in class if the instructor does not talk about them.

Reading for Learning

We all know *how* to read. You are proving it by reading these words. Hopefully, you are also realizing some ideas as a result of reading. If you are only reading words, please WAKE UP! STOP DAYDREAMING!

We can read a variety of things: newspapers, movie reviews, novels, magazines, and textbooks. Textbooks are unlike all printed materials and must be read with a strategy all their own. There are many reading and studying strategies, and all of them work to an extent. Perhaps you learned one or more in the course of going to high school. Perhaps you even took a how-to-study course when you entered college. If so, you probably learned one or two of these systems. If you have one you like that works for you, keep it. If you are interested in learning a new one, read on.

The PQ4R Method

One of the most successful and most widely used methods of studying written material is the SQ3R method, which was first developed at Ohio State University. Researchers had noted that students who were more successful were more active readers. More recently, this method has been updated to the PQ4R method, which adds an additional step. This method teaches you the same skills that have made many thousands of students successful. If you use this method when you read and study, you will be more successful, too. I have outlined the steps as follows.

The P stands for PREVIEW. After you have read the overview or chapter outline and the list of learning objectives, you should survey (preview) the chapter in the text. This is also called *skimming*. Look at the headings and subheadings, and get the gist of the major points in the chapter. Check off each point in the outline of this Study Guide as you pass it in the pages of the text.

The Q stands for QUESTION. Reading is greatly enhanced if you are searching for the answers to questions. For this text, the Study Guide provides learning objectives that can serve as questions. For other texts, make up questions for yourself that are based on the chapter overview or on your own survey of the chapter. Be sure that you have at least one question for each major unit in the chapter; you will be less efficient at studying those units for which you do not have questions.

The first of the four Rs is for READ. As you read, look for the answers to the questions you posed or to the study or learning objectives furnished for you. When you find material that answers these questions, put a mark (X) or a sticky note in the margin next to that material. This will help now, as you are actively involved, and later, when you review. It is a good idea to wait to underline or highlight lines of text until after you have read the entire chapter at least once, so you will know what is and what is not most important. (In fact, while some "authorities" suggest you underline or highlight no more than 10% of what you are reading, I find that when most of us begin to underline or highlight, we wind up doing it to most of the chapter—I suggest not doing it at all because it becomes too passive, which counteracts your attempts to read actively.)

The second R stands for REFLECT. As you read, stop occasionally and reflect on the material to increase its meaningfulness. This includes analyzing the material, thinking about how to apply it to your life, interpreting the information, and connecting it with information you already have in your long-term memory.

The third R is for RECITE. One of the oldest classroom techniques in the world (Aristotle used it) is recitation. In the classroom version, the teacher asks the questions and the students answer them. Unless you can get your instructor to study with you regularly, you'll have to play both roles. Periodically, stop in your reading and say aloud (if possible) what the author is telling you. Try to put the information in your own words, but be sure to use technical terms as you learn them. If you are not in a situation where you can recite out loud, do it in writing. Just thinking it is not enough. When should you pause to recite? A good rule of thumb is that each time you come to the end of a major subheading, you should recite. One professor encourages his students to recite at least one sentence at the end of each paragraph, and two or three or more sentences at the end of each subunit (when you come to a new heading).

People who do not use recitation usually forget half of what they read after 1 hour, and another half of the half they remembered by the end of the day. People who use recitation often remember from 75 to 90% of what they studied. This technique pays off. (By the way, if anyone questions why you are talking to yourself, tell them that a psychologist recommended it.)

The fourth R is for REVIEW. You should review a chapter soon after you have studied it (using the PQ and the first 3 Rs). You should review it again the day or evening before the test. It is not usually helpful to cram the night before a test, and particularly not the day of the test. That type of studying does not produce good memory and is likely to make you more anxious during the test itself, which brings us to our next topic.

Taking Tests

One of the things students fear most is failure. Failure signifies that things are not going well and alerts us to the possibility that we may not achieve our goals. Unfortunately, many students see tests and exams as opportunities to fail, rather than as opportunities to shine. They prepare by becoming anxious and fearful and by trying to cram as much information as possible into their short-term memories right before the exam. These students rarely do well on the exam. They often fail, thus accomplishing just what they feared.

Taking tests requires strategy and planning. First, it is helpful to know what type of test you will have. Your instructor probably told you this information during the first class meeting, or it may be in the class syllabus or course outline. If you do not know, ask.

If you are going to be taking essay exams, the best way to prepare is by writing essays. Before you do this, it is a good idea to find out what types of questions the instructor asks and what is expected in a response. Again, it is helpful to ask the instructor for this information. Perhaps you can even see some examples of essay questions from previous years—some instructors have copies of their exams on file in the department office or in the library. By finding out what is expected, you can formulate a model against which you can evaluate your answers.

Now, using the learning objectives—or some essay questions you wrote—actually sit down and write out the answers. I have prepared at least two essay questions for each chapter in this Study Guide. (HINT: If you usually feel more anxious during a test, it may help you to practice writing your essays in the room in which the test will be given. Simply find a time when the room is vacant, then make yourself at home.)

If your instructor gives multiple-choice tests, then you should practice taking multiple-choice tests. For each chapter, either use questions provided in the Study Guide or make up your own. You may find it helpful to work out an arrangement to pool questions with other students, thereby reducing the amount of work you have to do and developing a network of friends. Or, you may ask your professor if he or she would allow students to write some of the exam questions—some of my professors did that in my undergraduate classes, and I sometimes have my students do it as well.

Whichever way you do it, the important thing is to prepare for tests and exams. Preparation is about 95% of the secret to getting a good grade. (Yes, there is some actual luck or chance involved in test scores, as even your instructor will admit!) Preparation is not only a good study and review technique, but it also helps to reduce anxiety.

Dealing with Test Anxiety

Anxiety can be a helpful response when it occurs at low levels. In 1908, Yerkes and Dodson showed that the amount of anxiety that could benefit performance was a function of the difficulty and complexity of the task. As the difficulty of the task rose, anxiety became less helpful and more likely to interfere with performance.

If you have ever been so anxious in a test situation that you were unable to do well, even though you knew the information, you have test anxiety. If you get your exams back and are surprised that you marked wrong answers when you knew the correct answers, or if you can only remember the correct answers after you leave the examination room, you may have test anxiety.

Strategy 1: Effective Study

Use study habits that promote learning and make the best use of time. Strategies, such as scheduling your time and using the PQ4R method, reduce anxiety by increasing confidence. As you realize that you know the material, your confidence rises and anxiety retreats.

Strategy 2: Relaxation

Each of us develops a different pattern of relaxation. Some people relax by going to a specific place, either in person or mentally. Others relax by playing music, by being with friends, by using autogenic relaxation phrases (e.g., You are relaxed. You feel prepared and confident.), or by meditating. Whatever you do, be aware of it and try to practice relaxation techniques. If you are not good at relaxing, try thinking about those situations that make you anxious and relax while you think of them. To do this, allow yourself to think only briefly (15 to 30 seconds at a time) of the situation that makes you anxious, and then relax again. After several such pairings, you will find that thinking about that situation no longer makes you anxious. At this point, you may be surprised to find that the situation itself also no longer produces anxiety. You may find it helpful to think about these anxiety-provoking situations in a sequence from those that produce little anxiety to those that are more anxiety-evoking. Such a list—from low to high anxiety—might look something like this:

1. Your instructor announces that there will be a test in 4 weeks.
2. Your instructor reminds you of the test next week.
3. As you study, you see on the course outline the word "test," and remember next week's test.
4. One of your friends asks you if you want to study together for the test, which is the day after tomorrow.
5. You choose not to go out with your friends because of the test tomorrow.
6. As you get up in the morning, you remember that today is the day of the test.
7. You are walking down the hall toward the classroom, thinking about what questions might be on the test.
8. The instructor enters the classroom carrying a sheaf of papers in hand.
9. The instructor distributes the papers and you see the word "test" or "exam" at the top.

10. After reading the first five questions, you have not been able to think of the answer to any of them.

If you work at it gradually and consistently, pairing these types of thoughts (briefly) with relaxation and remembering to let go and relax after each one, you will dispel test anxiety and make test taking a more productive and successful experience.

Strategy 3: Thinking Clearly

Most students who have test anxiety think in unclear and unproductive ways. They say to themselves things like: "I can't get these answers correct," or "I don't know this stuff . . . I don't know anything at all," or "I'm going to fail this test. I'm probably going to flunk out of school. I'm just an idiot." These thoughts share two unfortunate characteristics: they are negative and they are absolute. They should be replaced.

When we tell ourselves negative and absolute thoughts, we find it impossible to focus on the test material. The result is that we miss questions even when we know the answers. Our thinking prevents us from doing well.

A good strategy for replacing these negative and absolute thoughts is to practice thinking positive and honest thoughts, such as:

- "I may not know all of the answers, but I know some of them."

- "I don't know the answer to that right now, so I will go on to the next one and come back to that."

- "I don't have to get them all right. I studied hard and carefully, and I can get some of them correct."

- "I am a serious student and have some abilities."

- "Hmm. This is a hard question, so I'll skip it, come back, and look for any clues in other questions that might help me answer this one."

- "I am prepared for this test and know many of the answers."

- "This test is important, but it is not going to determine the course of my entire life, and if I don't do well it doesn't mean I'm a horrible person or a dummy."

By thinking clearly, honestly, and positively, we quiet the flood of anxiety and focus on the task at hand. Students who use this technique invariably do better on tests. It takes practice to think clearly, but it is worth the effort. After awhile, you will find that it becomes natural and does not take any noticeable effort. And as anxiety is reduced, more energy is available for studying and doing well on exams. The eventual outcome is more enjoyment with learning, better learning, more success in college, and the achievement of your goals.

Strategy 4: Guided Imagery

I often have my students relax before a test (see Strategy 2), close their eyes, and visualize themselves walking into a tall building. They go into the elevator in the building and take it to the top floor, which is 56 stories up. They walk out of the elevator and go to the stairwell, then climb to the top of the building. There is no railing on top of the building. I direct them to walk over to the side of the building and put their toes at the edge, then look down. I ask them to pay attention to how they are feeling—physically and emotionally—as they look down onto the street from the top of this building. I then instruct them to back away from the edge, take a deep breath, and imagine that they can fly—just spread out their arms and fly. Then they are directed back to the edge of the building, knowing that they can fly. Again they put their toes on the edge, look down, then spread their arms and fly, eventually floating down to land safely on the ground below.

Next I have them visualize themselves in the classroom; on the desk before them is their test. They look at the test and see themselves reading the questions, saying, "I know the answer. Yes, I remember learning that." They visualize themselves being successful, answering all the questions correctly, feeling good about themselves. Then I have them visualize getting their tests back with a big "A" staring them in the face.

Some students are much better able to visualize than others. You can try combining Strategy 2 with this strategy to help you improve your visualization because it can be an effective success strategy. (After the guided relaxation, I remind my students they really *can't* fly, so please don't try!)

Strategy 5: Do the Easy Ones First

One technique I learned while studying for the GRE (Graduate Record Exam) was to read each question, answer the ones I knew, then go back to the harder ones. Two things to watch out for with this technique are first, be sure you get the answers in the right place—sometimes when we skip a question or two, we wind up marking the wrong space, so check that your answer to question 10 is in space 10; second, you may find that you're stumped by the first several questions—don't let that throw you, just keep going because there is bound to be one you jump on and say, "Yes! I know that one!" Answer the easy ones first, then go back to the others after you've built up your confidence seeing that you *do* know "stuff." Then, always go back over the whole test to be sure you answered every question. (The exception here is if you have a professor who takes more than one point off for wrong answers—in that case, it's better not to answer than to answer wrong, but I don't know anyone who does that.)

Strategy 6: State-Dependent Learning

Research has found that we remember information best when we are in the same "state" we were in when we first learned the information. So, for example, you might remember a certain song when prompted by a specific stimulus (seeing someone who reminds you of your "first true love"); or, we remember things we learned when we were particularly happy if we are again in that mood. This goes for physical contexts as well—so we have an advantage if we take an exam in the same room where we learned the information in the first place (though we have little control over this because exams may be scheduled in a room that was not our classroom).

This strategy also correlates to physical context in terms of our bodies—if you drink coffee or caffeine-laden sodas when you study, try to do the same before your exam. On the other hand, if you don't consume caffeine when you study, by all means, *do not* suddenly have a cup of coffee before your exam. Because of the power of this phenomenon, you may want to create a particular mental context for yourself when you study so that you can put yourself into the same mental context when you take your exams.

Strategy 7: Take a Break

If you find yourself getting stressed out during the test, take a break. Put your pencil down and breathe deeply. You may even want to put your head down on the desk (but please, do not fall asleep). Use the relaxation techniques or the guided imagery strategy; visualize yourself looking at the test and suddenly realizing that you *do* know the answers to at least most of the questions. Then go back to taking the test.

Remember that with all of these test-taking strategies, if you don't do Strategy 1, none of the others will help. Passing the course requires that you actively study the material!

Memory Techniques

No matter how much you read, it won't help you if you don't remember *what* you read. The most critical factor in remembering is being able to apply what you have learned. Of course, some things, such as people's names or certain dates or statistical information, are not easily applied to your life, so you'll have to use other techniques for that information. But first, let's talk about the "easy way."

Apply It to Your Life

If you can take the material you are learning and use it in your everyday life, you will remember it without any problem. For example, if you have a 2-year-old child, then you read what Piaget said about how 2-year-olds think, or what Erikson said about the need for children to gain a sense of autonomy over their bodies, or what the information-processing theorists say about how much a 2-year-old can remember, then you can see how (and if) these theories apply to your child. Of course, not everyone has a 2-year-old child, but we all were 2 years old at some point in our lives, or we may know children who are that age. Watch children, and see how the theories work by observing what these children do. The same goes for observing infants, teenagers, adults, and, particularly, yourself!

Another method of applying the material to your life is to connect it with what you already know, either from life experience or other courses you have taken. Sometimes what you are learning fits nicely with what you already know, sometimes it contradicts what you learned before, and sometimes it appears to be brand new. This is an opportunity for you to look at how the new information fits in with the old—were there new research findings? Or, is it merely a difference of opinion? Make these associations—don't keep the information for any class neatly compartmentalized—if you do, you'll have a hard time trying to find it when you need it.

Teach It to Someone Else

When we start teaching something to someone else, we find we *have to* learn it, and by trying to explain the material to another person, we examine it and think about it differently. So, take the material you are learning in this class (or any class) and teach it to someone else. When they ask you questions, you can look them up and find the answers, think them out together, or ask someone else. As you explain these concepts to someone else (e.g., your children, your friends, or even your dog or cat), you will suddenly see the concepts in a totally different light.

Mnemonic Techniques

Some things are really difficult to apply to your life. Dates, names, places, statistics, and such may not have a great deal of meaning for you. In that event, use the tricks that memory specialists use: mnemonics. There are many different types. (For example, one famous mnemonic is an acronym for remembering the Great Lakes: HOMES = Huron, Ontario, Michigan, Erie, and Superior; the colors of the spectrum is someone's name: ROY G. BIV = red, orange, yellow, green, blue, indigo, and violet.) You can make up your own acronyms by taking the first initial of any term, person, and so forth. It's easiest, though, if it's something that makes sense to you.

Another mnemonic technique is called the *method of loci*, and I've been told that it's the method medical students use to remember body parts. You list the things you need to remember, then visualize yourself walking around a familiar place (like your living room), putting one item on a particular piece of furniture, another item on the next piece, and so on. Then when you need to remember those items, you go through your "living room" to see where each one is. Say, for example, you need to remember the theorists in Chapter 2 of this text. You might put Piaget on the piano, Freud on the sofa, Skinner in the television (i.e., a "box"), and so on. (They don't have to be on the object that starts with the same letter as their name, although that might be an additional mnemonic technique; or you might put them on objects that you associate with their work.) Because you also need to associate the theorists with their theories, you might imagine that Piaget is thinking about how to play the piano; Freud has hidden unacceptable thoughts under the sofa; Skinner has been reinforced for sitting so nicely in front of the television, and so forth.

One other mnemonic technique is the *story method*. Take the information you need to remember and put it into a story. So, you may make up a story about how Piaget came up with his four stages of development. (Because he relied so heavily on his own three children, you might want to incorporate them into the story, but it's your story—do it the way you want.)

There are many other mnemonic techniques. You might want to check out a book on memory strategies from the library to find some that work well for you.

Be an "Information Dropper"

This technique is similar to the suggestion to teach, but less formal. Ask your friends to "indulge" you by listening to what you learned in your life-span development class (or any other class). Then *tell* them what you are learning. You may, in fact, find that you have managed to help one of your friends by sharing this information—wouldn't that be a nice feeling!

Rote Memory

If you can remember back to grade school, when you learned to multiply, somehow the only way that seems to happen is by repeating the multiplication tables over and over and over again. Personally, I think this method is the worst way to learn anything, but for some things (like multiplication tables), it works. The flashcards that are available on the McGraw-Hill Web site for the text (www.mhhe.com/santrock/ld8) are one way to help you learn through repeating the material you don't know. I hope you will then go further and apply the information to other areas of your life.

Ask the Professor

Previously in this Letter to the Student I talked about the PQ4R Method of Studying. Recall that the Q stands for "Question"; that is, before you read each section, make up a question then search for the answer as you read. I find that as I read just about anything, questions just naturally pop into my head—I'd like to suggest that you try to do the same (please, don't just accept everything that's put before you in black and white!). You can also create questions before you do any of the self-tests, then see if you and the professor who wrote the questions (such as for this Study Guide) were thinking in the same direction or if you came up with questions that weren't asked (bear in mind that in any study guide, we can only present a limited number of questions). By developing your own set of questions (and answers), you will deepen your understanding of the material and help prepare yourself for upcoming exams. Now, here's the fun part: see if you can come up with questions that either you *can't* answer or that you think are unique or "tricky" (bearing in mind that most instructors really do try to stay away from "trick questions"), then pose those questions to your own instructor. Or, if you'd like, feel free to e-mail me (arosenfield@esedona.net) to see if I can answer your question(s). I may just give you a hint and see where you go with it, but I'm always happy to "dialogue" with my students, whether in my own classroom or those who use my study guides. So give it a try and see what you can come up with.

A Final Thought

Remember this: Professors don't actually "teach" their students. Rather, they facilitate learning so students end up teaching themselves. Although we try hard to motivate our students, keep them interested, and present information in a way that helps students to understand, the ultimate responsibility for learning rests with the students. Some students have learned *despite* their professors, whereas others don't learn even with the best professors. So, keep your goals in mind, study hard, ask questions, and aim for success.

If you have thoughts you'd like to share with me—or other ideas for how to study and learn, things that worked for you or didn't work for you—you may reach me through my e-mail address: arosenfield@esedona.net.

    With good thoughts for your continued success,

    Anita Rosenfield, Ph.D.

Two Important Notes About Getting Permission

In each chapter of this Study Guide, you will find suggested Research Activities. Some of these activities involve working with children, and many involve requesting participation by people (e.g., children, adolescents, and/or adults) who are not members of your Child Development class. Whenever you work with persons under the age of 18, you must obtain written permission from a parent or guardian (even if that is not specifically mentioned in the particular Research Activity); also, *always* ask the person assisting you if he or she is willing to help you with your project, despite that person's age. (A sample form is included as follows.)

If the parent, guardian, or participant indicates a reluctance to participate, thank them anyway and move on to someone else. If, at any point during the project, participants indicate a desire to discontinue participation, stop immediately and thank them for their help up to that point. Participation in research is *always* voluntary; no one should ever be coerced into involvement and, once having begun, participants *always* have the right to discontinue their participation if they so desire.

Further, each institution (college, university, etc.) has its own standards for conducting research. Before engaging in any of the suggested Research Activities, check with your instructor to determine whether you need to obtain approval from your school's Institutional Review Board (IRB). If approval is necessary, be sure to plan sufficient time for completing your project that includes time for getting your proposal reviewed.

SAMPLE CONSENT FORM

Child Development—Psychology

In partial fulfillment of the requirements of this course, I will need to [**fill in what you will need to do, for example**: *observe a child who is between 5 and 10 years of age. I will need to have this child perform three tasks and answer questions about . . . During the observations I will assess the child's ability to complete various tasks, including:*
- *Discussing whether various items (such as a car or an egg) are alive.*
- *Telling me if the child thinks certain shapes look like boys or girls.]*

I will compile a summary report based on these observations, and I will submit this report to my psychology professor. In my report, I will include information about the child's age and gender, but I will not disclose the child's identity. The child's performance on these tasks cannot be used to speculate about the child's potential, and I will make no speculations about the child based on these observations. I will read the previous statements to the parents of the child I will observe.

Date	Student's Signature
The previous statements were read to me. I understand that my child will be observed in the manner described. I agree to allow my child to participate in these observations. I understand that I can withdraw this agreement at any time. If I have any further questions, I understand that I may contact (professor of psychology at phone #).	Child's Name/Age: Parent's Name Printed Parent's Signature/Date

CHAPTER 1: INTRODUCTION

CHAPTER OUTLINE	REACH YOUR LEARNING GOALS

CHAPTER OUTLINE

HOW CAN CHILDREN'S LIVES BE
    IMPROVED?
    Health and Well-Being
    Families and Parenting
    Education
    Sociocultural Contexts: Culture,
        Ethnicity, and Socioeconomic Status
    Gender
    Social Policy

WHAT ARE SOME HISTORICAL VIEWS
    OF CHILD DEVELOPMENT?
    Early Views of Children
    The Modern Study of Child Development
    Early Modern Theorists

WHAT ARE THE DEVELOPMENTAL
    PROCESSES AND PERIODS?
    Biological, Cognitive, and Socioemotional
    Processes
    Periods of Development

WHAT ARE THE CORE ISSUES IN CHILD
    DEVELOPMENT?
    Nature and Nurture
    Continuity and Discontinuity
    Early and Later Experience
    Evaluating the Developmental Issues

WHAT ARE THE MAIN CAREERS IN
    CHILD DEVELOPMENT?
    Education and Research
    Clinical and Counseling
    Medical, Nursing, and Physical
        Development
    Families and Relationships
    Web Site Connections for Careers
        in Child Development

REACH YOUR LEARNING GOALS

1. HOW CAN CHILDREN'S LIVES BE IMPROVED?

Health & Well-Being	Education	Gender
Families & Parenting	Sociocultural Contexts: Culture, Ethnicity, & Socioeconomic Status	Social Policy

2. WHAT ARE SOME HISTORICAL VIEWS OF CHILD DEVELOPMENT?

Early Views of Children	The Modern Study of Child Development	Early Modern Theorists

3. WHAT ARE THE DEVELOPMENTAL PROCESSES AND PERIODS?

Biological, Cognitive, & Socioemotional Processes	Periods of Development

4. WHAT ARE THE CORE ISSUES IN CHILD DEVELOPMENT?

Nature & Nurture	Early & Later Experience
Continuity & Discontinuity	Evaluating the Developmental Issues

5. WHAT ARE THE MAIN CAREERS IN CHILD DEVELOPMENT?

Education & Research	Medical, Nursing, & Physical Development	Web Site Connections for Careers In Child Development
Clinical & Counseling	Families & Relationships	

Learning Goals

By the time you have completed this chapter, you should be able to reach the following goals:

1. Identify six areas in which children's lives can be improved.
2. Characterize how children were viewed historically and by early theorists.
3. Discuss the most important developmental processes and periods.
4. Describe three key developmental issues.
5. Summarize the possible career paths that involve working with children.

What do psychologists mean by the term *development*?	Explain the difference between the terms *gender* and *sex*.
What role does *context* play in development?	What is the relationship between *social policy* and child development research?
Explain the term *culture*. What role does it play in terms of development?	Explain the *original sin* notion of childrearing. During what period was it particularly dominant?
What are cross-cultural studies? What is a special concern in comparing the United States with other cultures?	Who proposed the *tabula rasa* view of child-rearing? What does this view say?
Describe the difference between the terms *ethnicity* and *ethnic identity*.	Which philosopher presented the *innate goodness* view of childrearing? Explain this philosophy.
What are the implications of *socioeconomic status*?	What is *genetic epistemology*?

Gender: involves the psychological and sociocultural dimensions of being female or male. *Sex*: the biological dimension of being female or male.	*Development*: the pattern of movement or change that begins at conception and continues through the human life span.
Social policy: refers to the laws, regulations, and government programs that influence the welfare of a country's citizens. Comprehensive social policy often grows out of concern over broad social issues.	*Context*: refers to the setting in which development occurs; it is influenced by historical, economic, social, and cultural factors.
Original sin view: perceives children as basically bad, being born into the world as evil beings. It was particularly dominant during the Middle Ages.	*Culture*: refers to the behavior patterns, beliefs, and all other products of a particular group of people that are passed on from generation to generation; the group's culture influences the identity, learning, and social behavior of its members.
Tabula rasa view: proposed by English philosopher John Locke. Argues that children are not innately bad, but instead are like a "blank tablet" influenced by their experiences; parents need to spend time with and guide them.	*Cross-cultural studies*: compare one culture with one or more other cultures; offer information about how development is similar (universal) across cultures, or culture specific; while the United States is an achievement-oriented culture with a strong work ethic, Japanese children are better at math, and spend more time working on math in school and doing homework.
Innate goodness view: proposed by Swiss-born French philosopher Jean Jacques Rousseau. Stresses that children are inherently good and thus should be permitted to grow naturally, with little parental monitoring or constraint.	*Ethnicity*: rooted in cultural heritage, nationality characteristics, race, religion, and language. *Ethnic identity*: a sense of membership in an ethnic group, based on shared language, religion, customs, values, history, and race.
Genetic epistemology: a term that James Mark Baldwin used to refer to the study of how children's knowledge changes over the course of their development.	*Socioeconomic status (SES)* refers to the grouping of people with similar occupational, educational, and economic characteristics. It implies certain inequalities based on occupational prestige, level of educational attainment, economic resources, and level of power to influence community institutions.

Define the term *biological processes*. Give some examples of biological processes.	What is the time span of *middle* and *late childhood*? What are the primary characteristics of this period of development?
Define the term *cognitive processes*. What are some examples of cognitive processes?	What is the time span of *adolescence*? What milestones characterize this period of development?
Define the term *socioemotional processes*. What are some examples of socioemotional processes?	Define the *nature-nurture issue*.
How long is the *prenatal period*? What occurs during the prenatal period?	What is the *continuity-discontinuity issue*?
How long does the period of *infancy* last? What limitations and activities characterize this period of development?	Describe the debate concerning the *early-later experience issue*. Which cultures are more likely to support each side of this issue?
What is the time span of *early childhood*? What achievements and activities characterize this period of development?	Explain why it is important to evaluate the developmental issues of nature/nurture, continuity/discontinuity, and early and late experience.

Middle and late childhood: developmental period extending from about 6 to 11 years of age (elementary school years). Mastery of fundamental skills (reading, writing, arithmetic), formal exposure to larger world, self-control increases.	*Biological processes*: produce changes in an individual's body. Examples: genes inherited from parents; development of brain, height, weight, motor skills, and hormonal changes in puberty.
Adolescence: developmental period of transition from childhood to early adulthood (approximately 10–12 to 18–20 years of age). Rapid physical changes, changes in body contour, development of sexual characteristics, prominent development in independence and identity, abstract thought.	*Cognitive processes*: refer to changes in an individual's thought, intelligence, and language. Examples: watching a colorful mobile, putting together a two-word sentence, memorizing a poem, solving a math problem.
Nature-nurture issue: Debate about whether development is primarily influenced by nature (biological inheritance) or nurture (environmental experiences).	*Socioemotional processes*: involve changes in an individual's relationships with other people, changes in emotions, and changes in personality. Examples: an infant's smile in response to mother's touch, a child's aggressive attack on a playmate.
Continuity-discontinuity issue: the extent to which development involves gradual, cumulative change (continuity) or distinct stages (discontinuity).	*Prenatal period*: the time from conception to birth (approximately 9 months). Growth from single cell to a human organism complete with a brain and behavioral capabilities.
Early-later experience issue: focuses on the degree to which early experiences (especially infancy) or later experiences are key determinants of a child's development. Early: Western cultures; Later: Asian cultures	*Infancy*: developmental period extending from birth to 18 to 24 months. A time of extreme dependence on adults and beginning of psychological activities (e.g., language, symbolic thought, sensorimotor coordination, social learning).
The issues of nature/nurture, continuity/discontinuity, and early/later experiences influence public policy decisions about children and how each of us lives through the human life span, depending on which position one takes on each of them.	*Early childhood*: developmental period extending from the end of infancy to about 5 or 6 years of age (also called the preschool years). Increase in self-sufficiency, develop school-readiness skills (e.g., reading), spend time playing with peers.

Self-Test A: Multiple-Choice Questions

1. Which of the following is NOT a reason the text gave to study children?
   a. The more you learn about children, the better you can guide them.
   b. You may gain insight into your own history.
   c. It is a requirement for such fields as nursing, psychology, and child development.
   d. As a parent or teacher, you may have responsibility for children.

2. The pattern of movement or change that begins at conception and continues through the human life span is referred to as:
   a. maturation.
   b. development.
   c. biology.
   d. physiological development.

3. Tiffany Field (2001) found that massage can:
   a. overstimulate infants, causing them to be hyperactive.
   b. overstimulate infants, causing them to become ill.
   c. facilitate weight gain in premature infants.
   d. help mothers bond with their premature infants.

4. A problem with passing parenting practices and child-care strategies from one generation to the next is:
   a. it is too difficult to learn that way.
   b. what worked for previous generations won't work for children today.
   c. children are more likely to learn the undesirable practices and strategies than those that are desirable.
   d. both desirable and undesirable practices and strategies are passed on.

5. _____ has/have been increasingly advocated as a strategy for improving the academic achievement of adolescents at risk for academic failure.
   a. Mentoring programs
   b. Tutoring
   c. Summer school
   d. Remedial classes

6. The important concepts involved in sociocultural contexts of development are:
   a. context, culture, ethnicity, and socioeconomic status.
   b. biological, cognitive, and socioemotional processes.
   c. nature-nurture, continuity-discontinuity, and stability-change issues.
   d. ethnicity, race, and religion.

7. Culture refers to:
   a. the setting in which development occurs that is influenced by historical, economic, and social factors.
   b. the behavior patterns, beliefs, and other products of a group that are passed on from generation to generation.
   c. one's heritage, nationality characteristics, race, religion, and language.
   d. activities engaged in only by the elite members of a group.

8. Assuming these fourth-graders are typical of children in their country, cross-cultural studies suggest which child would have the highest math achievement?
   a. Momoko, a Japanese girl
   b. Alexei, a Russian boy
   c. Jean, a Swiss boy
   d. Larry, an American boy

9. A researcher assessing the occupational, educational, and economic characteristics of a group of people is evaluating their:
   a. financial status.
   b. socioeconomic status.
   c. demographics.
   d. cultural factors.

10. Marian Wright Edelman says that:
a. the United States is doing an excellent job of providing children with good health care and safe schools.
b. parenting education for parents over the past 15 years has led to fewer problems in children's behavior.
c. among industrialized nations, the United States is one of the worst in terms of social neglect of its children.
d. computer use is among the most critical issues for children in the U.S. today.

11. The family policies of the United States for improving the well-being of families and their children:
a. overwhelmingly focus on treating problems.
b. try to enhance parental competence.
c. try to enhance children's competence.
d. focus on preventing and treating problems.

12. Carlo and Lucia believe their role as parents is to help their children overcome their evil nature and achieve salvation. This indicates they accept which philosophy of child rearing?
a. *tabula rasa*
b. innate goodness
c. laissez-faire
d. original sin

13. Since Marcel and Isabel adhere to the fundamental premise of Jean-Jacques Rousseau's "innate goodness" argument, we would expect them to:
a. reject the need to "teach" language since speech is inherited.
b. provide their children with little discipline or constraints.
c. view their children as intellectually indistinguishable from themselves.
d. believe their children's minds are like "blank slates" on which experience will write its lessons.

14. The major shift that took place in the study of child development during the late 1800s was:

a. a switch from a strictly philosophical perspective to one that includes direct observation and experimentation.
b. a switch from an experimental perspective to one that is primarily philosophical.
c. moving from direct observation to a philosophical perspective.
d. moving from highly complex to more simplified techniques for studying children and adolescents.

15. Which theorist argued that adolescence is a time of "storm and stress"?
a. Arnold Gesell
b. Sigmund Freud
c. G. Stanley Hall
d. John B. Watson

16. Genetic epistemology refers to the study of:
a. how children's knowledge changes over the course of their development.
b. hereditary factors that affect an individual's development.
c. the interplay between genetic and environmental influences on development.
d. the role of genetic mutations on development.

17. Which of the following would involve a socioemotional process?
a. increased manual dexterity as a child ages
b. increased memory function over time
c. changes in personality over time
d. improved ability at problem solving

18. What is TRUE concerning the biological, cognitive, and socioemotional processes?
a. Each is distinct from the others.
b. The cognitive is more closely related to the socioemotional than to the biological.
c. They are intricately interwoven.
d. They are more obvious in the early years than later in life.

19. Amber is in a time of extreme dependence on her parents. She is just beginning to use language, symbolic thought, and sensorimotor coordination. She is in which stage of development?
a. perinatal
b. infancy
c. early childhood
d. dependent

20. Sonny is learning to read, write, and do arithmetic as she is being formally exposed to the world outside her family. She is in which period of development?
a. early childhood
b. middle-late childhood
c. pre-pubertal
d. adolescent

21. Graham is 15 years old. We would expect to see all of the following occurring in his life EXCEPT:
a. increased illogical thought processes.
b. pursuit of independence.
c. dramatic gains in height and weight.
d. a deepening of his voice.

22. Advocates of the "nature" position believe that _____ produce(s) commonalities in growth and development.
a. environmental stimuli
b. a genetic blueprint
c. the biological environment
d. parenting practices

23. Anthony is 6 months old and has been diagnosed as retarded. His parents believe that providing intellectual stimulation and emotional support for him will increase his intelligence as well as his chances to live a normal life. They are proponents of the _____ view of development.
a. nature
b. nurture
c. discontinuity
d. maturation

24. Professor Lepidopter believes that infants are like caterpillars and will eventually develop into "butterfly adolescents," demonstrating which view of development?
a. nature
b. nurture
c. continuity
d. discontinuity

25. Yeh and Li are from a traditional Asian background. They are more likely than persons from Western cultures to believe that:
a. early childhood experiences are critical in determining a child's development.
b. early childhood experiences are important, but can be offset by later experiences.
c. childhood experiences before age 6 or 7 have little importance compared with later experiences.
d. experiences throughout a person's life are critical to their ongoing development.

26. With regard to life experience, Sigmund Freud would most likely suggest that:
a. experiences early in life are critical in determining a child's development.
b. experiences early in life are important, but can be offset by later experiences.
c. experiences occurring before age 6 or 7 have little importance compared with later experiences.
d. experiences throughout a person's life are critical to their ongoing development.

27. By and large, developmental psychologists today generally tend to agree that:
a. nature plays a greater role than nurture in development.
b. nurture plays a greater role than nature in development.
c. both nature and nurture are intricately interwoven and together play an important role in development.
d. it is inappropriate to debate this issue.

28. After meeting with his departmental advisor, David decides he wants to become a college professor who teaches child development. To do so, he will most likely need at least:
a. an associate's degree.
b. a bachelor's degree.
c. a master's degree.
d. a Ph.D.

29. The child developmentalist most likely to counsel parents and children when the children have school problems, and who will administer psychological tests to children, is the:
a. school psychologist.
b. counseling psychologist.
c. child clinical psychologist.
d. social worker.

30. Dr. Harkins has a Psy.D. She does psychological testing and psychotherapy in her private practice. Dr. Harkins is a
a. social worker.
b. clinical psychologist.
c. life specialist.
d. personal life coach.

Self-Test B: Matching

Match the following persons with the statement or theory that most closely reflects their perspective:

1. Marian Wright Edelman   a. Found massage therapy facilitates weight gain in premature infants.
2. John Locke   b. Children are innately good.
3. Jean-Jacques Rousseau   c. Both early and later life experiences contribute to development.
4. Sigmund Freud   d. Children are like blank slates and grow through experience.
5. Tiffany Field   e. Characteristics "bloom" with age because of biological blueprint.
6. Jerome Kagan   f. The United States ranks very low in the treatment of children.
7. Arnold Gesell   g. Children think in a qualitatively different manner than adults.
8. Alfred Binet   h. Adolescence is a time of "storm and stress."
9. G. Stanley Hall   i. Collaborated in developing the first modern test of intelligence.
10. Jean Piaget   j. The bulk of mental life is unconscious.

Self-Test C: True-False

T/F   1. Sociocultural contexts do not influence children's development as much as ethnicity.

T/F   2. Gender refers to the biological dimension of being female or male.

T/F   3. Philosophical views of childhood, such as notions of original sin and *tabula rasa,* were prominent prior to the nineteenth century.

T/F   4. Most developmental psychologists today support G. Stanley Hall's theory that adolescence is a period of storm and stress.

T/F   5. Development is influenced by an interplay of biological, cognitive, and socioemotinoal processes.

T/F   6. Smiling is an example of a socioemotional process.

T/F 7. In the debate between the impact of nature and nurture on development, the current thinking among developmental researchers is that nature has a greater influence than nurture.

T/F 8. Asian cultures place the heaviest emphasis on the first six years of life in terms of child development.

T/F 9. To be a psychiatrist, an individual must first receive a medical degree.

T/F 10. Marian Wright Edelman believes that standing up for children is the most important mission in the world.

Self-Test D: CD

1. Brooks-Gunn says that the _____ has lifted more children out of poverty than any other policy.

2. According to Brooks-Gunn, which period of life should be the primary focus for developing healthy children?
   - a. infancy
   - b. the first year
   - c. the first five years
   - d. birth through adolescence

3. T/F Eccles believes that closer contact with teachers would help stem the drop off in school motivation when children move from junior high or middle school to high school.

4. T/F There are no biological differences between identical twins because they develop from the same embryo.

Essay Questions

1. One evening at a family gathering your uncle corners you and says, "Your Mom says you're on the County Commission to Improve Education. What a waste of money that is! Everyone knows that good, old-fashioned reading, writing, and 'rithmetic need to be taught the same way they've been taught for the last 200 years. We're just throwing our money away with all these extra programs that try to coddle kids. And these mentoring programs you were talking about are just a waste of money, too. Kids today just need a swift kick now and then to make them learn." How do you respond to him?

2. The "nature-nurture controversy" has been around for a long time. When having coffee in the cafeteria, you get into a discussion about this issue with two of your friends. One of them stubbornly states that nature is the only thing that matters; your other friend just as stubbornly asserts that nurture is the only thing that is important in terms of who we are, how we develop, and what our lives will be like. Knowing you are taking this class in Child Development, they turn to you to tell them who is right. Discuss this issue with them, being sure to incorporate into your answer all you know about the biological, cognitive, and socioemotional processes.

Key to Self-Test A: MultipleChoice

1. c (LG1)	11. a (LG1)	21. a (LG3)
2. b (LG1)	12. d (LG2)	22. b (LG4)
3. c (LG1)	13. b (LG2)	23. b (LG4)
4. d (LG1)	14. a (LG2)	24. d (LG4)
5. a (LG1)	15. c (LG2)	25. c (LG4)
6. a (LG1)	16. a (LG3)	26. a (LG4)
7. b (LG1)	17. c (LG3)	27. c (LG4)
8. a (LG1)	18. c (LG3)	28. c (LG5)
9. b (LG1)	19. b (LG3)	29. a (LG5)
10. c (LG1)	20. b (LG3)	30. b (LG5)

Key to Self-Test B: Matching

1. f
2. d
3. b
4. j
5. a
6. c
7. e
8. i
9. h
10. g

Key to Self-Test C:True-False

1. False. Ethnicity is one of the four components of sociocultural contexts (contexts, culture, ethnicity, and socioeconomic status).
2. False. Gender refers to the psychological and sociocultural dimensions of being female or male; sex refers to the biological dimension of being female or male.
3. True
4. False. Although some adolescents go through a period of "storm and stress," most do not experience such extremes in their emotions and behavior.
5. True
6. True
7. False. Most psychologists today consider both nature and nurture—and the interplay between them—as critical elements of development.
8. False. People in Asian countries are more likely to believe that experiences occurring after age 6 or 7 are more important to development than are earlier experiences.
9. True
10. True

Key to Self-Test D:CD

1. increased earned income tax credit
2. c
3. True
4. False. Differences may develop from such factors as positioning and nutrition in the womb.

Key to Essay Questions

1. Acknowledge your uncle's concerns and advise him of some of the current issues that are being discussed with regard to education, such as length of school day and school year; whether the curriculum should be changed; accountability of schools, teachers, and students; whether more demands should be made on children; and whether schools should focus on knowledge and cognitive skills or whether they should also include concern for socioemotional and physical development. Try to educate him a bit about the issues of diversity, including such things as how context, culture, ethnicity, and gender affect children's ability to learn and how our country would benefit by being able to educate all of its citizens. Then explain exactly what mentoring programs are and let him know how effective these programs have been in reducing unexcused absences from school, improving classroom performance, and creating better relationships between mentored children and their parents.
2. A proper answer should first explain what "nature" and "nurture" are in terms of biological predisposition and environmental influence, then look at the interaction between the two.

Research Project 1: Child Abuse Prevention

There are many excellent reasons to study child development, as outlined by the author of your text. These include being better able to deal with children by learning about them, gaining insight into your own history, and because you may (either at present or in the future) have responsibility for children. Another reason may not be as obvious as the others: to reduce the incidence of child abuse. The main issue here is that when parents' expectations of their children are inconsistent with what the child may be able to do at any given developmental stage, the parents may become frustrated, lose patience with the child, and engage in abusive behavior (emotionally and/or physically). Check out resources on the Internet (e.g., those listed in the "Additional Resources" section); in your public library; at local hospitals; from federal, state, and local government agencies; and from private agencies to plan an intervention that can be used to educate parents about what they can expect from their children as they develop and what they can do to deal with feelings of frustration and avoid abuse. This would include information on not only *how* and *what* skills children develop as they grow, but also techniques to help parents work with their children as well as information about local resources available for parents.

Research Project 2: Influencing Social Policy

A primary concern of all persons involved in child development, no matter which subspecialty, is social policy. Throughout Chapter 1, Santrock provides numerous examples of the importance of providing a safe and healthful environment to children, both for their own sake and for the sake of society (e.g., the story of Jeffrey Dahmer, the quote from Aristotle, the work of Marian Wright Edelman). Select one area that particularly concerns you, then clearly define the problem, design an effective plan that could be implemented, and state what outcome you anticipate would result from implementing your plan. Once you have completed this project, submit it to whatever person(s) and/or agency(ies) you believe would be able to use your intervention effectively. Report on the results of your endeavor to your class.

Personal Application 1: Reflecting on What You Learned

Consider what you read in Chapter 1, then answer the following questions:

1. What information in this chapter did you already know?

2. How can/do you use that information in your own life?

3. What information in this chapter was totally new to you?

4. How can you use that new information in your own life?

5. What information in this chapter was different from what you previously believed?

6. How was this information different?

7. How do you account for the differences between what you believed and what you learned in the chapter?

8. What is the most important thing you learned from reading this chapter?

Personal Application 2: Consider Your Own Development

Reveiw your life thus far. Using your own reflections and input from family members, reconstruct your development from as early as you can remember up to who you are today. Consider the developmental issues of nature-nurture, continuity-discontinuity, and early versus later experience. Describe which parts of you (e.g., aspects of your personality, your intellect, your values and beliefs, your basic behavior patterns) you believe result from each of these six elements. You may use the following chart, create a pie chart, or come up with some other graphic aid to help you visualize which elements have played the strongest role in shaping you into the person you are now. How would you explain your findings?

Aspect of Your Self	Nature-Nurture	Continuity-Discontinuity	Early-Later Experience
Personality traits (describe)			
Intellect (describe)			
Values & beliefs (describe)			
Behavior patterns (describe)			
Other (describe)			

Internet Projects

Check out the McGraw-Hill Web site for this text (www.mhhe.com/santrockc9). The site contains numerous activities, in particular, information that will help you research the answers and complete the exercises in the "Taking It to the Net" section at the end of the textbook chapter. Please note that all Web site addresses in this Study Guide have been checked and are correct at the time of publication; however, Web sites may be discontinued or addresses may change, so when you search a given site it may no longer be viable. If that occurs, I apologize for the inconvenience and would appreciate you notifying me so I can make appropriate revisions in future editions of this Study Guide.

Internet Project 1: Beginning to Search Online

Go to www.psychology.org, Encyclopedia of Psychology, sponsored by Jacksonville University, and conduct a search for any of the terms in the Key Terms section of the text. How many links[1] did you find? How many of those links referred you to professional journal articles? How many were someone's personal opinion? Compare the information you got from these different sources of information. What other types of links came up on the screen? How helpful was the information you found?

Internet Project 2: Careers in Life-Span Development

There are several sections in Chapter 1 where the author talks about careers in developmental psychology, most particularly the last section, for Learning Goal 5. The Internet offers many job sites, some more general and others more specific. The two sites that are particularly geared toward psychologists are sponsored by the American Psychological Association (APA at www.apa.org) and the American Psychological Society (APS at www.psychologicalscience.org). Both of these sites (and their print publications) have excellent articles on relevant topics for anyone interested in the social sciences and higher education; they also have job postings. Go to each of these sites and check out listed positions that are relevant to child development ("career info" and "employment ads," respectively). Then answer the following questions:

1. Which site is easier to navigate?
2. Which site offers the most positions in general?
3. Which site offers the most positions in child development?
4. How many positions did each site have that related to child development?
5. Which site offers positions that are most relevant to your interests?
6. How would you go about applying for a job that you found on each of these sites?
7. Did you learn anything about child development from exploring these sites?
8. What else did you learn from exploring these sites?

- APA site: www.apa.org
(Note there is a special "classified ads" link in the student section under the "Career Center" link for resources, publications, and other helpful links.)
- APS site: www.psychologicalscience.org
(Note that if you add "apssc" after the "org" you will get to the student section.)

---

[1] For those of you who are not familiar with the Internet, a link is either a topic or a Web address (such as those given here, such as www.apa.org) and will be a color such as blue or purple. If you point the screen cursor on the link and click the left side of the mouse, you will go to the Web site for that link. If you want to get back to where you were before, *usually* left-clicking the "back" key at the top left of the screen will do it

Additional Internet Resources

American Academy of Pediatrics at http://www.aap.org/research.html offers a variety of links for information on children's well-being.

Children's Defense Fund (CDF): http://www.childrensdefense.org—The Web site for CDF, the organization headed by Marian Wright Edelman to promote child welfare (discussed in Chapter 1 of the text).

Mayo Clinic's Health Site can be found at http://www.mayoclinic.com—Check out "baby health" and "children's health" at the Health Center links on the left.

Medscape: http://www.medscape.com/homepage—Free database of medical articles, plus access to medical dictionaries, drug databases, and breaking medical news (you may have to register, but it's free).

National Alliance to End Homelessness: http://www.endhomelessness.org/.

National Institutes of Health: http://www.nih.gov—Starting point for getting into any subagency of NIH.

National Institute of Mental Health: http://www.nimh.nih.gov—Excellent resource for policy statements, NIMH research, and grants.

New England Journal of Medicine: http://content.nejm.org/ —Abstracts to articles, full text on letters and commentaries (there is a fee for full articles)

Psychological Tutorials and Demonstrations: http://psych.hanover.edu/Krantz/tutor.html—An excellent source of links on a wide variety of psychology-related topics provided by Professor John H. Krantz of Hanover University; you may also find his Web site useful: http://psychlab1.hanover.edu/.

Scientific American: http://www.sciam.com—General scientific resource.

Scirus: For Scientific Research Only: http://www.scirus.com/srsapp/ —A veritable wealth of information on scientific topics with an enormous database, including genetics and psychology.

Society for Research in Child Development (SRCD): http://www.srcd.org—The Web site for SRCD, an organization whose purposes are to promote multidisciplinary research in the field of human development, to foster the exchange of information among scientists and other professionals of various disciplines, and to encourage applications of research findings.

CHAPTER 2: THE SCIENCE OF CHILD DEVELOPMENT

CHAPTER OUTLINE

HOW IS CHILD DEVELOPMENT A SCIENCE?
The Importance of Research in Child Development
The Scientific Research Approach

WHAT ARE THE MAIN THEORIES OF CHILD DEVELOPMENT?
Psychoanalytic Theories
Cognitive Theories
Behavioral and Social Cognitive Theories
Ethological Theory
Ecological Theory
An Eclectic Theoretical Orientation

WHAT ARE THE MAIN RESEARCH METHODS IN CHILD DEVELOPMENT?
Methods for Collecting Data
Research Designs
Time Span of Research
Research Journals

WHAT ARE SOME CHALLENGES IN CHILD DEVELOPMENT RESEARCH?
Conducting Ethical Research
Minimizing Bias
Thinking Critically about Research on Children's Development

REACH YOUR LEARNING GOALS

1. **HOW IS CHILD DEVELOPMENT A SCIENCE?**

The Importance of Research in Child Development	The Scientific Research Approach

2. **WHAT ARE THE MAIN THEORIES OF CHILD DEVELOPMENT?**

Psychoanalytic Theories	Behavioral & Social Cognitive Theories	Ecological Theory
Cognitive Theories	Ethological Theory	An Eclectic Theoretical Orientation

3. **WHAT ARE THE MAIN RESEARCH METHODS IN CHILD DEVELOPMENT?**

Methods for Collecting Data	Time Span of Research
Research Designs	Research Journals

4. **WHAT ARE SOME CHALLENGES IN CHILD DEVELOPMENT RESEARCH?**

Conducting Ethical Research	Thinking Critically about Research on Children's Development
Minimizing Bias	

Learning Goals

By the time you have completed this chapter, you should be able to reach the following goals:

1. Discuss the importance of research in child development and the scientific method.

2. Describe the main theories of child development.

3. Explain how research on child development is conducted.

4. Summarize challenges in child development research.

Differentiate between *scientific research* and the *scientific method*.	What is the *Oedipus complex*?
What is a *theory*? What is a *hypothesis*? How do theories differ from hypotheses?	What are the specific crises in each of Erikson's eight stages of development? Match each stage with its age group.
How does *psychoanalytic theory* describe development?	How does *assimilation* differ from *accommodation*? Which theory do these processes fit?
Name and describe the three structures of personality according to Freud's psychoanalytic theory.	Describe Piaget's four stages of cognitive development and summarize what occurs in each stage.
What role does *fixation* play in development of the adult personality?	Describe Vygotsky's *sociocultural cognitive theory*.
Describe the five psychosexual stages of development, including approximate age spans and the primary focus of pleasure.	Explain *information-processing theory*.

The *Oedipus complex* is the Freudian concept that the young child develops an intense desire to replace the same-sex parent and enjoy the affections of the opposite-sex parent (based on the Greek myth).	The *scientific method* attempts to discover accurate information by conceptualizing the problem, collecting data, drawing conclusions, and revising theories. *Scientific research*, which is objective, systematic, and testable, is based on the scientific method.
Trust/Mistrust: 1st year; need comfort, minimal fear. *Autonomy/Shame & Doubt*: 1–3; independence. *Initiative/Guilt*: 3–5; purposeful behavior. *Industry/Inferiority*: 6–puberty; master intellect. *Identity/Identity Confusion*: achieve identity as teen. *Intimacy/Isolation:* early adult; intimate relations. *Generativity/Stagnation*: mid-adult; help young folk. *Integrity/Despair*: older adult; evaluate one's life.	*Theory*: an interrelated, coherent set of ideas that helps explain data and make predictions. *Hypothesis*: specific testable assumptions and predictions derived from theories. Theories are broader explanations that need to be narrowed down into testable hypotheses.
Assimilation: occurs when new information is incorporated into existing knowledge *Accommodation*: occurs when new information does not fit into existing information, so individuals must adjust to the new information. These are part of Piaget's theory of cognitive development.	*Psychoanalytic theory* describes development as primarily unconscious (beyond awareness) and heavily colored by emotion.
Sensorimotor: birth–2; coordinate sensory experiences with physical motoric actions to understand the world. *Preoperational*: 2–7; represent the world symbolically (words, images, drawings). *Concrete operational*: 7–11; perform operations; (concrete) logic replaces intuition. *Formal operational*: begins between age 11–15; abstract, idealistic, logical thought.	*Id*: Freudian personality structure that consists of instincts (the reservoir of psychic energy). *Ego*: Freudian personality structure that deals with the demands of reality. *Superego*: Freudian personality structure that is the moral branch.
Vygotsky's *sociocultural cognitive theory* emphasizes how culture and social interaction guide cognitive development.	When conflicts between the early sources of pleasure and the demands of reality are not resolved, the individual may become *fixated* at a particular stage of development because needs are under- or overgratified.
Information-processing theory: Emphasizes that individuals manipulate information about their world, monitor it, and strategize about it; gradually increasing capacity for processing information allows us to acquire increasingly complex knowledge and skills.	*Oral*: first 18 months; pleasure centers around the mouth. *Anal*: 1-1/2 to 3; pleasure involves anus, eliminative functions. *Phallic*: 3–6; focus on genitalia. *Latency*: 6–puberty; sexuality repressed; social/intellectual skills develop. *Genital*: puberty on; sexual reawakening; adult sexuality, sexual pleasure focused on someone outside the family.

Contrast Pavlov's *classical conditioning* with Skinner's *operant conditioning*.	Describe two *psychophysiological measures* used to assess the functioning of the central nervous system (CNS), autonomic nervous system (ANS), and the endocrine system.
What are the three key factors of Bandura's *social cognitive theory*? What is its primary difference from behaviorism?	Explain how *correlational research* differs from *descriptive research*. What is a *correlation coefficient*?
What does ethological theory say about development? Explain *imprinting, critical periods,* and *sensitive periods*.	What is an *experiment*? How does the *independent variable* differ from the *dependent variable*?
Describe the five systems of *ecological theory*.	Compare and contrast *cross-sectional* and *longitudinal approaches*.
What is an *eclectic theoretical orientation*?	What are the four important research ethics issues discussed in the text?
Name some of the scientific methods researchers use when gathering data about development.	What is *ethnic gloss*?

Magnetic resonance imaging (MRI) uses a magnetic field and radio waves to construct images of a person's tissues and biochemical activities, and the *electroencephalogram (EEG),* records the brain's electrical activity.	Pavlov's *classical conditioning:* a neutral stimulus acquires the ability to produce a response originally produced by another stimulus. Skinner's *operant conditioning:* the consequences of a behavior produce changes in the probability of the behavior's occurrence.
Correlational research: goal is to describe the strength of the relationship between two or more events/characteristics. *Descriptive research*: aims to observe and record behavior *Correlation coefficient:* a number based on a statistical analysis used to describe the degree of association between to variables (−1.00 to +1.00).	*Social cognitive theory*: emphasizes the interactions among behavior, environment, and person/cognition in development; explains that organisms learn from observing the consequences of other organisms' behavior; its emphasis on cognition differentiates it from strict behaviorism.
Experiment: carefully regulated procedure in which factors believed to influence behavior are manipulated and other factors are held constant *Independent variable*: manipulated, influential, experimental factor in the experiment *Dependent variable*: the factor (outcome) measured to assess any change resulting from changes in the independent variable.	*Ethology*: behavior strongly influenced by biology and evolution. *Imprinting*: rapid, innate learning within a critical period for attachment to first moving object seen. *Critical period*: fixed time period early in development during which certain behaviors optimally emerge. *Sensitive period:* longer, more flexible period for emergence of behaviors.
Both are time span inquiries. *Cross-sectional*: individuals of different ages are compared at one time. *Longitudinal*: the same individuals are studied over a period of time, usually several years.	*Microsystem*: setting in which individual lives, e.g., family *Mesosystem*: involves relations between microsystem or connections between contexts *Exosystem*: social setting where person is not active influences person's immediate environment *Macrosystem*: culture in which person lives *Chronosystem*: patterns of environmental events and transitions over life course; sociohistorical circumstances.
Research ethics issues: informed consent (participants must know what their participation involves/risks that might develop), *confidentiality* (researchers keep all data confidential and, when possible, anonymous), *debriefing* (inform participants of the purpose and methods used after the study is over), and *deception* (ensure that deception will not harm participant & participant is debriefed when study is completed).	*Eclectic theoretical orientation*: selects and uses whatever is considered the best in each theory, since no single theory can entirely explain the complexity of development by itself.
Ethnic gloss is using an ethnic label, such as African American or Latino, in a superficial way that makes an ethnic group look more homogeneous than it really is.	*Methods for collecting data:* laboratory observation (a controlled setting); naturalistic observation (real-world setting); surveys and interviews (open- or closed-ended questions); standardized tests (uniform procedures for administration and scoring); psychophysiological measures; and case studies (in-depth look at a single individual).

Self-Test A: Multiple-Choice Questions

1. Science is defined by:
   a. what it investigates.
   b. how it investigates.
   c. experience.
   d. scientists.

2. Scientific research is all of the following, EXCEPT:
   a. objective.
   b. systematic.
   c. intuitive.
   d. testable.

3. The first step of the scientific method is:
   a. conceptualize a problem.
   b. collect information.
   c. draw conclusions.
   d. revise conclusions.

4. An assumption or prediction that can be tested to determine its accuracy is a/an:
   a. theory.
   b. hypothesis.
   c. scientific fact.
   d. independent variable.

5. Biological processes are important in whose theory?
   a. Freud's
   b. Piaget's
   c. Vygotsky's
   d. Watson's

6. A psychoanalytic researcher would be primarily interested in _____ processes.
   a. learned
   b. unconscious
   c. biologically based
   d. social

7. When you think to yourself, "I feel guilty about eating that last piece of chocolate," which part of your personality is at work?
   a. id
   b. est
   c. ego
   d. superego

8. Sara was extremely strict while toilet training her 2-year-old son, Harris. She scolded him and made him sit on a "potty chair" for an hour if he soiled his pants. Later in life, Harris became extremely stingy and obsessively clean. In Freudian terms, Harris had _____ during the anal stage.
   a. projected
   b. fixated
   c. become motivated
   d. overdeveloped

9. During which stage would Freud say pleasure focuses on eliminative functions?
   a. oral
   b. anal
   c. phallic
   d. genital

10. Erik Erikson's theory assumes human behavior to be primarily motivated by
    a. sexual energy.
    b. biological maturation.
    c. changes in cognitive processes.
    d. affiliation with other people.

11. Dr. Rostand, a cognitive theorist, would be concerned with children's:
    a. unconscious thoughts.
    b. conscious thoughts.
    c. memories.
    d. behavior.

12. Which statement does NOT represent an important contribution of the psychoanalytic theories?
    a. Early experiences play an important part in development.
    b. Personality can be better understood if it is examined developmentally.
    c. It is important to consider unconscious aspects of the mind.
    d. Individuals actively construct their understanding of the world.

13. Four-year-old Priscilla has always been surrounded by loving adults. She has now met Mr. Scrooge, who is unfriendly and scares Priscilla. In terms of Piaget's theory, Priscilla will change her view of adults through the process of:
    a. assimilation.
    b. accommodation.
    c. operations.
    d. cognitive processing.

14. Vygotsky claimed that knowledge involves all of the following EXCEPT:
    a. it is situated and collaborative.
    b. it is generally constructed through interaction with other people and objects, not from within the individual.
    c. it has it origins in social relations and is embedded in a sociocultural backdrop.
    d. it is best analyzed individually, by looking at the child, not the child's context.

15. The information-processing approach to development emphasizes:
    a. the quality of thinking among children of different ages.
    b. manipulation, monitoring, and strategizing about information.
    c. age-appropriate experiences of sexual energy.
    d. overcoming certain age-related problems or crises.

16. From B. F. Skinner's point of view, behavior is explained by paying attention to:
    a. consequences of that behavior.
    b. the self-produced consequences of that behavior.
    c. individuals' cognitive interpretations of their environmental experiences.
    d. the biological processes that determine maturation.

17. According to Bandura, interactions among _____ reciprocally influence each other and development.
    a. personal, behavioral, and environmental factors
    b. punishment, reward, and reinforcement
    c. memory, problem solving, and reasoning
    d. cognition, reward, and observation

18. One of the most important applications of the ethological perspective for human development involves:
    a. imprinting.
    b. attachment.
    c. critical periods of development.
    d. its emphasis on cognition.

19. The aspects of Anil's setting in which the most direct interactions with social agents, such as his family, peers, school, and neighborhood, take place are his:
    a. microsystem.
    b. exosystem.
    c. mesosystem.
    d. chronosystem.

20. The term _____ is used to describe an orientation simultaneously consisting of several different theoretical perspectives.
    a. nondescript
    b. eclectic
    c. quasi-experimental
    d. pseudoscientific

21. If Cynthia wants to have as much control over the variables in her research as possible, she should collect her data:
    a. in a laboratory.
    b. through naturalistic observation.
    c. by interviewing her participants.
    d. using the case study method.

22. The easiest way to get information from a lot of people quickly it to use which method?
    a. a survey.
    b. naturalistic observation.
    c. a case study.
    d. an experiment.

23. The most convenient method for evaluating the relationship between attachment and parenting styles is:
    a. correlational.
    b. experimental.
    c. survey.
    d. longitudinal.

24. Experimental designs are superior to correlational designs when dealing with:
    a. concepts not previously studied.
    b. variables that are difficult to manipulate.
    c. variables that are unethical to manipulate.
    d. isolating cause and effect.

25. Professor Tucker wants to see the effect of smiling on students. He smiles at half of his students when they ask questions, and not at the others. In this experiment, smiling is the:
    a. independent variable.
    b. dependent variable.
    c. control variable.
    d. confounding variable.

26. To see if smiling at students when they ask questions will encourage them to ask more questions, an effective research method places students in the experimental group (get smiles) or control group (no smiles) through the process of:
    a. random selection.
    b. cross-sectional selection.
    c. random assignment.
    d. first-come/first-placed.

27. Talal is interested in children's motor abilities. Working with children ranging in age from 5 months to 5 years, he observes how they grasp drawing utensils. After a month of observation and data collection, he has completed his _____ study.
    a. longitudinal
    b. sequential
    c. cross-sectional
    d. correlational

28. To protect research participants from mental and physical harm, the American Psychological Association advocates all of the following EXCEPT:
    a. informed consent.
    b. payment for participation.
    c. confidentiality.
    c. debriefing.

29. Mr. Killen is researching sex differences in regard to achievement expectations. In his study he finds that 70% of the males scored high on achievement expectations compared with only 65% of the females. What conclusion could correctly be drawn from this finding?
    a. This difference suggests a statistically significant difference between males and females in achievement expectations.
    b. Mr. Killen has erroneously engaged in ethnic gloss.
    c. Males have higher achievement expectations than females.
    d. This difference may be statistically insignificant and might disappear if the study is repeated.

30. As a wise consumer of information about children's development, Selena would:
    a. consider the source of the information and evaluate its credibility.
    b. assume that group research applies to individuals.
    c. understand that correlational studies allow us to make causal conclusions.
    d. rely on what is reported in the popular media.

Self-Test B: Matching

Match the following persons with the statement or theory that most closely reflects their perspective:

1.	Sigmund Freud	a.	Russian physiologist; discovered the principle of classical conditioning.
2.	Erik Erikson		
3.	Jean Piaget	b.	Five environmental systems have continuing importance to development.
4.	Lev Vygotsky		
5.	Ivan Pavlov	c.	Language is a tool that helps children plan activities and solve problems.
6.	B. F. Skinner		
7.	Albert Bandura	d.	Behavior is strongly influenced by biology.
8.	Konrad Lorenz	e.	Believed personality has three structures: id, ego, superego.
9.	Urie Bronfenbrenner	f.	Gender differences, if found, are often unduly magnified.
10.	Florence Denmark	g.	Rewards and punishments shape individuals' development.
		h.	Suggested that humans develop in psychosocial stages.
		i.	People cognitively represent others' behavior and sometimes adopt it themselves.
		j.	Children actively construct their understanding of the world in four stages.

Self-Test C: True-False

T/F 1. Information based on personal experience is objective.

T/F 2. Scientific research is objective, systematic, and testable.

T/F 3. Cognitive theories describe development as primarily unconscious and as heavily colored by emotion.

T/F 4. A contribution of cognitive theories is their emphasis on the active construction of understanding.

T/F 5. Classical conditioning, operant conditioning, and social cognitive theory are all versions of the behavioral approach.

T/F 6. Ethology stresses that behavior is strongly influenced by biology, is tied to evolution, and is characterized by critical or sensitive periods.

T/F 7. Correlational research involves conducting an experiment, which can determine cause and effect.

T/F 8. The dependent variable is the manipulated, influential, experimental factor in an experiment.

T/F 9. Random assignment involves researchers assigning participants to experimental and control groups by chance.

T/F 10. Researchers' ethical responsibilities include obtaining informed consent, ensuring confidentiality, debriefing participants, and avoiding unnecessary deception.

Self-Test D: OLC

1. Jean Piaget says that children _____ their own cognitive worlds.

2. Which of the following theorists believed that knowledge is constructed through interaction with other people and objects in one's culture?
    a. Erikson
    b. Piaget
    c. Vygotsky
    d. Skinner

3. T/F   Social cognitive theorists believe that children acquire behaviors, thoughts, and feelings through observing the behavior of others.

4. T/F   Imprinting refers to the unique characteristic of an individual's fingerprints.

Essay Questions

1. One of your good friends works at a day-care center and, knowing you are taking a class in child development, he has asked you to talk to the parents about the types of behaviors they might expect from their children as they develop. He told you the parents have many questions and concerns about Sigmund Freud's theories and his emphasis on sexuality, but they have heard good things about Jean Piaget's theories. Your friend has also recently learned about the Russian educator Lev Vygotsky, and would like you to cover all three of these, plus any others you think are important. How would you inform these parents about these theories and what they can expect from their children?

2. Your professor has told the class that your final project for this class is to look at similarities and differences among children with respect to a variable (or variables) of your choice. She has said that you must consider at least three different aspects of diversity that you are studying in this child development class. She has also cautioned you about ethical concerns. What methods of data collection would you consider, which do you think would be best for purposes of the assignment, and why would that be the best? Explain which research method you would choose and why you would choose that design. Discuss how a cross-sectional design would be more practical for this assignment than a longitudinal design. Describe which elements of diversity you would explore and why, and discuss the particular ethical issues that would be a concern in this study.

Key to Self-Test A: Multiple Choice

1. b (LG1)	11. b (LG2)	21. a (LG3)
2. c (LG1)	12. d (LG2)	22. a (LG3)
3. a (LG1)	13. b (LG2)	23. a (LG3)
4. b (LG1)	14. d (LG2)	24. d (LG3)
5. a (LG2)	15. b (LG2)	25. a (LG3)
6. b (LG2)	16. a (LG2)	26. c (LG3)
7. d (LG2)	17. a (LG2)	27. c (LG3)
8. b (LG2)	18. b (LG2)	28. b (LG4)
9. b (LG2)	19. a (LG2)	29. d (LG4)
10. d (LG2)	20. b (LG2)	30. a (LG4)

Key to Self-Test B: Matching

1. e
2. h
3. j
4. c
5. a
6. g
7. i
8. d
9. b
10. f

Key to Self-Test C: True-False

1. False. Information based on personal experience tends to be subjective.
2. True
3. False. Cognitive theories emphasize conscious thoughts; psychoanalytic theories describe development as primarily unconscious and heavily colored by emotion.
4. True
5. True
6. True
7. False. Correlational research is aimed at describing the strength of the relationship between two or more events or characteristics; experimental research involves conducting experiments to determine cause and effect.
8. False. An independent variable is the manipulated, influential, experimental factor; a dependent variable is a factor that can change in an experiment in response to changes in the independent variable.
9. True
10. True

Key to Self-Test D: OLC

1. actively construct
2. c
3. True
4. False. Imprinting is the rapid, innate learning within a limited critical period of time that involves attachment to the first moving object seen.

Key to Essay Questions

1. A proper answer describes the basic elements of Freud's, Piaget's, and Vygotsky's theories. With regard to Freud, include the importance of unconscious motives to behavior, development of the three parts of the personality (id, ego, superego), and the developmental stages, noting what types of behavior one might expect in each (e.g., toilet training would take place most easily in the anal stage when the child is focusing on the anal region as a source of pleasure). Note that Piaget was interested in the process of *how* children think and saw children as little scientists who need a sufficiently simulating environment to develop their cognitive abilities. Discuss his four stages of development and his concepts of assimilation and accommodation. While Vygotsky (like Piaget) believed children actively construct their knowledge, he emphasized the importance of social relations in the child's development, and he said that a child's cognitive skills, to be understood, must be analyzed and interpreted developmentally (they build on each other); he also believed that cognitive skills are mediated by language. Suggest how parents might see evidence of these theories (e.g., when a child begins to "identify" with the same-sex parent by imitating that parent's behaviors) and how they can use the information for their child's healthy development (e.g., don't expect a child to be toilet trained until the child is ready). Then select one of the other theories and select those aspects of that theory that you think would be particularly helpful for parents in providing a healthy environment for their children.

2. First, you will need to discuss the different methods for collecting data and the different research methods, such as observation, interviews or surveys, standardized tests, psychophysiological

measures, and case studies, as well as looking at correlational studies and experiments, then explain which of these you would select and why that one would be the best for purposes of this short study. Compare cross-sectional and longitudinal designs and explain that having only a short period of time makes a cross-sectional design more appropriate. Then look at the different elements of diversity, such as age, gender, culture, and ethnicity and discuss how you would guard against bias in any of these, both in terms of the research itself and in analyzing and reporting your results. Finally, you need to address such ethical issues as informed consent (with any participants under age 18 you are required to obtain parental consent; it is also appropriate to ask the children to agree to participate and NEVER force any child into participating against his/her will), ensuring confidentiality, debriefing, and avoiding unnecessary deception of participants.

Research Project 1: How Well Do the Theories Fit?

Note that some of the theories in Chapter 2 pertain primarily to child development (e.g., Freud, Piaget), whereas others take more of a life-span perspective (e.g., Erikson, information processing). For this project, first chart the different theories presented in Chapter 2 so you have a clear idea of each of them (use charts in the text). Then choose a location where you can sit inconspicuously and, for 30 to 60 minutes, observe a child or a group of children. Accurately record what you observe, being careful to record only behaviors, oral communications, and interactions with others rather than your own inferences or interpretations. (Remember to observe only, do not interact or communicate.) On the basis of these observations, indicate the following:

1. What theory do you think best explains development of the child? Explain your reasons for choosing this theory.
2. What hypothesis would you make that could help you test development at this level? How would you go about testing that hypothesis?
3. What other theories do you think fit the behaviors you observed? How are they helpful? Explain how these fit.
4. Were there aspects of behavior not explained by the theory(ies) you chose? Explain.
5. What hypothesis would you make that could help you test development at this level? How would you go about testing that hypothesis?
6. What other theories do you think fit the behaviors you observed? Explain how these fit.
7. Based on your observations and application of the theory, do you believe that any of these theories is a "perfect fit"? Explain how they did fit and how they did not fit.
8. Describe how you would design your own theory to describe child development.

Research Project 2: Using What You Have Learned

Check out several service groups in your local community to see which of them may benefit from learning about the various developmental theories (e.g., Head Start programs, PTA, YMCA, Girl Scouts and Boy Scouts). Assess their particular needs (e.g., as parents, educators, teens who are likely someday to become parents) and ask what specific questions they have. Based on what you have learned in this chapter, supplemented by your own review of the literature (see Additional Internet Resources), prepare a talk for one or more of those groups to help them understand development from the perspective of the different theories presented. It will help to have charts and handouts that show each theory separately and then compare them on the issues you present.

Personal Application 1: Reflecting on What You Learned

Consider what you read in Chapter 2, then answer the following questions:

1. What information in this chapter did you already know?
2. How can/do you use that information in your own life?
3. What information in this chapter was totally new to you?
4. How can you use that new information in your own life?
5. What information in this chapter was different from what you previously believed?
6. How was this information different?
7. How do you account for the differences between what you believed and what you learned in the chapter?
8. What is the most important thing you learned from reading this chapter?

Personal Application 2: How Are the Theories Reflected Through Your Own Development?

Reflect on your own development and, using your own reflections and input from family members, reconstruct your development from as early as you can, up to who you are today. Consider the developmental theories discussed in the chapter and decide which best applies to your own experiences. Feel free to use more than one theory to describe different aspects of your development, or as overlapping explanations.

Aspect of Your Self	Theory (or Theories) and Explanation of How It Applies (or They Apply)
Personality traits (describe)	
Intellect (describe)	
Values and beliefs (describe)	
Behavior patterns (describe)	
Other (describe)	

1. When looking at this chart, what patterns do you see?
2. What theory or theories best describe how you came to be the person you are today?

3. Which theories don't fit your own development?
4. From looking at how the theories do or do not apply to your own development, how do they help you (or not help you) understand development generally?
5. How would you describe your own theory of development if you were to create one?
6. In what ways do you think theories are useful? In what ways might they limit how we view development or any other issue?

Internet Projects

Check out the McGraw-Hill Web site for this text (www.mhhe.com/santrockc9). You'll find numerous activities there, in particular, information that will help you research the answers and complete the exercises in the "Taking It to the Net" section at the end of the textbook chapter. Please note that all Web site addresses in this Study Guide have been checked and are correct at the time of publication; however, Web sites may be discontinued or addresses may change, so when you search a given site it may no longer be viable. If that occurs, I apologize for the inconvenience, and would appreciate you notifying me so I can make appropriate revisions in future editions of this Study Guide.

Internet Project 1: Psychological Theories and Other Hidden Treasures

Bookmark this site: http://psychclassics.yorku.ca/topic.htm or put it on a post-it attached to your computer or write it inside the front cover of this Study Guide or your textbook. This site, developed by Christopher D. Green at York University in Toronto, Canada, is a treasure trove of old classics in psychology. For purposes of this project, look at the different sections, from ancient to modern philosophical thought, the various theories presented, and other topics such as personality, perception, social psychology, and women and psychology. Thinking about the theories presented in Chapter 2 of your textbook, which ones do you find at this Web site, which aren't there, and what approaches do you see at this Web site that aren't discussed in the text? Why do you think some are included in the text and not on the Web site, or on the Web site and not in the text? The articles posted on this site are all classics in psychology. Read some of them, such as Watson's 1913 paper, "Psychology as the Behaviorist Views It," Binet's 1905 article on diagnosing the "intellectual level of subnormals" (revised 1916), and Freud's history of psychoanalysis. What can you learn from reading the original "masters"? How have they helped create the psychology of development that you are currently studying? Look, too, at the section on neuropsychology, noting that the first articles dates back to 1861. Did you realize that this field was almost 150 years old? Another article to savor is Harry Harlow's 1958 APA presidential address ("The Nature of Love")—you may want to read it now, or save it for Chapter 8 when you read about attachment. Keep going back to this site over and over again to learn what the founders of psychology have to teach us today.

Internet Project 2: Child Advocacy

Many different Web sources deal with the welfare of children. Some are based on empirical research, some are voices of advocacy, some are biased, and others more balanced. Even on the same site you might find a mixture. Explore some of these sites and describe each of them in terms of the type of information provided, the source of the information, how useful it is, how emotionally laden it is, how balanced or biased the site appears to be, and any other comments you might have concerning each site. Try some of the following:

- Street Kids International: http://www.streetkids.org/—Offers a first-hand look at children's issues around the world, including photo galleries.

- Children's Defense Fund: http://www.childrensdefense.org—The Web site for CDF, the organization headed by Marian Wright Edelman to promote child welfare (discussed in Chapter 1 of the text).
- National Alliance to End Homeless: http://www.endhomelessness.org/—A major resource on all aspects of homelessness, including homeless children.
- Society for Research in Child Development (SRCD): http://www.srcd.org—The Web site for SRCD, an organization whose purposes are to promote multidisciplinary research in the field of human development, to foster the exchange of information among scientists and other professionals of various disciplines, and to encourage applications of research findings.

Additional Internet Resources

American Psychological Association (APA): http://www.apa.org—Particularly, go to the "Public Publications" link and check out the "Database Info" and "Print and Media" offerings.

American Psychological Society (APS): http://www.psychologicalscience.org

Carl Jung: http://www.cgjungpage.org—Discusses Carl Jung, his writings and his theories, including the collective unconscious.

The Child Development Web site: http://childstudy.net—Information and tutorials on child development.

Erik Erikson's Eight Stages of Psychosocial Development:
http://facultyweb.cortland.edu/~ANDERSMD/ERIK/welcome.HTML—Offers a Web tutorial on Erikson's theory and work.

Developmental Psychology Links: http://www.socialpsychology.org/develop.htm

Psychological Resources on the Net: http://psych.hanover.edu/Krantz/lists.html—A fountain of information and useful links.

Jean Piaget Society: http://www.piaget.org—Explores Piaget's theories as well as cognitive differences in children and adults.

Scientific American: http://www.sciam.com—General scientific resource with some fascinating, free full-text articles and innumerable abstracts (full-text can be ordered for a fee).

Sigmund Freud and the Freud Archives: http://users.rcn.com/brill/freudarc.html—Discusses Freudian theories and explores the psychoanalytic paradigm.

CHAPTER 3: BIOLOGICAL BEGINNINGS

CHAPTER OUTLINE

WHAT IS THE EVOLUTIONARY PERSPECTIVE?

Natural Selection and Adaptive Behavior
Evolutionary Psychology

WHAT ARE THE GENETIC FOUNDATIONS OF DEVELOPMENT?

The Genetic Process
Genetic Principles
Chromosome and Gene-Linked Abnormalities

WHAT ARE SOME REPRODUCTIVE CHALLENGES AND CHOICES?

Prenatal Diagnostic Tests
Infertility and Reproduction Technology
Adoption

THE NATURE-NURTURE DEBATE: HOW DO HEREDITY AND ENVIRONMENT INTERACT?

Behavior Genetics
Heredity-Environment Correlations
Shared and Nonshared Environmental Experiences
The Epigenetic View
Conclusions About Heredity-Environment Interaction

REACH YOUR LEARNING GOALS

1. **WHAT IS THE EVOLUTIONARY PERSPECTIVE?**

   Natural Selection and Adaptive Behavior

   Evolutionary Psychology

2. **WHAT ARE THE GENETIC FOUNDATIONS OF DEVELOPMENT?**

   The Genetic Process

   Chromosomal and Gene-Linked Abnormalities

   Genetic Principles

3. **WHAT ARE SOME REPRODUCTION CHALLENGES AND CHOICES?**

   Prenatal Diagnostic Tests

   Adoption

   Infertility and Reproductive Technology

4. **HOW DO HEREDITY AND ENVIRONMENT INTERACT? THE NATURE-NURTURE DEBATE**

   Behavior Genetics

   Conclusions About Heredity-Environment Interaction

   Shared and Nonshared Environmental Experiences

   Heredity-Environment Correlations

   The Epigenetic View

Learning Goals

By the time you have completed this chapter, you should be able to reach the following goals:

1. Discuss the evolutionary perspective on development.

2. Describe what genes are and how they influence human development.

3. Identify some important reproductive challenges and choices.

4. Characterize some of the ways that heredity and environment interact to produce individual differences in development.

Explain the concepts of *natural selection* and *adaptive behavior*.	What is the role of *fertilization* in the reproductive process? What is a *zygote*?
What is the basis of *evolutionary psychology*?	What is the difference between a *genotype* and a *phenotype*?
Describe Bandura's notion of *bi-directional evolutionism*.	Explain the *dominant-recessive gene principle*.
What are *chromosomes*? How many do we (usually) have? Where do we get our chromosomes?	What is *X-linked inheritance*? When does *genetic imprinting* occur?
What is *DNA*? What are *genes*?	Explain the concept of *polygenic inheritance*.
Explain the processes of *mitosis* and *meiosis*.	Explain the connection between *chromosomal abnormalities* and *Down syndrome*.

In the process of reproduction, *fertilization* occurs when an egg and sperm fuse to create a single cell, a *zygote*. A *zygote* is a single cell formed through fertilization; the unpaired chromosomes from the egg and the sperm combine to form one set of paired chromosomes.	*Natural selection* is the evolutionary process that favors individuals of a species that are best adapted to survive and reproduce (Darwin). *Adaptive behavior* is behavior that promotes the organism's survival in the natural habitat (e.g., attachment between caregiver and baby assures the infant's closeness for feeding).
Genotype: the person's genetic heritage, the actual genetic material. *Phenotype*: observable characteristics; the way an individual's genotype is expressed in observed and measurable physical and psychological characteristics; for each genotype, a range of phenotypes can be expressed.	*Evolutionary psychology* emphasizes the importance of adaptation, reproduction, and "survival of the fittest." The evolutionary process of natural selection favors behaviors that increase reproductive success, i.e., the ability to pass on one's genes to the next generation.
Dominant-recessive gene principle: If one gene of a pair is dominant and one is recessive, the dominant gene exerts its effect, overriding the potential influence of the other, recessive gene. A recessive gene exerts its influence only if the two genes of a pair are both recessive.	*Bidirectional view:* environmental and biological conditions influence each other, e.g., evolutionary pressures created changes in biological structures for the use of tools, which enabled organisms to manipulate, alter, and construct new environmental conditions; then environmental innovations produced new selection pressures for specialized biological systems for consciousness, thought, and language.
X-linked inheritance: Inheritance of an altered (mutated) gene carried on the X chromosome. Males only have one X chromosome, so they have no "backup" copy and an alteration in the X chromosome may thus carry an X-linked disease. *Genetic imprinting*: Genes altered in either parent have different effects depending on whether they are inherited from the mother or the father.	*Chromosomes* are threadlike structures that come in 23 pairs, one member of each pair coming from each parent. Chromosomes contain the genetic substance deoxyribonucleic acid (DNA). Chromosomes are subdivided into smaller segments called genes.
Polygenic inheritance: A genetic principle describing the interaction of many genes to produce a particular characteristic (psychological disorders, for example, are not merely from one gene but from several that interact).	*DNA (deoxyribonucleic acid)*, a complex molecule containing genetic information; has a double-helix shape, like a spiral staircase. *Genes,* units of hereditary information, are short segments composed of DNA that direct cells to reproduce themselves and assemble proteins, which are the building blocks of cells and regulate the body's processes.
Chromosomal abnormalities: When a gamete is formed, the sperm and ovum do not have their normal set of 23 chromosomes. *Down syndrome*: Genetically transmitted form of mental retardation caused by an extra copy of chromosome 21.	*Mitosis*: The cell's nucleus (including the chromosomes) duplicates itself and divides. *Meiosis:* Cell division in which a cell from the testes or ovaries duplicates its chromosomes, then divides twice, forming four eggs or sperm, each of which has only half the genetic material of the parent cell (i.e., 23 unpaired chromosomes).

Describe the sex-linked chromosomal abnormalities of *Klinefelter syndrome*, *fragile X syndrome*, *Turner syndrome*, and *XYY syndrome*.	Discuss the three most common high-tech assisted reproduction techniques used in the United States.
What are the causes and results of the gene-linked abnormalities *phenylketonuria* and *sickle-cell anemia*?	Describe some of the positive and negative characteristics of adopted children and adolescents as compared with their non-adoptive siblings.
Describe the gene-linked abnormalities of *cystic fibrosis*, *spina bifida*, and *Tay-Sachs disease*.	What is *behavior genetics*? Compare the primary methods used by behavior geneticists to study the influence of heredity on behavior: *twin studies* and *adoption studies*.
What has been accomplished so far by the *Human Genome Project*? What are future hopes for the project?	Explain *passive genotype-environment correlations*; *evocative genotype-environment correlations*; and *active (niche-picking) genotype-environment correlations*.
What methods are commonly used for prenatal testing to determine whether a fetus is developing normally?	How do *shared environmental influences* differ from *nonshared environmental influences*?
Define *infertility* and explain its possible causes.	Discuss the *epigenetic view* in terms of heredity-environment interaction.

In vitro fertilization (IVF): Eggs and sperm combined in laboratory dish; if any egg is fertilized, resulting embryo(s) is (are) transferred to the woman's uterus. *Gamete intrafallopian transfer (GIFT)*: Doctor inserts eggs and sperm directly into a woman's fallopian tube. *Zygote intrafallopian transfer (ZIFT)*: Eggs are fertilized in laboratory, then resulting zygotes are transferred to a woman's fallopian tube.	*Klinefelter syndrome*: Males have extra X chromosome (XXY); testes are undeveloped, breasts are enlarged; *fragile X syndrome* results from constricted X chromosome, which often breaks, leads to mental deficiency; *Turner syndrome*: females miss an X chromosome (XO); short stature, webbed neck; *XYY syndrome*: males have extra Y; the belief that it contributes to violence/aggression is not supported.
The most positive outcomes are for children adopted early in life. Negative characteristics include more psychological, physical, and school-related problems, greater use of illicit drugs, greater tendency to engage in delinquent behavior. Positive outcomes include more prosocial behavior (e.g., altruism and support of others) and less chance of being withdrawn.	*Phenylketonuria (PKU)*: Inability to metabolize protein properly; untreated, it results in mental retardation and hyperactivity. *Sickle cell anemia*: Affects red blood cells and occurs most often in African Americans.
Behavior genetics: Studies the influence of heredity and environment on individual differences in human traits and development; *twin studies* compare behavioral similarity of identical twins with that of fraternal twins; *adoption studies* seek to discover whether the behavior and psychological characteristics of adopted children are more like their biological or adoptive parents (heredity vs. environment); also look at adoptive and biological siblings.	*Cystic fibrosis:* Glandular dysfunction that interferes with mucus production; breathing and digestion are hampered, shortening lifespan. *Spina bifida*: Neural tube disorder that causes brain and spine abnormalities. *Tay-Sachs disease*: Deceleration of mental and physical development caused by accumulation of lipids in the nervous system.
Passive genotype-environment correlation: Biological (genetically-related) parents rear their child. *Evocative genotype-environment correlation:* A child's characteristics elicit certain types of environments. *Active (niche-picking) genotype-environment correlation:* Children seek out environments they find compatible and stimulating.	The *Human Genome Project* found that humans have only about 20,000-25,000 genes. The Project has linked specific DNA variations with increased risk of many diseases and conditions. Among future hopes are identifying why genetic abnormalities occur and discovering cures for them.
Shared environmental influences: Siblings' common experiences, such as parents' personalities and intellectual orientation, family's socioeconomic status, and neighborhood in which they live. *Nonshared environmental influences*: Siblings' unique experiences within and outside the family that are not shared by another sibling; even experiences that occur within the family can be part of the "nonshared" environment.	*Ultrasound sonography*: High-frequency sound waves are directed into pregnant woman's abdomen. *Chorionic villi test sampling*: Sample of placenta removed between weeks 8 and 11. *Amniocentesis:* Sample of amniotic fluid withdrawn by syringe and tested for abnormalities (weeks 15–18). *Maternal blood test (triple screen)*: Assesses alpha-fetoprotein, estriol, and human chorionic gonadotropin for birth defects and Down syndrome.
The *epigenetic view*: Development is the result of an ongoing, bi-directional interchange between heredity and environment.	*Infertility* is the inability to conceive a child after 12 months of regular intercourse without contraception. Common causes for **women**: not ovulating, production of abnormal ova, blocked fallopian tubes; or disease that prevents implantation of the ova; **men**: low sperm production, sperm lack motility, or blocked passageways.

Self-Test A: Multiple-Choice Questions

1. Criticisms of the Minnesota identical twins study have included all of the following concerns, EXCEPT:
   a. the twins would be expected to have many similarities because of their shared genes.
   b. some of the separated twins were together several months prior to their adoption.
   c. some of the twins had been reunited prior to their testing.
   d. adoption agencies often place twins in similar homes.

2. The evolutionary process that favors individuals of a species that are best adapted to survive and reproduce is:
   a. genetic transmission.
   b. species superiority.
   c. natural selection.
   d. evolutionary exclusion.

3. _____ emphasizes the importance of adaptation, reproduction, and "survival of the fittest" in shaping behavior.
   a. Evolutionary psychology
   b. Social cognitive theory
   c. *The Bell Curve*
   d. The Human Genome Project

4. Which of the following is NOT an idea proposed by evolutionary developmental psychologists?
   a. Many aspects of childhood function as preparations for adulthood.
   b. Humans have an extended juvenile period so our brains can develop and learn the complexity of human social communities.
   c. Environmental and biological conditions influence each other.
   d. Evolved mechanisms are not always adaptive in contemporary society.

5. Albert Bandura:
   a. proposes a bidirectional view in which evolutionary pressures create biological changes, which, in turn, produce new selection pressures.
   b. proposes a one-sided evolutionism that suggests social behavior is the product of evolved biology.
   c. totally rejects evolutionary psychology.
   d. believes that just as evolution shapes our physical features, it also pervasively influences cognition, aggression, and mating patterns.

6. The nucleus of each human cell contains:
   a. 23 chromosomes.
   b. 46 chromosomes.
   c. 46 pairs of chromosomes.
   d. 23 sets of genes.

7. The specialized form of cell division in which a cell of the testes or ovaries duplicates its chromosomes, then divides twice (to form four eggs or sperm), with half of the genetic material of the parent cell is:
   a. reproduction.
   b. mitosis.
   c. meiosis
   d. separation.

8. Nancy is 5'5", weighs 120 lbs, has brown hair and green eyes, and she has an outgoing personality. These observable characteristics are manifestations of her
   a. biological destiny.
   b. genotype.
   c. phenotype.
   d. physiological inheritance.

9. Mort and Milly have brown eyes and their son Murray has blue eyes, so
   a. Mort must have two recessive genes for blue eyes.
   b. Milly must have two recessive genes for blue eyes.
   c. Mort and Milly must each have a recessive gene for blue eyes.
   d. either Mort or Milly (or both) is not Murray's biological parent.

10. _____ occurs when genes have differing effects depending on whether they are inherited from the mother or the father.
   a. Genetic imprinting
   b. X-linked inheritance
   c. Genetic mutation
   d. Hemophilia

11. The most recent research from the Human Genome Project suggests that there are about _____ human genes.
   a. 10,000 to 15,000
   b. 20,000 to 25,000
   c. 30,000 to 35,000
   d. 100,000

12. Cassandra has a form of mental retardation caused by the presence of an extra copy of chromosome 21. Cassandra has:
   a. Down syndrome.
   b. fragile X syndrome.
   c. Turner syndrome.
   d. Klinefelter syndrome.

13. Linden was born with an extra X chromosome. He has undeveloped testes and enlarged breasts. He would be diagnosed with:
   a. fragile X syndrome.
   b. Turner syndrome.
   c. XO syndrome.
   d. Klinefelter syndrome.

14. Which of the following is NOT a sex-linked chromosome abnormality?
   a. Klinefelter syndrome
   b. fragile X syndrome
   c. phenylketonuria
   d. XYY syndrome

15. D'Andre has a gene-linked abnormality that occurs most often in people of African descent. This disorder causes failure of misshapen red blood cells to carry oxygen to the body's cells and results in early death. He has:
   a. sickle-cell anemia.
   b. phenylketonuria (PKU).
   c. Down syndrome.
   d. Tay-Sachs disease.

16. Bob and Mary have sought the services of a genetic counselor, who will:
   a. help them decide how likely they are to have a genetically defective baby.
   b. administer in vitro fertilization.
   c. counsel them on how to raise a baby born with genetic abnormalities.
   d. suggest whether they should terminate Mary's pregnancy if tests show the fetus to have genetic defects.

17. Which prenatal diagnostic test involves removal of a small sample of the placenta to check for the presence of birth defects?
   a. the triple screen
   b. ultrasound
   c. amniocentesis
   d. chorionic villi sampling

18. Veronica and her husband have been engaging in regular intercourse without contraception for 6 months and have not yet conceived a child. Veronica's ob/gyn is most likely to tell her that:
   a. she is infertile.
   b. the problem may be due to her husband's low sperm motility.
   c. if, after 6 more months, she is still not pregnant, they can begin exploring why the couple is infertile.
   d. she most likely has a problem either with abnormal ova or with her fallopian tubes.

19. In an attempt to get pregnant, Sarah's egg and Leon's sperm were combined in a laboratory dish and after fertilization the embryo was transferred to Sarah's uterus. This process is called:
   a. zygote intrafallopian transfer.
   b. gamete intrafallopian transfer.
   c. in vitro fertilization.
   d. cloning.

20. Studies of children born using new reproductive technologies have found that these children:
    a. do not differ from naturally conceived children in various psychological characteristics.
    b. have higher rates of psychological problems than other children.
    c. have lower rates of psychological problems than other children.
    d. do not differ from naturally conceived children in psychological characteristics, but there are noted differences in other areas of development.

21. Research has found all of the following concerning adoption, EXCEPT:
    a. adopted adolescents are referred for psychological treatment two to five times as often as their non-adopted peers.
    b. adopted children show lower levels of prosocial behaviors than non-adopted children.
    c. the later adoption occurs, the more problems the adopted children have.
    d. the vast majority of adopted children adjust effectively.

22. Dick and Jane adopted a little girl they named Sally. Suggestions to follow to ensure Sally's healthy development as she moves from childhood through adolescence include all of the following EXCEPT:
    a. talk to Sally in simple ways about her adoption status when she begins to ask "Where did I come from?"
    b. recognize Sally's ambivalence about being adopted.
    c. provide her with support for coping with adoption-related tasks.
    d. try to make themselves look as perfect as possible to Sally.

23. Behavioral geneticists believe that behaviors are determined by:
    a. only biological factors.
    b. only environmental factors.
    c. biological factors at birth and environmental factors throughout life.

d. a continuous interaction between biological and environmental factors.

24. Dr. Fulbright believes that heredity is a critical component of specific behaviors he is studying. If he is correct in his assumption, we would expect to find the following from his twin studies:
    a. Dizygotic twins express the behavior more similarly than monozygotic twins.
    b. There is little similarity in expression of the behavior in either monozygotic or dizygotic twins.
    c. Monozygotic twins express the behavior more similarly than fraternal twins.
    d. Behavior is expressed similarly by monozygotic and dizygotic twins.

25. Dr. Green's major focus of research is in adoption studies. One way she may gather data is to compare:
    a. dizygotic twins with each other.
    b. children living in different adoptive families.
    c. adoptive siblings and biological siblings.
    d. monozygotic twins with dizygotic twins.

26. Cherie's parents encourage her musical abilities and include her in their chamber quartet. Cherie's appreciation and pursuit of music can be seen as a:
    a. shared environment.
    b. active (niche-picking) genotype-environment correlation.
    c. evocative genotype-environment correlation.
    d. passive genotype-environment correlation.

27. Children who are highly active, easily distracted, and move very fast often elicit adult attempts to quiet them down, punishment for lack of concentration, and angry warnings to slow down. This would describe which genotype-environment correlation?
    a. passive
    b. evocative
    c. active
    d. niche-picking

28. Larry and Anita grew up in the same home, with the same parents, and went to the same schools. Larry is two years older than his sister Anita. It is likely that the extreme differences in their personalities are due to:
    a. nonshared environmental experiences.
    b. shared environmental experiences.
    c. niche-picking experiences.
    d. heritability.

29. Professor Sentient adopts an epigenetic view of development. We would thus expect her to believe that development is the result of:
    a. primarily hereditary influences.
    b. primarily environmental influences.
    c. an ongoing, bi-directional interchange between heredity and the environment.
    d. the biological unfolding of developmental processes.

30. All of the following are criticisms of Judith Harris' assertions that parents have little impact on their children's and adolescents' behavior EXCEPT:
    a. There is a complex interaction between peer contexts and developmental trajectories.
    b. Peers actually have little influence on children and adolescents.
    c. In the early years parents play an important role in selecting children's peers.
    d. In the early years parents play an important role in influencing children's development.

Self-Test B: Matching

Match the following persons with the statement or theory that most closely reflects their perspective:

1. David Buss
2. Thomas Bouchard
3. Charles Darwin
4. Albert Bandura
5. Steven Jay Gould
6. Holly Ishmael
7. Judith Harris
8. Robert Plomin
9. Ellen Pinderhughes
10. Sandra Scarr

a. Describes three ways that heredity and environment are correlated.
b. Describes challenges and offers suggestions for adoptive parents at different points in their adoptive children's development.
c. What parents do does not make a difference in children's behavior.
d. Children reared in the same environment often have different personalities.
e. Conducted the Minnesota Study of Twins Reared Apart.
f. Rejects the notion of social behavior as the product of evolved biology.
g. Proposed the concepts of natural selection and survival of the fittest.
h. Genetic counseling combines science orientation and human contact.
i. Evolution pervasively influences our fears, our aggressions, and how we make decisions.
j. In most domains of human functioning, biology allows a broad range of cultural possibilities.

Self-Test C: True-False

T/F   1. Natural selection is the process that favors individuals of a species that are best adapted to survive and reproduce.

T/F   2. Ecological psychology holds that adaptation, reproduction, and "survival of the fittest" are important in shaping behavior.

T/F   3. Bandura argues that there is a bi-directional link between biology and environment.

T/F   4. The nucleus of each human cell contains 23 chromosomes.

T/F   5. It is impossible for two brown-eyed parents to give birth to blue-eyed offspring.

T/F   6. Down syndrome is the result of a chromosomal abnormality caused by the presence of an extra chromosome 21.

T/F   7. Other genes or developmental events can sometimes compensate for genetic disorders.

T/F   8. Adopted children are more likely than their non-adopted counterparts to have emotional and behavioral problems.

T/F   9. Behavior geneticists have found twin studies and adoption studies to be highly unreliable in determining the nature of heredity's influence on development.

T/F   10. Many behavior geneticists argue that differences in siblings' development are due to nonshared environmental experiences and heredity rather than shared environmental experiences.

Self-Test D: OLC

1. _____ refers to an individual's actual hereditary constitution, and _____ refers to an individual's observable and measurable characteristics.

2. All three of the Brodsky children grew up in the same house, went to the same school, and observed their parents' dedication to charitable work. These experiences constitute the children's
   a. shared environmental influences.
   b. nonshared environmental influences.
   c. niche-picking experiences.
   d. heritability.

3. T/F   Mitosis is the process by which cells divide into gametes for cell growth and repair.

4. T/F   The human genome is made up of many collaborative genes that work together.

Essay Questions

1. Imagine that you are a genetic counselor and a couple has come to you because they are concerned about whether they should have children. The wife is 40 years old and comes from an Eastern European Jewish background. Her husband is a 42-year-old African American. What potential problems might this couple's children have? How would you counsel them?

2. As you join some friends over coffee one day, you hear one of your male friends saying, "The evidence is really clear. Men are preprogrammed to have many women in their lives so they can ensure that their genes survive in the gene pool. And, besides that, men are preprogrammed to find the most attractive mate they can!" The women in the group immediately jump on this "sexist" notion and say that the evidence clearly demonstrates that only nonhuman animals are dominated by their hormones, and that humans are not preprogrammed in any way. Knowing you are taking this class in Child Development, they turn to you for your enlightened perspective. What do you tell them?

Key to Self-Test A: Multiple Choice

1. a (INTRO)	11. b (LG2)	21. b (LG3)
2. c (LG1)	12. a (LG2)	22. d (LG3)
3. a (L1G1)	13. d (LG2)	23. d (LG4)
4. c (LG1)	14. c (LG2)	24. c (LG4)
5. a (LG1)	15. a (LG2)	25. c (LG4)
6. b (LG2)	16. a (LG2)	26. d (LG4)
7. c (LG2)	17. d (LG3)	27. b (LG4)
8. c (LG2)	18. c (LG3)	28. a (LG4)
9. c (LG2)	19. c (LG3)	29. c (LG4)
10. a (LG2)	20. a (LG3)	30. b (LG4)

Key to Self-Test B: Matching

1. i
2. e
3. g
4. f
5. j
6. h
7. c
8. d
9. b
10. a

Key to Self-Test C: True/False

1. True
2. False. Ecological theory emphasizes the role of social contexts in development; the definition in this question refers to evolutionary theory.
3. True
4. False. The normal human cell nucleus contains 23 *pairs* of chromosomes, for a total of 46.
5. False. If both parents have recessive genes for blue eyes and both pass their recessive genes on to their child, then the child will have blue eyes.
6. True
7. True
8. True
9. False. Behavioral geneticists rely heavily on twin studies and adoption studies.
10. True.

Key to Self-Test D: OLC

1. genotype; phenotype
2. a
3. False. Mitosis is the process by which the cell's nucleus duplicates itself with two new cells being formed, each containing the same DNA as the parent cell, arranged in the same 23 pairs of chromosomes.
4. True

Key to Essay Questions

1. First you would need to look at the potential risk factors for Tay-Sachs (mother's background), Down syndrome (mother's age), and sickle-cell anemia (father's background). Discuss how you might do this (look at family history, genetic testing). In terms of counseling on how they should proceed, you would help them consider their own wishes and options (What kinds of tests would you suggest? What other options/procedures might be available?). What personal issues (e.g., the couple's ethical and religious beliefs) might you consider?

2. You will need to address the ideas proposed by evolutionary developmental psychologists, particularly the fact that humans have evolved differently from other animals. As a student of child development, you should also include such issues here as evolution of the extended juvenile period that is needed so the brain can develop and learn the complexity of human social communities, how some aspects of childhood are preparation for adulthood although others are not, and how some evolved mechanisms are not always adaptive in contemporary society. It is important also to bring up Bandura's bi-directional view, that environmental and biological conditions influence each other. Expand this to discuss what Scarr says about the three ways that heredity and environment are correlated (passive genotype-environment correlations, evocative genotype-environment correlations, and active [niche-picking] genotype-environment correlations) and how they change over time, as well as criticisms that Scarr's view overemphasizes heredity. Also, look at the shared and nonshared environmental experiences and address the epigenetic view, which emphasizes that (consistent with Bandura) development is the result of an ongoing, bi-directional interchange between heredity and the environment. This discussion is likely to conclude with a more balanced view that our sexual/mate selection is both biologically and socioculturally influenced.

Research Project 1: Heritability of Eye Color

To help you understand the concept of heritability (and the dominant-recessive genes principle), collect data from your own family and from one other family that is willing to participate. (Look only at blood relatives, not relatives by marriage.) Record the eye color of all family members, using the tables provided as follows, then answer the following questions:

1. What patterns did you notice for members of each family in terms of eye color?
2. Which eye color seems most prominent for each family?
3. Describe how the dominant-recessive genes principle would explain the patterns you found.
4. Are your observations consistent with what this principle would predict? Explain.

(Note that if there are fewer of one category of siblings, aunts, uncles, and/or cousins, but more of another, feel free to change category names, e.g., from "siblings" to "cousins.")

	Family 1	Family 2
# with brown eyes		
# with blue eyes		
# with green eyes		
# with other color (describe)		

Family 1		Family 2	
Family Member	**Eye Color**	**Family Member**	**Eye Color**
Self			
Mother		Mother	
Father		Father	
Maternal Grandmother		Maternal Grandmother	
Maternal Grandfather		Maternal Grandfather	
Paternal Grandmother		Paternal Grandmother	
Paternal Grandfather		Paternal Grandfather	
Sibling		Sibling	
Sibling		Sibling	
Sibling		Sibling	
Maternal Aunt		Maternal Aunt	
Paternal Aunt		Paternal Aunt	
_____ Aunt		_____ Aunt	
Maternal Uncle		Maternal Uncle	
Paternal Uncle		Paternal Uncle	
_____ Uncle		_____ Uncle	
Maternal Cousin		Maternal Cousin	
Maternal Cousin		Maternal Cousin	
Paternal Cousin		Paternal Cousin	
Paternal Cousin		Paternal Cousin	

Research Project 2: Charting Chromosomal and Gene-Linked Abnormalities

Referring back to the section on chromosomal and gene-linked abnormalities, chart each of them, indicating the description, risk factors (e.g., mother's age, parents' ethnic background), treatment, incidence, and type (i.e., chromosome, sex-linked, gene-linked). Note that most, but not all, of this information is included in tables in the chapter. What other information would be helpful for you to know about each of these disorders? If you were counseling a couple who were planning to have a baby, what specific information would you need to elicit from them to ensure the best chances for a healthy child?

Disorder	Description	Type	Risk Factors	Incidence	Treatment
Down syndrome					
Klinefelter syndrome					
Fragile X syndrome					
Phenylketonuria					
Sickle-cell anemia					
Diabetes					
Hemophilia					
Huntington disease					
Tay-Sachs disease					
Cystic fibrosis					
Spina bifida					
Others					

Personal Application 1: Reflecting on What You Learned

Consider what you read in Chapter 3, then answer the following questions:

1. What information in this chapter did you already know?

2. How can/do you use that information in your own life?

3. What information in this chapter was totally new to you?

4. How can you use that new information in your own life?

5. What information in this chapter was different from what you previously believed?

6. How was this information different?

7. How do you account for the differences between what you believed and what you learned in the chapter?

8. What is the most important thing you learned from reading this chapter?

Personal Application 2: How Can This Chapter Help You Understand Your Own Reproductive Choices?

Reflect on your own background and, using your own reflections and input from family members, reconstruct your development from as early as you can remember up to who you are today. Consider the research and theories discussed in Chapter 3 and decide which best apply to your own experiences. Incorporate more than just one theory or research study to describe different aspects of your personal development, or as overlapping explanations.

Aspect of Your Self	Arguments Presented	Describe How the Information Applies to Your Life
Personality traits (describe)		
Intellect (describe)		
Physical characteristics (e.g., height, eye color) (describe)		
Physical disorders (e.g., diabetes, Klinefelter syndrome) (describe)		
Other (describe)		

From looking at your own chart, based on the information in the chapter (and any other information you may have gathered), explain:

1. Does the information in the chapter and in your chart provide you with a better understanding of yourself? In what way?
2. How can you use this information in your own life?
3. In what way (if any) will this information affect your decisions concerning family planning?
4. Was any of this information frightening to you, or did it make you feel less fearful? Explain.
5. What other insights have you gained from preparing this chart?

Internet Projects

Check out the McGraw-Hill Web site for this text (www.mhhe.com/santrockc9). You'll find numerous activities there, in particular, information that will help you research the answers and complete the exercises in the "Taking It to the Net" section at the end of the textbook chapter. Please note that all Web site addresses in this Study Guide have been checked and were correct at the time of publication; however, Web sites may be discontinued or addresses may change, so when you search a given site it may no longer be viable. If that occurs, I apologize for the inconvenience and would appreciate you notifying me so I can make appropriate revisions in future editions of this Study Guide.

Internet Project 1: Biological Beginnings

Go to http://www.webmd.com and do a search for "reproductive challenges." How many links did you find? How many of those links referred you to professional journal articles? How many were about an individual involved in this area? How diverse were the results you found? What kind of information did you find that expanded on or was not included in the chapter (there is NO WAY an author can possibly include ALL information in a single textbook chapter)? Compare the information you got from these different sources of information. What other types of links came up on the screen? How helpful was the information you found? How can this information help you make wise decisions in your own life, or help you provide useful information for a friend or family member?

Internet Project 2: Prenatal Testing

Go to http://www.howstuffworks.com/prenatal-testing.htm[1] and check out the section on how prenatal testing works. What different types of tests did you learn about? Which tests were discussed in the text? Were there tests that were not presented in the text? When would you use each of these tests, and why would each be used? Were there chromosome or gene-linked disorders discussed at the Web site that weren't in the text? Describe them. Select a link that interests you from the end of the article and summarize what you learned from that site.

Additional Internet Resources

American Psychological Association (APA): http://www.apa.org—Particularly, go to the "Public Publications" link and check out the "Print and Media" offerings.

American Psychological Society (APS): http://www.psychologicalscience.org.

The Child Development Web site: http://childstudy.net—Provides information on children's topics; encourages social activism.

Genetic Science Learning Center: http://gslc.genetics.utah.edu—Offers activities, notification of upcoming events and workshops for teachers, and downloadable *Teaching Tips and Classroom Resources*, the GSLC newsletter. The main Web site offers online multimedia tutorials and activities covering topics such as basic genetics, chromosomes, genetic disorders, cloning, stem cells, and genetic testing.

---

[1] How Stuff Works is a wonderful site that gives clear explanations about how almost anything you can think of works. If something you're interested in is not on the site, suggest it and they will most likely research it and publish what they've learned on their site.

Human Genome Project Information: http://www.ornl.gov/hgmis—Provides the latest updates on the Human Genome Project with excellent graphics and detailed explanations of this fascinating area of study.

Ivillage Web site for health issues provides links to a variety of different topics including reproductive/gynecological issues and sexually transmitted diseases at http://www.ivillage.com.

National Down Syndrome Society: http://www.ndss.org—Provides comprehensive, online information about Down syndrome, including education, research, and advocacy.

Nature Genome Web site: http://www.nature.com/genomics—Presents a variety of sources on genome projects—human and nonhuman—around the world.

National Institutes of Health: http://www.nih.gov—Starting point for getting into any subagency of NIH.

National Institute of Mental Health: http://www.nimh.nih.gov—Excellent resource for policy statements, NIMH research, and grants.

Professor Lawrence M. Hinman of University of San Diego: http://ethics.acusd.edu/applied/bioethics/index.asp—Another excellent site that provides good subject matter for discussion on the ethical and legal issues surrounding reproductive technology, including cloning.

Scientific American: http://www.sciam.com—General scientific resource.

Serendip: http://serendip.brynmawr.edu/serendip—Interactive exhibits, articles, links on the topics covered in this chapter.

Society for Research in Child Development (SRCD): http://www.srcd.org is the Web site for SRCD, an organization whose purposes are to promote multidisciplinary research in the field of human development, to foster the exchange of information among scientists and other professionals of various disciplines, and to encourage applications of research findings.

University of Chicago Press Journals: http://www.journals.uchicago.edu/pub-alpha.html offers links to numerous professional journals.

University of Kansas Medical Center, Genetics Education Center: http://www.kumc.edu/gec—Excellent resource on Human Genome Project as well as exhibits, links, articles, search engines, and other useful information on genetics.

CHAPTER 4: PRENATAL DEVELOPMENT

CHAPTER OUTLINE

WHAT IS THE COURSE OF PRENATAL DEVELOPMENT?

The Germinal Period
The Embryonic Period
The Fetal Period

WHAT ARE EXPECTANT PARENTS' EXPERIENCES LIKE DURING PRENATAL DEVELOPMENT?

Confirming the Pregnancy and Calculating the Due Date
The Three Trimesters and Preparation for the Birth
The Expectant Mother's Nutrition, Weight Gain, and Exercise
Culture and Prenatal Care

WHAT ARE SOME POTENTIAL HAZARDS TO PRENATAL DEVELOPMENT?

Some General Principles
Prescription and Nonprescription Drugs
Psychoactive Drugs
Environmental Hazards
Infectious Diseases
Incompatible Blood Types
Other Parental Factors

REACH YOUR LEARNING GOALS

1. **WHAT IS THE COURSE OF PRENATAL DEVELOPMENT?**

The Germinal Period	The Fetal Period
The Embryonic Period	

2. **WHAT ARE EXPECTANT PARENTS' EXPERIENCES LIKE DURING PRENATAL DEVELOPMENT?**

Confirming the Pregnancy and Calculating the Due Date	The Expectant Mother's Nutrition, Weight Gain, and Exercise
The Three Trimesters and Preparation for the Baby's Birth	Culture and Prenatal Care

3. **WHAT ARE SOME POTENTIAL HAZARDS TO PRENATAL DEVELOPMENT?**

Some General Principles	Psychoactive Drugs	Infectious Diseases
	Other Parental Factors	
Prescription and Nonprescription Drugs	Environmental Hazards	Incompatible Blood Types

Learning Goals

By the time you have completed this chapter, you should be able to reach the following goals:

1. Discuss the three periods of prenatal development.
2. Characterize expectant parents' experiences during prenatal development.
3. Describe potential hazards during prenatal development.

Describe the *germinal period* of prenatal development.	Describe the changes that occur during the *fetal period*.
Differentiate between the *blastocyst* and *trophoblast* and relate them to the germinal period. Explain *implantation*.	What are the signs of pregnancy? How is pregnancy tested? How is the due date calculated?
Describe the *embryonic period* of prenatal development and the three layers of the embryo.	Describe the major events during the *first trimester* of pregnancy.
Define the *amnion* and its importance during prenatal development.	Describe the major events during the *second trimester* of pregnancy.
What are the *placenta* and the *umbilical cord*?	Describe the major events during the *third trimester* of pregnancy.
Explain *organogenesis*.	How does the pregnant mother's "profile" change during the two weeks before the baby's birth?

During the *fetal period* (2 to 9 months after conception), fetus becomes active, moves its arms and legs, opens and closes mouth, moves head, skin structures form, coordinates movements, respiration and organ systems become regulated; grows from less than 1 inch to about 20 inches and from less than 1 ounce to about 7 pounds.	*Germinal period*: First two weeks after conception: creation of zygote, continued cell division, attachment of zygote to uterine wall.
Early signs of pregnancy: Missed menstrual period, breast changes, fullness/aching in lower abdomen, fatigue, drowsiness, faintness, nausea/vomiting, frequent urination, increased vaginal secretions. *Tests*: Check urine/blood for HCG. *Due date calculated* not from time of conception, but from first day of woman's last menstrual period (average of 280 days or 40 weeks).	*Blastocyst*: Inner layer of cells that develops during the germinal period; later develops into embryo. *Trophoblast*: Outer layer of cells that develops during the germinal period; later provides nutrition and support for the embryo. *Implantation*: About 10 days after conception, the zygote attaches to the uterine wall.
First trimester: Prenatal organ systems are formed and begin to function; for pregnant woman, a time of physical and emotional adjustment to pregnancy; fatigue, and possibly nausea and vomiting ("morning sickness").	*Embryonic period*: 2 to 8 weeks after conception; rate of cell differentiation intensifies, support systems for cells form, organs appear. *Endoderm*: Inner layer of cells that develop into digestive and respiratory systems; *ectoderm*: outer layer becomes nervous system, sensory receptors, skin parts; *mesoderm*: middle layer becomes circulatory, excretory and reproductive systems, bones and muscles.
Second trimester: mother's nausea and fatigue lessen or disappear; uterus expands into abdominal cavity; fundus reaches the navel; colostrum present in the milk glands; pregnancy may become more of a reality for the mother's partner.	*Amnion*: Life-support system; a bag or envelope containing a clear fluid (*amniotic fluid*) in which the developing embryo floats; amniotic fluid provides temperature, humidity, and pressure control and helps cushion and protect the fetus against physical shocks and trauma.
Third trimester: Mother's uterus expands to just below her breastbone; crowding by uterus and high levels of progesterone may cause heartburn and indigestion, shortness of breath; abdominal pressure; decreased blood flow and progesterone may cause varicose veins, hemorrhoids, swollen ankles. Adjustments in sexual activity.	*Placenta*: Life-support system consisting of a disc-shaped group of tissues in which small blood vessels from mother and offspring intertwine (but do not join). *Umbilical cord*: Life-support system with two umbilical arteries and one umbilical vein connecting baby to placenta.
About two weeks before birth: Fetus descends into pelvic cavity; mother may feel less pressure on diaphragm—easier to breathe and eat; with head pressing on mother's bladder, she may need to urinate more often; mother may feel "nesting urge," resulting in preparing for baby's arrival; toward end of pregnancy, Braxton Hicks contractions increase; as birth nears, cervix is softer and thinner.	*Organogenesis*: The process of organ formation that takes place during the first two months of prenatal development.

What are normal and ideal weight gain patterns during pregnancy? How do the pregnant woman's nutritional needs change?

Describe the disorder that a child may acquire if the mother consumes alcohol during pregnancy.

How much exercise and what type of exercise may be undertaken during pregnancy?

What are the potential effects on the unborn child when the pregnant mother smokes or is exposed to *nicotine*, is addicted to *heroin* or is treated with *methadone*, or uses *marijuana*, *methamphetamine*, or *cocaine*?

What are some factors that may explain why the United States has a higher percentage of low-birthweight infants than other industrialized nations?

What *environmental toxins* have been shown to endanger the fetus and what problems might they cause?

Describe some of the areas of cultural variation in prenatal care. Why are these considered important to health care providers in the United States?

What are the potential effects for the child when the mother is exposed to the following diseases: *rubella*, *syphilis*, *genital herpes*, *AIDS*?

Explain the concept of *teratology*. What is a *teratogen*? What factors influence the severity of damage and type of defect that occurs?

What role do *blood type* and *Rh factor* play in the health of a woman's offspring?

What are some of the prescription drugs that function as teratogens? What is the controversy with the drug *thalidomide*? Which nonprescription drugs can be harmful to the unborn child?

What parental behaviors and characteristics are of particular importance during the prenatal period?

Fetal alcohol syndrome (FAS): A cluster of abnormalities appearing in the offspring of mothers who drink alcohol during pregnancy; may result in facial deformities, defective limbs, face, and heart; below-average intelligence/mental retardation;100% avoidable by avoiding alcohol during pregnancy. Even moderate drinking can result in children being less attentive and alert.	*Optimal weight gain*: Depends on mother's height, bone structure, prepregnant nutritional state; best outcomes average 25 to 35 lbs; 2 to 4.4 lbs in first trimester, 1 lb/week thereafter. *Nutrition:* Eat at least 3 small meals/day; snack on fruit, cheese, milk; 4 to 6 8-oz glasses of water, 8 to 10 8-oz cups of fluid daily; greatly increased need for protein, iron, vitamin D, folacin, calcium, phosphorous, magnesium.
Nicotine: Fetal/neonatal death; preterm births, low birth weight, respiratory problems, SIDS; *cocaine*: low length/length; neurological/cognitive deficits (may be from associated factors); *marijuana*: impaired attention, smaller babies, cognitive deficits; *methamphetamine*: infant mortality, low birthweight, developmental/behavioral problems; *heroin/ methadone*: behavioral difficulties and withdrawal.	*Exercise*: Depends on course of pregnancy, mother's fitness and usual activity level; low impact (e.g., swimming) is safer than jogging; short time intervals; decrease intensity as pregnancy progresses; avoid prolonged overheating; avoid high-risk activities; warm up, stretch before exercising, cool down, lie on left side 10 min. after; stop/see MD if dizzy etc.; wear supportive shoes/bra; reduce activity last 4 weeks.
Environmental toxins: radiation: gene mutation; chromosomal abnormalities; pollutants & toxic wastes (e.g., carbon monoxide and lead) affect mental development; mercury: brain & nervous system defects; PCBs: smaller, preterm infants, slow reactions, less effective short term memory, lower verbal intelligence & comprehension.	Pregnant women in the U.S. do not receive the uniform prenatal care that women in many Scandinavian and Western European countries receive; no national policy of health care to assure high-quality assistance for pregnant women; many women do not receive prenatal care in first trimester; some receive none at all.
Rubella: Mental retardation, blindness, deafness, heart defects. *Syphilis:* Damages organs after formed; eye lesions (can cause blindness); skin lesions; at birth: CNS and gastrointestinal tract problems. *Genital herpes:* May cause death, brain damage. *AIDS*: Can transmit HIV to child.	Cultural variations in prenatal care: If pregnancy is viewed as a natural occurrence, prenatal care may be a low priority. Health care providers need to assess whether cultural practices pose a threat to the expectant mother and her fetus: prevalence of traditional home care remedies and folk beliefs, importance of indigenous healers, influence of professional health care workers.
Incompatible blood type is a risk to prenatal development. If pregnant woman's *Rh factor* is positive and fetus's is negative, antibodies in the mother may attack the fetus, resulting in miscarriage or stillbirth, anemia, jaundice, heart defects, brain damage, or death soon after birth.	*Teratology*: The field of study that investigates the causes of birth defects. *Teratogen*: Agent (e.g., environmental hazards, drugs, exposure to disease) causing a birth defect. The dose, time of exposure to a particular agent, and genetic susceptibility influence the severity of damage and type of defect that occurs.
Mother's nutrition: Malnourished: infant malformation, low birthweight (obese: late fetal death); lack of folic acid: neural tube defects. *Mother's age*: Infants born to adolescents are often premature, high mortality rates; after 30: increased risk of Down syndrome and low birthweight; fetal death increases for women over 35. *Father's age*: Risk of birth defects, Down syndrome, dwarfism, Marfan syndrome. *High stress*: Prematurity, irritability, slow adjustment.	*Prescription drugs* that can be harmful are antibiotics, antidepressants, certain hormones, and Accutane. *Thalidomide*, a tranquilizer used in 1961, often resulted in stunted fetal limb growth; banned in the U.S., it is now being used for other diseases, making it available and again potentially harmful. *Non-prescription drugs* such as diet pills, aspirin, and caffeine can also be harmful to the unborn child.

Self-Test A: Multiple-Choice Questions

1. The period of prenatal development that occurs in the first two weeks after conception is called the _____ period.
    a. fetal
    b. germinal
    c. embryonic
    d. blastocystic

2. The inner layer of cells that develops during the germinal period is called the:
    a. blastocyst.
    b. zygote.
    c. trophoblast.
    d. embryo.

3. Which of the following events does NOT occur during the embryonic period?
    a. rate of cell differentiation intensifies
    b. fingernails and toenails form
    c. organs appear
    d. support systems for the cells form

4. The _____ produces internal body parts.
    a. exoderm
    b. ectoderm
    c. mesoderm
    d. endoderm

5. A skin defect might be traced to an initial problem with the embryo's _____ cells.
    a. mesoderm
    b. ectoderm
    c. microderm
    d. endoderm

6. Which statement is NOT true?
    a. The placenta and umbilical cord keep all harmful substances away from the fetus.
    b. Most bacteria are too large to pass through the placental wall.
    c. Oxygen, water, salt, food from the mother's blood, carbon dioxide, and the embryo's digestive wastes pass back and forth through the umbilical cord.
    d. No one completely understands the mechanisms governing transfer across the placental barrier.

7. During the second trimester, the amniotic sac is filled mainly with:
    a. blood.
    b. mucus.
    c. urine.
    d. air.

8. The process of organ formation that takes place during the first two months of prenatal development is called:
    a. germinal development.
    b. genesis.
    c. organogenesis.
    d. fetal development.

9. A growth spurt in the fetus's lower body parts occurs during the _____ month.
    a. seventh
    b. sixth
    c. fifth
    d. fourth

10. What is the first time a fetus has a chance of surviving outside the womb?
    a. three months
    b. five months
    c. seven months
    d. eight and a half months

11. When Abigail takes a pregnancy test, her urine or blood will be checked for:
    a. estrogen.
    b. progesterone.
    c. acetylcholine.
    d. human chorionic gonadotropin.

12. Raul and Elena learn that Elena is pregnant. Their "due date":
    a. is calculated according to the first date of Elena's last menstrual period.
    b. cannot be calculated because they are not sure when the baby was conceived.
    c. is calculated according to the first time they had sexual intercourse after Elena's last menstrual period.
    d. has a one-month range, depending on when the baby was conceived.

13. Which of the following is NOT typical of changes a woman experiences during her first trimester of pregnancy?
    a. nausea and vomiting
    b. enlargement of breasts
    c. increased mood stability
    d. increase in spontaneous sexual activity

14. The time for an expectant mother to prepare her breasts for breast feeding is:
    a. before she becomes pregnant.
    b. during the first trimester.
    c. during the second trimester.
    d. immediately after the baby is born.

15. Maternal weight gains that are associated with the best reproductive outcomes are:
    a. 10 to 20 pounds.
    b. 25 to 35 pounds.
    c. 30 to 45 pounds.
    d. 35 to 60 pounds.

16. Marybeth is having a normal pregnancy. She should follow all of these guidelines for exercise EXCEPT:
    a. exercise for short time intervals.
    b. avoid prolonged overheating.
    c. warm up and stretch before exercising, cool down afterwards.
    d. lie on her right side for 10 minutes after exercising.

17. The high incidence of low-birthweight occurrence in the United States is explained by all of the following, EXCEPT:
    a. pregnant women in the United States do not receive the uniform prenatal care that women in other countries receive.
    b. the quality of care provided by medical practitioners in the United States is substandard.
    c. more than 25% of American women of prime child-bearing age do not have insurance to cover hospital costs.
    d. The United States lacks a national health care policy to assure high-quality assistance for pregnant women.

18. Maria Jesus is from a strongly traditional Mexican-American family. A health care worker working with her during pregnancy should not be surprised if Maria Jesus seeks advice from:
    a. an herbalist.
    b. a medicine woman.
    c. a curandero.
    d. a root doctor.

19. Which phrase best defines a *teratogen*?
    a. a life-support system that protects the fetus
    b. an agent that causes birth defects
    c. an abnormality of infants in alcoholic mothers
    d. an agent that stimulates the formation of organs

20. The severity of the damage and the type of defect that occurs from a teratogen is influenced by all of the following, EXCEPT:
    a. location of the teratogenic agent.
    b. dose of the teratogenic agent.
    c. time of exposure.
    d. genetic susceptibility.

21. Daria was born with no arms and with fingers jutting out of her shoulders because her mother had taken a prescribed drug for morning sickness that was later banned in the U.S. in 1961. This drug is:
    a. thalidomide.
    b. bromide.
    c. marijuana.
    d. Vioxx.

22. To be absolutely sure that there will be no negative effects on the fetus, what does the text suggest in terms of guidelines for alcohol use during pregnancy?
    a. no more than one 4-ounce glass of wine a day; no other alcoholic beverages
    b. no more than one 4-ounce glass of any alcoholic beverage a day
    c. no more than three 4-ounce glasses of wine or one 4-ounce glass of other alcoholic beverage a day
    d. no alcohol during pregnancy

23. Audrey and her husband each smoke a pack of cigarettes a day. They should be concerned that their unborn child is at risk for all of the following EXCEPT:
    a. deformed limbs.
    b. respiratory problems.
    c. sudden infant death syndrome (SIDS).
    d. cancer.

24. Marijuana is not recommended for use by pregnant women because:
    a. it has been linked with cognitive and attention impairments.
    b. it may result in large birthweight babies.
    c. it can cause addiction in the newborn baby.
    d. it has been linked to tremors, irritability, and disturbed sleep in newborn babies.

25. All of the following are environmental hazards to prenatal development, EXCEPT:
    a. NSAIDs.
    b. PCBs.
    c. radiation.
    d. prolonged exposure to heat.

26. Maternal diseases or infections can produce defects in the baby by:
    a. lowering the mother's immune system.
    b. crossing the placental barrier.
    c. interfering with delivery of nutrients.
    d. reducing the amount of oxygen flowing to the baby.

27. Sally has AIDS. To reduce the risk of transmitting HIV to her unborn baby, she should:
    a. have a cesarean delivery.
    b. refrain from sex during her pregnancy.
    c. take AZT during pregnancy and delivery.
    d. take megadoses of vitamins during pregnancy.

28. When a woman has a negative Rh factor in her blood, her partner has a positive Rh factor, and the fetus's blood is Rh positive:
    a. antibodies in the mother provide the fetus with extra immune substances that most other children do not have.
    b. antibodies in the mother may attack the fetus, resulting in miscarriage, anemia, heart defects, brain damage, or death soon after birth.
    c. the first pregnancy will be at-risk, but by subsequent pregnancies the mother will have developed antibodies to protect the fetus.
    d. the mother will need to have a blood transfusion after each Rh positive child is born.

29. With regard to how a pregnant woman's emotional state affects the unborn child, researchers have found that:
    a. this has largely been an old wives' tale.
    b. certain frightening experiences can leave birthmarks on the child.
    c. women under stress are about four times more likely to have longer pregnancies.
    d. women under stress are about four times more likely to deliver prematurely.

30. With regard to prenatal development, Santrock suggests that it is important to:
    a. keep in mind that for most pregnancies, prenatal development does not go awry.
    b. be constantly vigilant to avoid any and all types of behaviors or environments that could harm the unborn child.
    c. take a somewhat negative perspective of potential problems in order to avoid any harm to the unborn child.
    d. take the most positive perspective possible and minimize any concerns about potential problems in order to avoid harm to the unborn child.

Self-Test B: Matching

Match the following terms with the statement that matches best:

1. germinal period
2. embryonic period
3. fetal period
4. endoderm
5. mesoderm
6. ectoderm
7. teratogen
8. fetal alcohol syndrome
9. Christine Dunkel-Schetter
10. National Institute of Drug Abuse

a. Abnormalities in offspring of mothers who drink alcohol heavily during pregnancy.
b. Mothers' marijuana use during pregnancy produces smaller babies.
c. An agent that causes birth defects.
d. Linked premature births with high level of mother's stress.
e. Developmental period from two to eight weeks after conception.
f. The inner layer of cells, which develops into digestive and respiratory systems.
g. The middle layer of cells, which becomes the circulatory, excretory, and reproductive systems and the bones and muscles.
h. The outer layer of cells, which becomes the nervous system, sensory receptors, and skin parts.
i. Developmental period that begins two months after conception and lasts through birth.
j. Two week period of development after conception.

Self-Test C: True-False

T/F 1. The germinal period is from conception until about 10 to 14 days later.

T/F 2. The embryonic period is the longest period of development.

T/F 3. During the second trimester, fetal urine is the main source of amniotic fluid.

T/F 4. The length of pregnancy is computed from the last time the woman had sexual intercourse.

T/F 5. The nausea that many women experience during the first trimester occurs primarily in the morning.

T/F 6. After exercising, a pregnant woman should lie on the left side for 10 minutes to improve circulation and promote placental function.

T/F 7. Among the industrialized nations, the United Stateshas one of the lowest rates of low-birthweight infants.

T/F 8. A teratogen is any agent that causes birth defects.

T/F 9. The U.S. Surgeon General has determined that a pregnant woman can safely consume one alcoholic drink each day during her pregnancy without harming her unborn child.

T/F 10. High stress in the mother during pregnancy is linked to premature delivery.

Self-Test D: OLC

1. _____ takes place when one sperm from the male unites with an _____ from the female.
2. How does the placenta/umbilical cord life-support system prevent harmful bacteria from invading a fetus?
   a. Most bacteria are too large to pass through the placenta's walls.
   b. The placenta generates antibodies that attack and destroy bacteria.
   c. Most bacteria become trapped in the maze of blood vessels of the umbilical cord.
   d. No one understands how this life-support system keeps bacteria out.
3. T/F   Fetal alcohol syndrome can produce abnormalities in the babies of mothers who drink alcohol heavily during pregnancy.
4. T/F   Cigarette smoking by pregnant women can lead to preterm births and lower birthweights.

Essay Questions

1. The principal of a local high school asks you to talk to the senior class about potential hazards to prenatal development. She asks that you honestly discuss alcohol and other drugs as well as environmental hazards and maternal diseases, including the different agents that can cause problems, the problems they may cause, and how these problems can be avoided. What will you tell the students about teratogens and prenatal care?
2. One of your cousins has recently gotten married and is now talking about becoming pregnant. She knows you are taking this class in child development and asks for your input on what she should expect to happen to her during pregnancy, and what she should do to ensure that her baby is healthy. What advice can you give her?

Key to Self-Test A: Multiple Choice

1. b (LG1)	11. d (LG2)	21. a (LG3)
2. a (LG1)	12. a (LG2)	22. d (LG3)
3. b (LG1)	13. c (LG2)	23. a (LG3)
4. d (LG1)	14. c (LG2)	24. a (LG3)
5. b (LG1)	15. b (LG2)	25. a (LG3)
6. a (LG1)	16. d (LG2)	26. b (LG3)
7. c (LG1)	17. b (LG2)	27. c (LG3)
8. c (LG1)	18. c (LG2)	28. b (LG3)
9. d (LG1)	19. b (LG3)	29. d (LG3)
10. c (LG1)	20. a (LG3)	30. a (LG3)

Key to Self-Test B: Matching

1. j
2. e
3. i
4. f
5. g
6. h
7. c
8. a
9. d
10. b

Key to Self-Test C: True/False

1. True
2. False. The embryonic period lasts from about two to eight weeks after conception.
3. True
4. False. The length of pregnancy is computed from the first day of the woman's last menstrual period.
5. False. "Morning sickness" can occur at any time of the day.
6. True
7. False. Among the industrialized nations, the United States has one of the highest rates of low-birthweight infants.
8. True

9. False. It is suggested that pregnant women drink no alcohol during their pregnancy (this also extends to when they are breast feeding their babies).
10. True

Key to Self-Test D: CD

1. Fertilization; ovum
2. a
3. True
4. True

Key to Essay Questions

1. An appropriate answer should include alcohol and other drugs, such as nicotine, marijuana, and cocaine, and their potential effects on the developing embryo/fetus, noting at which stage of development particular organs are most vulnerable (note that no amount of alcohol is considered safe at any point during pregnancy). You should also discuss what is known about the effects of certain diseases, such as rubella, syphilis, HIV/AIDS, etc., and about environmental hazards such as radiation, lead, secondhand smoke, etc. Explain how each of these problems can be avoided (e.g., do not consume alcohol or other drugs during pregnancy); then describe the type of prenatal care that a pregnant woman should get to ensure the health of her child.

2. Of course, the first thing you might want to tell her is that she and her husband should talk with her gynecologist or another person in the field who can provide them with all the information they need about pregnancy in general and help them with any issues that are specific to them (e.g., any health problems, weight issues, genetic concerns, etc.), and to ensure that she gets excellent prenatal care. Then, generally, explain that both she and her husband will be going through changes during the nine months of pregnancy (and, obviously, after the baby is born). Explain what happens to the developing baby during the three prenatal periods (germinal, embryonic, and fetal), then talk about the changes your cousin can expect physically and emotionally during the three trimesters, discuss appropriate weight gain, nutrition, and exercise, and how drugs, diseases, and environmental hazards can affect her unborn child. You might also bring up the issue of incompatible blood types. Be sure to let your cousin know the dangers of consuming alcohol during pregnancy (any amount may be unsafe) and the harmful effects of smoking on her baby, even secondhand smoke, and encourage her to do whatever she needs to do to reduce excessive stress in her life, including being sure to have a good support system. Finally, reassure her that most pregnancies go smoothly and she should enjoy the process.

Research Project 1: Women's Health Practices

The text discusses certain maternal behaviors that are potentially harmful to an unborn child, such as smoking or using alcohol and other drugs; it also discusses healthful practices, such as good nutrition, safe exercise, prenatal care, etc. Talk to women you know who are of child-bearing age to see how much they know about what is both harmful and healthful for their unborn child; assess the behaviors in which they engage; and for those who smoke, drink, or use other drugs, have them tell you why they do so, whether they will continue to do so when they are pregnant, how they plan to quit, and what they expect the consequences might be for their child if they continue. If they are unaware of the potential harmful effects of teratogens, explain these to them, then ask if they would engage in these practices while pregnant. Compare the responses you get to see if you can draw any conclusions. What type of campaign do you think might be useful to have women discontinue unhealthy behaviors and engage in healthful ones instead?

Research Project 2: Understanding Teratogens

The chapter describes various teratogens, environmental agents that are harmful to the unborn child. There are other potentially dangerous elements not included due to space limitations. Consider the list of teratogens that were included, then check out others that were not. Chart the teratogens described in the text, then add others from your own research. Indicate the period of development when each teratogen affects the unborn child, potential problems that may result, how (if at all) the problem can be treated, how to protect the pregnant mother and her child, and other information you think is important.

Teratogen & Its Source	Critical Period	Problems Caused	Treatment If Any	Protection	Other Relevant Information
Rubella (German Measles)					
Syphilis					
Alcohol					

1. Which of these teratogens are easily avoidable? How can they be avoided?
2. Which are difficult to avoid? What can be done to protect the mother and her unborn child?
3. What teratogens come from paternal factors?
4. Based on what you have learned, what is the best advice you can think of for a couple planning to have a child?

Personal Application 1: Reflecting on What You Learned

Consider what you read in Chapter 4, then answer the following questions:

1. What information in this chapter did you already know?
2. How can/do you use that information in your own life?
3. What information in this chapter was totally new to you?
4. How can you use that new information in your own life?
5. What information in this chapter was different from what you previously believed?
6. How was this information different?

7. How do you account for the differences between what you believed and what you learned in the chapter?
8. What is the most important thing you learned from reading this chapter?

Personal Application 2: How Can This Chapter Help You Understand Your Own Pregnancy Behaviors?

Your responses to this application will, of course, depend on your age and sex; think about these questions as appropriate:

- If you are beyond child-bearing age, consider your past behaviors (whether you have children or not)
- If you are a female who is currently of child-bearing age or will be in the future
- If you are a male who is presently in a position to father children or you will be at some point in the future

For any of these scenarios, reflect on your present or past behaviors, as well as those that you will have to assess when planning to/becoming pregnant (or, in the case of men, impregnating a female partner). Create a chart to look at your past and present behaviors that might affect the health of an unborn child, if you were to become pregnant (or men, if your partner were to become pregnant). What behaviors will you need to eliminate or change (and why that would be important)? What behaviors will you need to cultivate (and why that would be important)? What other aspects of your life would affect the unborn child?

	Behaviors	Whether It Needs to Be Changed	How It Can Be Changed	Effect on the Baby	Other Comments
Past/Present Nutrition					
Past/Present Drug Use					
Past/Present Exercise					
Past/Present Lifestyle					
Past/Present Other Behaviors					
Future Behaviors					
Other					

From looking at your chart, based on the information in the chapter (and any other information you may have gathered), explain:

1. Does the information in the chapter and in your chart provide you with a better understanding of yourself and your habits and how they could affect an unborn child? In what way?
2. How can you use this information in your own life?
3. In what way (if any) will this information affect your decisions concerning your lifestyle during your own child-bearing years, or (if you are not in that age range), how can you use this information to help someone you know who may/will be having children (male or female)?
4. Did focusing on your behaviors create any kind of concern for you, or did it make you feel less fearful? Explain.
5. What other insights have you gained from preparing this chart?

Internet Projects

Check out the McGraw-Hill Web site for this text (www.mhhe.com/santrockc9). You'll find numerous activities there, in particular, information that will help you research the answers and complete the exercises in the "Taking It to the Net" section at the end of the textbook chapter. Please note that all Internet addresses in this Study Guide have been checked and were correct at the time of publication; however, Web sites may be discontinued or addresses may change, so when you search a given site it may no longer be viable. If that occurs, I apologize for the inconvenience and would appreciate you notifying me so I can make appropriate revisions in future editions of this Study Guide.

Internet Project 1: Predicting the Baby's Sex

This is a fun project for predicting whether a child will be a boy or a girl. If you or your spouse is currently pregnant, try this for predicting your own child's sex; otherwise, interview someone you know who is pregnant by asking the questions on this Web site: www.childbirth.org and link to "Boy or girl?" quiz. If the parents-to-be already know the sex of the child, see if this prediction agrees with the doctor's prediction. Note that there is a lot of other information about pregnancy and childbirth on this site as well.

Somewhat related is an excellent site, Ultrasound Pictures, http://www.ob-ultrasound.net. Although it may be a bit overwhelming for those not yet initiated into interpreting ultrasound radiographs, it's an excellent introduction and many of the graphics have markers to help you understand what you are looking at; you may even figure out how to determine the baby's sex. Something to think about as you work through this site is, "Just how many different types of ultrasound are there?"

Internet Project 2: Preventing FAS

Fetal alcohol syndrome (FAS) is 100% preventable. How? By not consuming alcohol when the baby is being conceived or at any time during pregnancy (note, too, that a father's excessive consumption of alcohol can damage his sperm with resulting consequences to the baby). Once the damage is done, it can't be undone. There are, however, ways to work with children who have FAS (or related conditions such as the milder fetal alcohol effects [FAE], Alcohol-Related Neurodevelopmental Disorder [ARND], functional or mental impairments linked to prenatal alcohol exposure, and Alcohol-Related Birth Defects [ARBD], malformations in the skeletal and major organ systems). Go to the Web site for the National

Organization for Fetal Alcohol Syndrome, http://www.nofas.org, and research this topic. Try to answer the following questions:

1. What is fetal alcohol syndrome?
2. What characteristics does an FAS child have, cognitively and physically?
3. What are the major problems encountered by someone with FAS?
4. How does FAS differ from FAE?
5. What are ARND and ARBD and how do they differ from FAS?
6. How do these disorders occur and how can they be prevented?

After clicking on the link that discusses how to work with children who have fetal alcohol syndrome, design a program that you think would help maximize the abilities (and minimize the challenges) of an FAS child. How long-lasting do you think this intervention would be? Explain your reasoning. What type of campaign would you suggest to eliminate FAS, FAE, ARND, and ARBD altogether?

Additional Internet Resources

APA site: http://www.apa.org—Offers a multitude of options for learning about pregnancy, childbirth options, and other topics covered in this chapter. Particularly, go to the "Public Publications" link and check out the "Print and Media" offerings.

Abortion: http://www.religioustolerance.org/abortion.htm—All sides of the issue.

American Medical Association: http://www.ama-assn.org.

Child Development Web site: http://childstudy.net—Information on children's topics, particularly social activism.

Embryo Visualization: http://embryo.soad.umich.edu/carnStages/carnStages.html—Provides a sampling of the Carnegie stages of embryos (go to the site to learn what the Carnegie stages are, as well as postovulatory age).

Genetic Science Learning Center: http://gslc.genetics.utah.edu/units/stemcells/sctoday/—This site provides information about stem cell therapies, research, and applications, including an explanation of why umbilical cord blood stem cells are an excellent resource for transplant therapies.

Hanover College: http://psych.hanover.edu/Krantz/lists.html—Provides excellent resources on various topics in psychology.

Healthfinder: http://healthfinder.gov—A guide to reliable health information; try conducting a search on any of the topics covered in this chapter

Mayo Clinic's Health Site: http://www.mayoclinic.com—Offers reliable health information from one of the foremost medical centers in the country.

Medscape: http://www.medscape.com/px/urlinfo—Free database of medical articles, plus access to medical dictionaries, drug databases, and breaking medical news.

National Council on Alcoholism and Drug Dependence: http://www.ncadd.org—Provides education, information, and assistance to the public and promotes the prevention, intervention, and treatment of alcoholism and drug dependence.

National Institutes of Health: http://www.nih.gov—Starting point for getting into any subagency of NIH.

National Institute of Mental Health: http://www.nimh.nih.gov—Excellent resource for policy statements, NIMH research, and grants.

New England Journal of Medicine: http://content.nejm.org—Abstracts to articles, full text letters and commentaries.

Scientific American: http://www.sciam.com—General scientific resource from the well-respected magazine.

Society for Research in Child Development (SRCD): http://www.srcd.org—The Web site for SRCD, an organization whose purposes are to promote multidisciplinary research in the field of human development, to foster the exchange of information among scientists and other professionals of various disciplines, and to encourage applications of research findings; some interesting articles are available at the site for non-members.

Ultrasound Pictures: http://www.ob-ultrasound.net—May be a bit overwhelming for those not yet initiated into interpreting ultrasound radiographs, but it's an excellent introduction and many of the graphics have markers to help you understand what you are looking at.

Web MD: http://www.webmd.com—Offers a wide variety of information for the medical profession and for consumers.

Weber State University in Ogden, Utah: http://faculty.weber.edu/tltr/Videotest.htm—Offers an excellent site with a myriad of information and short videos on childhood from conception through adolescence. You may need to download QuickTime from Apple.com, but it's free and will let you view the clips in the segment, as well as interviews with important people in the field of child development.

CHAPTER 5: BIRTH

CHAPTER OUTLINE

WHAT HAPPENS DURING THE BIRTH PROCESS?

Stages of the Birth Process
The Fetus/Newborn Transition
Childbirth Strategies and Decisions

HOW DO LOW BIRTH WEIGHT INFANTS DEVELOP?

Preterm and Small for Date Infants
Long-Term Outcomes for Low Birth Weight Infants
Nurturing Preterm Infants

WHAT ARE THREE MEASURES OF NEONATAL HEALTH AND RESPONSIVENESS?

WHAT HAPPENS DURING THE POSTPARTUM PERIOD?

Physical Adjustments
Emotional and Psychological Adjustments
Bonding

REACH YOUR LEARNING GOALS

1. **WHAT HAPPENS DURING THE BIRTH PROCESS?**

   Stages of the Birth Process

   Childbirth Strategies and Decisions

   The Fetus/Newborn Transition

2. **HOW DO LOW BIRTH WEIGHT INFANTS DEVELOP?**

   Preterm and Small for Date Infants

   Nurturing Preterm Infants

   Long-Term Outcomes for Low Birth Weight Infants

3. **WHAT ARE THREE MEASURES OF NEONATAL HEALTH AND RESPONSIVENESS?**

4. **WHAT HAPPENS DURING THE POSTPARTUM PERIOD?**

   Physical Adjustments

   Bonding

   Emotional and Psychological Adjustments

Learning Goals

By the time you have completed this chapter, you should be able to reach the following goals:

1. Discuss the stages, transitions, and decisions involved in birth.

2. Characterize the development of low birth weight infants.

3. Describe three measures of neonatal health and responsiveness.

4. Explain the physical and psychological aspects of the postpartum period.

What are the three stages of childbirth?	Differentiate among the three basic kinds of drugs used for labor in the United States.
Explain the term *anoxia*. How does anoxia develop and what problems are associated with its occurrence?	What is a *breech position*? What type of delivery would be used in the event of a breech birth? In what birthing instances might a cesarean delivery be performed?
Describe the *vernix caseosa*. What is its function?	What change has taken place over the past several decades with respect to the family's role in childbirth?
How does the childbirth setting typically differ between the United States and other countries around the world?	What special concerns exist for a child whose mother is expecting another baby, and how can these be handled?
Contrast *midwives* with *doulas*.	How can parents help a sibling who engages in regressive, attention-seeking behaviors after the birth of a new baby?
What are the methods of delivery described in the text?	Compare *low birth weight infants* with *preterm infants*.

Analgesia: Relieves pain; tranquilizers, barbiturates, narcotics; *anesthesia*: in late first-stage labor and during expulsion of baby to block sensation in an area of the body or to block consciousness (*epidural block* numbs sensation from waist down; *general anesthesia* blocks consciousness and is not generally used); *oxytocics*: synthetic hormones stimulate contractions (most common is pitocin).	*1st stage*: Lasts an average of 12 to 14 hours; uterine contractions 15 to 20 minutes apart; by end, contractions 2 to 5 minutes apart, cervix dilated to 4". *2nd stage*: Baby's head moves through cervix and birth canal (usually 45 to 60 min.). *Afterbirth*: Placenta, umbilical cord, and other membranes are detached and expelled (lasts a few minutes).
Breech position: Baby's buttocks is the first part to emerge from vagina; may cause respiratory problems; may necessitate *cesarean delivery*: removal of baby from uterus through an incision in mother's abdomen; performed in breech birth, or if baby is lying crosswise in uterus, baby's head is too large to pass through mother's pelvis, baby develops complications, or mother is bleeding vaginally.	*Anoxia*: A condition in which the fetus/newborn has an insufficient supply of oxygen; during contraction, placenta and umbilical cord are compressed as the uterine muscles draw together, decreasing the supply of oxygen; if delivery takes too long, anoxia can develop and may cause brain damage.
In the past several decades, *father's role* has changed: fathers have increasingly participated in childbirth, are more likely to go to obstetrician, attend childbirth preparation classes, learn about labor and birth, and be more involved in child care. *Siblings* often attend the birth or visit the mother shortly after.	The *vernix caseosa* is a protective skin grease consisting of fatty secretions and dead cells; it is thought to protect baby's skin against heat loss before and during birth.
Siblings and childbirth: If parents have a child and are expecting another, the older child must be prepared for the birth. Provide the child with realistic, age-appropriate information about pregnancy, birth, and life with a newborn.	*In U.S.*: 99% of births take place in hospitals; more than 90% are attended by physicians; increased use of birthing centers encourages father's participation. *Many other countries*: Babies more likely to be delivered at home and more likely to use midwives or doulas than physicians.
Regressive, attention-seeking behavior: Common after birth of a new baby; don't act disappointed; worry only if behavior persists after reasonable adjustment period; read books to child about living with a new baby; plan time alone with/give special time/gift to older child; "tell" baby how special sibling is in presence of sibling.	*Midwife*: Someone trained to assist in the delivery of babies, most are nurses with special training in delivery. *Doula*: A professional trained in childbirth who provides continuous physical, emotional, and educational support for the mother before, during, and after childbirth (Greek: a woman who helps).
Low birth weight infant: Weighs less than 5-1/2 lbs. at birth; *very low birth weight* is less than 3 lbs; *extremely low birth weight* weighs less than 2 lbs. *Preterm infant*: Born 3 weeks or more before pregnancy reaches full term. All are considered high-risk infants.	*Medicated*: Use of medication to reduce pain and/or to stimulate contractions. *Natural*: Reduce mother's pain by decreasing her fear via education and breathing/relaxation methods. *Prepared*: Similar to natural childbirth, but more detailed education regarding physiology *Cesarean*: Baby removed via incision in mother's abdomen.

Flashcards: Chapter 5-2

What is a *small for date (or small for gestational age) infant*? What are the main factors that lead to this condition?	What is the *postpartum period*? How long does it last?
What are some of the long-term problems faced by low birth weight infants? How can they be reversed?	Explain the process of *involution*.
Describe techniques that are currently used for nurturing preterm infants.	What are the possible causes of *emotional fluctuations* during the postpartum period? How would an *episiotomy* affect a couple's resumption of sexual intercourse?
What are three scales typically used to measure neonatal health and responsiveness?	What is *postpartum depression*? What are some signs that may indicate a need for professional help in treating postpartum adaptation?
When is the *Apgar scale administered?* What information does it provide?	What is *bonding*? What concerns do some pediatricians have about the relationship between bonding and administration of drugs during delivery?
When is the *Brazelton Neonatal Behavioral Assessment Scale (NBAS)* administered? What are its uses? What is the *Neonatal Intensive Care Unit Network Neurobehavioral Scale (NNNS)*?	State the *birth strategies* suggested at the end of the chapter that may benefit the baby and the mother.

Postpartum period: The period after childbirth or delivery when the woman's body adjusts, physically and psychologically, to the process of childbearing; lasts about 6 weeks or until the body has completed its adjustment and has returned to a near prepregnant state.	***Small for date (small for gestational age) infants***: birth weight is below normal when considering length of pregnancy (weighing less than 90% of babies of the same gestational age). The main factors in producing these infants are inadequate nutrition and smoking by the pregnant woman.
Involution: The process by which the uterus returns to its prepregnant size, 5 or 6 weeks after birth (uterus goes from 2–3 lbs after birth to 2–3.5 oz. by end of 5 or 6 weeks); nursing helps the uterus contract more rapidly.	***Low-birt weight problems***: Cerebral palsy and other forms of brain injury (related to low brain weight); increased risk for lung or liver disease; learning disability, ADHD, breathing problems. ***Intensive enrichment programs*** providing medical and educational services for parents and children may offset some of these problems.
Emotional fluctuations postpartum: Common; may be due to hormonal changes, fatigue, inexperience or lack of confidence with newborn babies, extensive time and demands of caring for a newborn. ***An episiotomy***, or surgical incision, used to enlarge the vaginal opening and help accommodate the emerging baby's head, requires stitches to close the cut; the mother's body needs special care to heal effectively.	***Appropriate stimulation*** based on infant's conceptual age, illness, individual makeup, and behavioral cues. ***Massage***: Stimulates musculoskeletal, nervous, and circulatory systems; promotes weight gain and improved immune functioning. ***Kangaroo care***: Technique for holding infant so there is skin-to-skin contact; improves heartbeat, temperature, breathing, sleep, weight gain, alertness.
Postpartum depression: Strong feelings of sadness, anxiety, or despair in new mothers that make it difficult for them to carry out daily tasks. ***Signs that professional help may be needed***: excessive worrying, depression, extreme changes in appetite, crying spells, and inability to sleep.	***Apgar Scale***: Administered 1 and 5 minutes after birth. ***Brazelton Neonatal Behavioral Assessment Scale (NBAS)***: Performed 24–36 hours after birth. ***Neonatal Intensive Care Unit Network Neurobehavioral Scale (NNNS)***: created to assess at-risk infants.
Bonding: Close connection, especially a physical bond, between parents and their newborn in the period shortly after birth. Some pediatricians argue that giving the mother drugs to make delivery less painful may contribute to lack of bonding by making the mother drowsy, interfering with her ability to respond to and stimulate the newborn.	***Apgar Scale***: at 1 and 5 minutes after birth; evaluates infants' heart rate, respiratory effort, muscle tone, body color, and reflex irritability; each scored on scale of 0 to 2; total score of 7 to 10 indicates good condition; 5 indicates there may be developmental difficulties; 3 or lower signals emergency and baby may not survive.
Birth strategies to benefit baby and mother: Take a childbirth class; become knowledgeable about different childbirth techniques; positive intervention for at-risk infants (e.g., massage); involve the family in the birth process; and know about the adaptation required in the postpartum period.	***NBAS***: Administered 24 to 36 hours after birth in 27 categories on 16 reflexes and reactions to circumstances; scored on scale of 0–2, based on baby's best performance; can indicate brain damage or brain stress; used in research studies and as a training tool for parents to stimulate responses/communication. ***NNNS***: provides a more comprehensive analysis for at-risk newborns

Self-Test A: Multiple-Choice Questions

1. Which statement about the first stage of birth is NOT correct?
   a. It is the longest of the three stages.
   b. At the beginning, uterine contractions are 15 to 20 minutes apart.
   c. The first stage is shorter for the first child than it is for later-born children.
   d. By the end of the first stage, the cervix is dilated to an opening of about 4 inches.

2. Mrs. Peters is bearing down hard with each contraction. She is in the _____ stage of labor.
   a. first
   b. second
   c. third
   d. final

3. If the placenta, umbilical cord, and other membranes are being detached and expelled:
   a. the mother is going through the normal phase called afterbirth.
   b. there was a problem with the birth and the baby is at risk.
   c. the mother is in danger of hemorrhaging.
   d. it would suggest that the delivery was a cesarean.

4. Which of the following can lead to anoxia during birth?
   a. if the delivery takes too long
   b. use of forceps to help ease the infant through the birth canal
   c. an episiotomy (surgically widening the vaginal opening)
   d. a cesarean delivery

5. Briana is typical of pregnant women in the United States. Consequently, we can expect that she will choose to have her baby:
   a. at home.
   b. in a hospital.
   c. in a flotation tank.
   d. in a birthing center that is not in a hospital.

6. Carol, a nurse who has been specially trained in delivering babies, is a midwife. She will most likely assist:
   a. with cesarean deliveries.
   b. in complicated deliveries.
   c. in uncomplicated vaginal deliveries.
   d. when attending physicians are overbooked.

7. Which statement has NOT been found to be true with respect to use of doulas during the childbirth process?
   a. Doula-supported mothers experience less pain during labor.
   b. Women using doulas during delivery have lower anxiety about birth.
   c. Women using doulas during delivery have increased sensitivity to their child's needs in the postpartum period.
   d. Doulas typically are used in place of midwives during delivery.

8. With regard to the use of medication during delivery, the American Academy of Pediatrics recommends:
   a. that medications only be used with cesarean deliveries.
   b. the least possible medication be used during delivery.
   c. the use of epidurals.
   d. general anesthesia to block consciousness during delivery.

9. Amanda was given oxytocin during delivery. It is most likely because:
   a. her contractions stopped.
   b. she was bleeding vaginally.
   c. she stopped ovulating.
   d. her placenta became partially detached.

10. Grantley Dick-Read believed that the _____ is an important dimension of reducing the mother's perception of pain during childbirth.
   a. type of drug administered
   b. doctor's relationship with the mother
   c. age of the mother
   d. use of forceps

11. Aisha and Malcolm have chosen to use a childbirth method that includes a special breathing technique to control pushing in the final stages of labor. They also learned a great deal about anatomy and physiology in preparing for the birth. Most likely they are using which method?
    a. medical
    b. natural
    c. prepared
    d. LeBoyer

12. Virtually all prepared childbirth methods emphasize all of the following EXCEPT:
    a. education.
    b. relaxation.
    c. breathing exercises.
    d. medication options.

13. Cesarean deliveries are usually performed in each of the following situations EXCEPT when the:
    a. head is the first part of the baby positioned to come out of the birth canal.
    b. baby is lying crosswise in the uterus.
    c. mother is bleeding vaginally.
    d. baby is in a breech position.

14. Compared to the number of cesarean deliveries in the year 2000, in 2001 the rate:
    a. remained pretty much the same.
    b. increased to almost 25% of all births.
    c. increased almost 25%.
    d. The figures have not yet been analyzed.

15. Dr. Herzig, an obstetrician, reflects the view of most health professionals today, so we would expect him to:
    a. discourage fathers from participating in the childbirth process.
    b. expect that expectant fathers should get in-depth training in childbirth procedures before participating in the birth process.
    c. encourage fathers to participate in the childbirth process.
    d. encourage the use of midwives more so than that of fathers.

16. Albert is planning to participate in the birth of his daughter. His participation is likely to include all of the following EXCEPT:
    a. providing his wife with support and encouragement.
    b. comforting his wife in difficult moments.
    c. assisting with the baby's delivery through the birth canal.
    d. helping his wife use breathing techniques they learned in preparation classes.

17. Three-year-old Jeremy had been toilet trained and had stopped sucking his thumb. Once his baby sister was brought home from the hospital, he started bed-wetting and sucking his thumb again. This behavior is:
    a. natural.
    b. an indicator of unresolved emotional problems that need therapy.
    c. serious, but should be ignored if his parents want it to go away.
    d. a sign that he is jealous and may cause harm to himself or to the baby.

18. John and Mary want to help their son cope with the arrival of his new sister. All of the following would be helpful EXCEPT:
    a. tell him he's grown up now and has to be nice to his little sister.
    b. read him books about living with a new baby before and after the baby is born.
    c. plan for time alone with him and do what he wants to do.
    d. use the time when the baby is asleep and John and Mary are both rested to give special attention to their son.

19. Which group is most at risk for having low birth weight babies in the United States?
    a. Asian Americans
    b. Euro-Americans
    c. African Americans
    d. Hispanic Americans

20. The leading cause of low birth weight in developed countries is:
    a. poor health.
    b. malnutrition.
    c. cigarette smoking.
    d. disease.

21. Momoko is a small for date infant. This means which of the following is true about Momoko?
    a. She weighed under 3 pounds when she was born.
    b. She was born three weeks or more before she was due.
    c. Her mother smoked during pregnancy.
    d. Her birth weight is below normal considering the length of her mother's pregnancy.

22. Low birth weight infants are more likely than normal birth weight infants to have all of the following problems, EXCEPT:
    a. brain damage.
    b. eating disorders.
    c. lung diseases.
    d. liver diseases.

23. The current belief about preterm infant care is:
    a. to bear in mind that "more is better."
    b. that it is too complex to be described only in terms of amount of stimulation.
    c. that stimulation is the primary mode of positive, health-promoting intervention.
    d. to avoid stimulating the baby.

24. Evidence suggests that _____ can lead to weight gain in preterm infants.
    a. a strong parental bond
    b. massage
    c. fat-free infant formulas
    d. exposure to parental voices

25. For two hours a day, either Maya's mother or father holds Maya, a preterm infant, wearing only a diaper, upright against their chest. This kangaroo care helps stabilize all of the following EXCEPT:
    a. heartbeat.
    b. temperature.
    c. muscle strength.
    d. breathing.

26. Two-day-old Terry's very low score on the Brazelton Neonatal Behavioral Assessment Scale may be a good indicator that:
    a. he has brain damage.
    b. his mother took heroin while she was pregnant.
    c. he will develop a "difficult" temperament.
    d. he is unlikely to bond with his primary caregiver.

27. Denise is going through the postpartum period. We would expect her to experience:
    a. a great deal of adjustment and adaptation.
    b. major depression.
    c. the greatest happiness of her life.
    d. anger toward her husband and her newborn.

28. Dorit gave birth to a baby five weeks ago. Her uterus is now returning to its prepregnant size through the process of:
    a. decompensation.
    b. decompression.
    c. involution.
    d. menarche.

29. During the postpartum period:
    a. fathers must undergo considerable adjustment.
    b. most mothers experience postpartum depression.
    c. babies typically experience eating problems.
    d. it is more important that sensitivity to the baby be developed by the mother than by the father.

30. Research suggests that:
    a. the newborn must have close contact with the mother in the first few days of life to develop optimally.
    b. bonding between infant and mother can occur only after standard childbirth.
    c. close contact with mothers is helpful to preterm infants.
    d. close contact with the mother is more important than close contact with the father.

Self-Test B: Matching

Match the following with the correct description:

1. Ferdinand Lamaze
2. Tiffany Field
3. Brazelton Neonatal Behavioral Assessment Scale
4. Barry Lester
5. Apgar Scale
6. Linda Pugh
7. Grantley Dick-Read
8. Doula
9. Kangaroo care
10. Involution

a. Co-developed the Neonatal Intensive Care Unit Network Neurobehavioral Scale (NNNS) with Brazelton and Tronick.
b. Used 1 and 5 minutes after birth to assess neonate's health.
c. English obstetrician who developed natural childbirth.
d. Explored the role of touch and massage in development.
e. French obstetrician who developed prepared childbirth.
f. Neonatal assessment of neurological development.
g. Neonatal nurse who researches interventions with low-income women.
h. A way of holding a preterm infant so there is skin-to-skin contact.
i. Process by which the uterus returns to its prepregnant size.
j. Caregiver who provides continuous physical, emotional, and educational support to the mother before, during, and just after childbirth.

Self-Test C: True-False

T/F 1. The last stage of birth occurs when the baby's head moves through the cervix.

T/F 2. Most births do not involve very much stress for the baby.

T/F 3. Most births in the United States occur in hospitals and are attended by physicians.

T/F 4. The trend in childbirth today is to use a natural method without any type of medication.

T/F 5. Small for date infants may be preterm or full term.

T/F 6. Most low birth weight babies have many health problems.

T/F 7. The Brazelton Neonatal Behavioral Assessment, performed within 24 to 36 hours after birth, can assess a newborn's neurological status.

T/F 8. All women who give birth experience a postpartum period.

T/F 9. Emotional fluctuation is common for women in the postpartum period.

T/F 10. Bonding with the mother soon after birth has been found to be critical for development of a competent infant or child.

Self-Test D: OLC

1. The Lamaze method of childbirth, a widely used form of prepared childbirth, focuses on breathing and _____. This method has increased the involvement of _____ in the entire process of childbirth.

2. In contrast to the Brazelton scales, the Apgar Scale primarily assesses a newborn's
   a. psychological status.
   b. reflexes.
   c. physiological health.
   d. responsibility to people.

3.   T/F   A doula, usually a woman, is part of the birthing team who provides continuous physical, emotional, and educational support for the mother before, during, and after childbirth.

4.   T/F   A low birth weight infant weighs less than 6-1/2 pounds.

Essay Questions

1. One of your friends has recently gotten married and has now confided in you that she is pregnant. She knows you're taking this Child Development class and asks for your input concerning what she can expect when giving birth. She also wants your suggestions concerning her childbirth options. What would you tell her about the three stages of birth, complications she might expect, options about the use of drugs and settings for childbirth, and the childbirth strategies that are available to her?

2. Your aunt's cousin's daughter had a baby. Your aunt tells you that the baby came earlier than expected and had some problems, but she's not sure what the problems were. She wants you to explain to her what might have happened and what you think her cousin's daughter should be doing to be sure the baby will thrive. What do you say?

Key to Self-Test A: Multiple Choice

1. c (LG1)	11. c (LG1)	21. d (LG2)
2. b (LG1)	12. d (LG1)	22. b (LG2)
3. a (LG1)	13. a (LG1)	23. b (LG2)
4. a (LG1)	14. b (LG1)	24. b (LG2)
5. b (LG1)	15. c (LG1)	25. c (LG2)
6. c (LG1)	16. c (LG1)	26. a (LG3)
7. d (LG1)	17. a (LG1)	27. a (LG4)
8. b (LG1)	18. a (LG1)	28. c (LG4)
9. a (LG1)	19. c (LG2)	29. a (LG4)
10. b (LG1)	20. c (LG2)	30. c (LG4)

Key to Self-Test B: Matching

1.   e
2.   d
3.   f
4.   a
5.   b
6.   g
7.   c
8.   j
9.   h
10. i

Key to Self-Test C: True/False

1. False. It is during the second stage that the baby's head moves through the cervix (and ends with the baby's complete emergence); the third stage is afterbirth.
2. False. Being born involves considerable stress but the baby is well prepared and adapted to handle the stress.
3. True
4. False. In the United States today the trend is toward using some medication during childbirth but keeping it to a minimum.
5. True
6. False. Although as a group low birth weight babies have more health and developmental problems than full-term babies, most are born normal and healthy.
7. True
8. True
9. True
10. False. Bonding has not been found to be critical in the development of a competent infant or child.

Key to Self-Test D: CD

1. education; father
2. c
3. True
4. False. A low birth weight infant weighs less than 5-1/2 pounds.

Key to Essay Questions

1. Describe the three stages of birth (e.g., first stage, the longest, lasts an average of 12 to 14 hours, with contractions first being 15 to 20 minutes apart); discuss possible complications (e.g., breech position); explain why your friend may or may not want to use drugs during childbirth, which drugs might be used, and potential consequences of using drugs for mother and child; and finally, describe the different childbirth strategies, such as standard childbirth, the Lamaze method, etc., and why your friend might prefer one over another. Be sure to discuss also the benefits of having her husband present during the birth process.
2. Since this "information" has come to you fourth-hand, you might suspect that you don't have the whole picture. However, to go bit-by-bit, begin with whether the baby actually was preterm (born 3 weeks or more before pregnancy reached full term) or if the date was somehow miscalculated. Discuss when the fetus would actually be viable and able to live, with or without assistance. Discuss, too, the issues of low birth weight and small for date babies, whether they are or are not preterm, differentiating between them, and exploring the potential risks for each. Note, though, that although low birth weight babies have more health and developmental problems than full-term babies, most are normal and healthy. Finally, discuss preterm infant care, noting that it will vary according to the child's conceptual age, illness, and individual makeup, and discuss massage therapy and kangaroo care.

Research Project 1: Generational Differences in Delivery Practices

This project looks at generational differences in delivery practices. Work with three other students in your class so you can pool your data after you have collected it. Present the following questions to your mother, your grandmother (if she's not alive, ask another woman you would be comfortable talking to who would be your grandmother's age), and a woman who has a child under 2 years of age, then circle the appropriate responses in the following table:

	Grandmother	Mother	Woman w/Baby
Was the delivery cesarean or vaginal?	C/V	C/V	C/V
Were medications used?	Y/N	Y/N	Y/N
Was the father present in the delivery room?	Y/N	Y/N	Y/N
Did the pregnant woman attend childbirth classes?	Y/N	Y/N	Y/N

After comparing responses with your group members, answer the following questions:
1. What might you conclude about the use of medication during delivery over the past three generations?

2. Has the percentage of cesarean deliveries relative to vaginal deliveries changed during that period?
3. What might you conclude about the presence of fathers during delivery over this period?
4. What change, if any, might be noted in terms of the percentage of women attending childbirth classes?
5. Are your findings consistent with the research described in the text? Explain.

Adapted from J. A. Simons. (1994). In J.W. Santrock, *Student Study Guide of Child Development*, 6th ed. Boston: McGraw-Hill.

Research Project 2: Assessing the Postpartum Period

Using your classmates, friends, family, or any other convenient source, locate a database of women who have given birth within the past month. (For reasons of sensitivity, avoid any who have had serious problems such as stillbirth or major medical problems of baby or mother and, of course, do get consent from all mothers who agree to participate.) Create a questionnaire to assess some of the postpartum issues you learned about in this chapter. First, look at such things as how many weeks it's been since the baby was born, how long the mother and child were in the hospital, the type of birth (e.g., natural, prepared, cesarean, etc.), and the physical condition of mother and child right after birth and when each left the hospital. If you can, see if you can get the Apgar score and, if given, the Brazelton Neonatal Assessment score. Then look at issues such as whether the mother experienced mood swings after the baby was born and, if so, how extreme they were and for what period of time, whether she had help (e.g., from family, midwife, friends, partner), how she would rate the bonding between her child and herself, how involved the baby's father has been in helping with the baby and with household chores, how supportive he has been of the baby's mother, etc. If there are other children in the house, interview them about their reactions to the new baby. Develop whatever other questions you believe are relevant and would provide you and your class with useful information about the postpartum period.

Note that when asking for a rating (such as how extreme mood swings were), you may ask the woman to rate them on a scale of 1 to 10, or use a Likert-type scale to rank them (you may assign numerical values to such responses as "Strongly Agree" to "Strongly Disagree" for purposes of statistical analysis), or any other form of ranking that works for you. Also feel free to interview others who are involved in this postpartum period (e.g., the baby's father). It is suggested that this be done as a group project, so lots of data can be collected, compared, and analyzed. Then answer the following questions:

1. What information did you learn that was consistent with the text?
2. What information did you learn that was not consistent with the text?
3. What information did you learn that could be helpful to you as a new parent?
4. What information did you learn that could be helpful to you as a health-care professional?

Personal Application 1: Reflecting on What You Learned

Consider what you read in Chapter 5, then answer the following questions:

1. What information in this chapter did you already know?
2. How can/do you use that information in your own life?
3. What information in this chapter was totally new to you?
4. How can you use that new information in your own life?
5. What information in this chapter was different from what you previously believed?
6. How was this information different?

7. How do you account for the differences between what you believed and what you learned in the chapter?
8. What is the most important thing you learned from reading this chapter?

Personal Application 2: Consider Your Choices

The chapter offers several different options for childbirth, such as natural or prepared childbirth, elective cesarean delivery, use of drugs (from local to general anesthetic), participation of fathers (and other family members), etc. You should also check out other possible options by checking the Internet, asking parents who have recently had a child, or checking hospitals and birthing centers. In the following chart, describe the options that are currently available (include those in the chapter as well as others that you can find), indicate the positive and negative aspects of each, then decide which would seem the best option for you if you were to have a child at this point in time. If you already have children, indicate which you used, why you chose that option (or, if you didn't choose the option yourself, who did?), and if you would choose a different one now that you have more information. What would be the major deciding factors for you in making this choice? This is *not* for women only—fathers are obviously a necessary part of procreation, so guys, think about this, too!

Type of Childbirth Option	Positive Aspects	Negative Aspects	Whose Choice Would This Option Be?	Deciding Factors for Choosing/Not Choosing
No. 1 Choice:				

Internet Projects

Check out the McGraw-Hill Web site for this text (www.mhhe.com/santrockc9). You'll find numerous activities there, in particular, information that will help you research the answers and complete the exercises in the "Taking It to the Net" section at the end of the textbook chapter. Please note that all Web site addresses in this Study Guide have been checked and were correct at the time of publication; however, Web sites may be discontinued or addresses may change, so when you search a given site it may no longer be viable. If that occurs, I apologize for the inconvenience and would appreciate you notifying me so I can make appropriate revisions in future editions of this Study Guide.

Internet Project 1: Having a Baby

What's it like to have a baby? Obviously this is a complicated question because only a woman who has had a baby can really explain the experience, and each woman's experience will be different (in fact, a woman may have different experiences with pregnancy and childbirth every time she gets pregnant!); however, an excellent site that provides interesting insights, personal experiences, graphics, and other useful information can be found at http://www.childbirth.org (some of the links are in conjunction with http://www.about.com). Check out this site for some of the terms used in Chapter 5 (e.g., *postpartum depression, cesareans*), and link to the pregnancy calendar. What type of information do you find there? What did you find that could help you in your own pregnancy or when a friend or family member (e.g., your wife, sister, daughter, niece) is pregnant? Check out the term *couvades*; in some cultures the focus in pregnancy is on the man, not the woman! Explore the links, search the terms, and compare what you learn at this site with what you learned from the text.

Internet Project 2: Assessing the Neonate

The text talks about the three scales for assessing the neonate's well-being, the Apgar Scale, the Brazelton Neonatal Assessment Scale (NBAS), and the Neonatal Intensive Care Unit Network Neurobehavioral Scale (NNNS). Although an acronym has been created to help remember what is assessed by the Apgar Scale (Activity/Pulse/Grimace/Appearance/Respiration), this scale is actually named for Virginia Apgar, the doctor who devised it in 1953. The Brazelton Neonatal Behavioral Assessment Scale (NBAS) was first developed in 1973 by Dr. T. Berry Brazelton; together with Barry Lester and Edward Tronick, Brazelton developed the newer NNNS in 2004. Compare the three scales in terms of what they measure and how they are used by reading the text and by exploring a couple of sites for each. For the Apgar, go to http://www.childbirth.org and type "Apgar" in the search box, then go to the site sponsored by Virginia Apgar's grandnephew, http://apgar.net/virginia. To explore the NBAS and the NNNS, go to http://www.brazelton-institute.com and http://www.brazelton.org/main.html (although this latter site is actually about the Brazelton Foundation with links to current articles, such as how to help children deal with catastrophic events).

In comparing the three scales, consider what you've learned about the doctors who created them, the information each can tell about the neonate's well-being, what other ways Brazelton and his colleagues have used his scales, and the changes that have been made to the original NBAS—how is it different from its predecessor and why were these changes made? Contemplate the importance of each of these measures and how they can be used to maximize the newborn's functioning.

Additional Internet Resources

American Academy of Pediatrics: http://www.aap.org.

American Medical Association: http://www.ama-assn.org.

APA site: http://www.apa.org—Offers a multitude of options for learning about pregnancy, childbirth options, and other topics covered in this chapter. Particularly, go to the "Public Publications" link and check out the "Print and Media" offerings.

Baby Center: http://www.babycenter.com/refcap/127.html—Learn about the baby's umbilical cord, such as its purpose, how to care for its stump after the baby is born, and signs of infection. You can then explore other links at this site for other information about conception, labor, delivery, and other relevant topics.

The Child Development Web site: http://childstudy.net—Information on children's topics.

Drkoop.com: www.drkoop.com—a Web site full of information on medical topics and links to many others.

Healthfinder: http://healthfinder.gov associated with http://www.health.gov, a portal to the Web sites of a number of multiagency health initiatives and activities of the U.S. Department of Health and Human Services and other federal departments and agencies.

International Confederation of Midwives: http://www.internationalmidwives.org/index.php?module=ContentExpress&func=display&ceid=34 — Provides information on midwifery, as well as updates on international conferences, links to other resources, and current articles relating to the activities and use of midwives.

Henry J. Kaiser Foundation: http://www.kff.org/—A good place to search for a vast amount of health information with special attention to the needs of the underserved (e.g., the poor, adolescents); although the site is extensive, check out information on pregnancy and childbirth.

Mayo Clinic's Health Site: http://www.mayoclinic.com.

Medscape: http://www.medscape.com/px/urlinfo—Free database of medical articles, plus access to medical dictionaries, drug databases, and breaking medical news.

National Institutes of Health: http://www.nih.gov—Starting point for getting into any subagency of NIH.

National Institute of Mental Health: http://www.nimh.nih.gov—Excellent resource for policy statements, NIMH research, grants; you might want to check out postpartum depression information at this site.

New England Journal of Medicine: http://www.nejm.org—Abstracts to articles, full text on letters and commentaries.

Scientific American: http://www.sciam.com—General scientific resource.

Society for Research in Child Development (SRCD): http://www.srcd.org—The Web site for SRCD, an organization whose purposes are to promote multidisciplinary research in the field of human development, to foster the exchange of information among scientists and other professionals of various disciplines, and to encourage applications of research findings.

Ultrasound Pictures: http://www.ob-ultrasound.net—May be a bit overwhelming for those not yet initiated into interpreting ultrasound radiographs, but it's an excellent introduction and many of the graphics have markers to help you understand what you are looking at.

Web MD: http://www.webmd.com—Offers a wide variety of information for the medical profession and for consumers.

CHAPTER 6: PHYSICAL DEVELOPMENT IN INFANCY

CHAPTER OUTLINE

HOW DO INFANTS GROW AND DEVELOP PHYSICALLY?

Where Growth Starts: Cephalocaudal and Proximodistal Patterns
Height and Weight
Brain Development
Sleep
Nutrition
Toilet Training
Health

HOW DO INFANTS DEVELOP MOTOR SKILLS?

The Dynamic Systems View
Reflexes
Gross Motor Skills
Fine Motor Skills

HOW CAN INFANTS' SENSORY AND PERCEPTUAL DEVELOPMENT BE CHARACTERIZED?

Defining Sensation and Perception
The Ecological View
Studying Infant Perception
Visual Perception
Other Senses
Intermodal Perception
Perceptual-Motor Coupling

REACH YOUR LEARNING GOALS

1. **HOW DO INFANTS GROW AND DEVELOP PHYSICALLY?**

Where Growth Starts: Cephalocaudal and Proximodistal Patterns	Brain Development	Nutrition
Height and Weight	Sleep	Toilet Training	Health

2. **HOW DO INFANTS' MOTOR SKILLS DEVELOP?**

Dynamic Systems Theory	Gross Motor Skills
Reflexes	Fine Motor Skills

3. **HOW CAN INFANTS' SENSORY AND PERCEPTUAL SKILLS BE CHARACTERIZED?**

Defining Sensation & Perception	Studying Infant Perception	Other Senses	Perceptual-Motor Coupling
The Ecological View	Visual Perception		Intermodal Perception

Learning Goals

By the time you have completed this chapter, you should be able to reach the following goals:

1. Discuss physical growth and development in infancy.

2. Describe infants' motor development.

3. Outline the course of sensory and perceptual development.

Contrast the *cephalocaudal* and *proximodistal patterns* of development.	What can be said about infants' patterns of sleep? What is *REM*?
What is *shaken baby syndrome?*	What is *SIDS*? What do we know about its possible causes? What advice is given for reducing the risk of SIDS?
What is the importance of *neurons*? Differentiate between *axons* and *dendrites*. What is the *myelin sheath* and what are its primary purposes?	Explain the advantages of breast feeding over bottle feeding.
What is the *forebrain*? Describe the *cerebral cortex* and its functions.	What is *marasmus* and what is its primary cause? What is *kwashiorkor* and what causes it?
Explain the location and primary functions of the *occipital lobe*, *temporal lobe*, *frontal lobe*, and *parietal lobe*.	What are two of the most important aspects of infant health? What are the most common accidents in infancy and early childhood?
What does the term *lateralization* describe with regard to the brain?	Describe *dynamic systems theory*.

Newborns sleep 16 to 17 hours a day, and some sleep more than others (range is 10 to 21 hours). The pattern may change from several long bouts (7 to 8 hours) to three or four shorter sessions; by age 1 month, most sleep longer at night; by 4 months they usually move closer to adult sleep patterns. *REM* (rapid eye movement) *sleep*: Recurring sleep during which vivid dreams occur; provides infants with self-stimulation and promotes brain development.	*Cephalocaudal pattern*: The sequence in which the greatest growth occurs at the top (head); physical growth and feature differentiation goes from top to bottom. *Proximodistal pattern*: The sequence in which growth starts at the center of the body and moves toward the extremities.
SIDS: Sudden infant death syndrome, occurs when an infant stops breathing, usually during the night, and suddenly dies without apparent cause; highest cause of infant death in the United States. *Risk factors*: Low-birthweight; sibling died of SIDS; sleep apnea; African-American/Eskimo; low SES; second-hand smoke; soft bedding. *Advice*: Place child *on back* to sleep.	*Shaken baby syndrome*: When a baby is shaken, the brain may swell and hemorrhage, resulting in brain damaged and/or death. Hundreds of babies in the United States are affected by shaken baby syndrome each year.
Advantages of breast feeding: Milk is clean and digestible, helps immunize the newborn; appropriate weight gain and lowered risk of obesity; fewer allergies; denser bones in childhood and adulthood; reduced childhood cancer/reduced incidence of breast cancer in mothers and female offspring; lower rates of SIDS; better neurological and cognitive development; better visual acuity; important for baby's health in poor countries.	*Neurons* are nerve cells that handle information processing at the cellular level. *Axons* are the part of the neuron that carries information away from the cell body to other cells; *dendrites* are the receiving parts of the neuron that collect information and route it to the cell body. The *myelin sheath,* a layer of fat cells encasing most axons, insulates nerve cells and helps the nerve impulse travel faster.
Marasmus: Wasting away of body tissues in the infant's first year caused by severe protein-calorie deficiency; *main cause*: early weaning from breast milk to inadequate nutrients (e.g., unsuitable and unsanitary cow's milk formula). *Kwashiorkor*: Deficiency in protein results in child's face, legs, abdomen swelling with water.	*The forebrain:* Highest level of the brain, consists of several structures including the cerebral cortex. *Cerebral cortex*: Covers the lower portions of the brain like a cap; divided into four lobes: frontal, occipital, temporal, and parietal; it plays critical roles in important human functions such as perception, language, and thinking.
Important aspects of infant health: Immunization and accident prevention; most common accidents: aspiration of foreign objects, suffocation, falls, poisoning, burns, motor vehicle accidents, bodily damage. *Major cause of death for children over 1*: automobile accidents; all infants (including newborns) should be secured in infant car seats.	*Frontal*: (at front of brain) involved in control of voluntary movement and intelligence. *Occipital*: (at rear of brain) involved in vision. *Temporal*: (lateral side of brain) involved in hearing. *Parietal*: (above temporal and occipital) involved in processing body sensations.
Dynamic systems theory: Proposed by Esther Thelen, seeks to explain how motor behaviors are assembled for perceiving and acting.	*Lateralization* is used to describe specialization in the brain's two hemispheres. Note that labeling people as "left-brained" (logical thinkers) or "right-brained" (creative thinkers) does not correspond to how the brain actually works—complex thinking in normal people results from communication between both sides.

What are *reflexes*? What are some of the reflexes that persist throughout life?	Define the *ecological view* of development.
What is the *Moro reflex*? What is its purpose?	What are *affordances*? Give some examples from the chapter.
Describe the *grasping*, *sucking,* and *rooting reflexes*.	Summarize Robert Fantz' research and the technique referred to as *visual preference method*.
What are *gross motor skills*? What is required for gross motor skills to develop?	What are *habituation* and *dishabituation*?
What is involved in *fine motor skills*? Explain the role of *perceptual-motor coupling* for fine motor coordination.	Contrast two elements of perceptual constancy: *size constancy* and *shape constancy*.
Contrast *sensation* and *perception*.	What is involved in *intermodal perception*?

Ecological view: People directly perceive information in the world around them; perception brings people in contact with the environment in order to interact with it and adapt to it (even complex things can be perceived directly without constructive activity). (Advocated by Eleanor and James J. Gibson)	*Reflexes*: Built-in reactions to stimuli; provide infants with adaptive responses before they have the opportunity to learn appropriate responses. *Examples of reflexes that persist throughout life* include breathing, coughing, blinking, salivating, yawning.
Affordances are opportunities for interaction offered by objects that are necessary to perform activities (e.g., a chair is appropriate for sitting, a solid surface is for walking, an object is within reach).	*Moro reflex*: A neonatal startle response that occurs in response to a sudden, intense noise or movement; when startled, the newborn arches its back, throws its head back, flings out its arms and legs, then rapidly closes arms and legs to the center of body. (Vestige from primate ancestry—to grab mother.)
Robert Fantz discovered that infants look at different things for different lengths of time; placed infants in a "looking chamber" with two visual displays and an experimenter viewed infants' eyes by looking through a peephole. *Visual preference method*: Developed by Fantz to determine whether infants can distinguish one stimulus from another by measuring the length of time they attend to different stimuli.	*Grasping reflex*: When something touches the infant's palms, the infant responds by grasping tightly. *Sucking*: Newborns automatically suck objects placed in their mouths (helps get nourishment before they associate a nipple with food). *Rooting*: When cheek is stroked or side of mouth is touched, infant turns its head toward the side that's touched (helps infant find something to suck).
Researchers study infant perception by presenting a stimulus several times and observing whether attention to the stimulus is reduced. *Habituation*: Decreased responsiveness to a stimulus after repeated presentations. *Dishabituation*: Recovery of habituated response after change in stimulation.	*Gross motor skills* involve large muscle activities such as moving one's arms and walking. Gross motor skills require postural control, control of head to stabilize the gaze and to track moving objects, and strength and balance in legs to walk.
Perceptual constancy: Sensory stimulation changes while perception of physical world remains constant. Two types are: *Size constancy*: Recognition that an object remains the same even though the retinal image of the object changes. *Shape constancy*: Recognition that an object remains the same even though its orientation to us changes.	*Fine motor skills* involve finely tuned movements, such as finger dexterity. *Perceptual-motor coupling* is the ability to coordinate proprioceptive cues with motor skills to coordinate such activities as grasping objects.
Intermodal perception: The ability to relate and integrate information about two or more sensory modalities, such as vision and hearing.	*Sensation*: Occurs when information interacts with sensory receptors (eyes, ears, tongue, nostrils, and skin). *Perception*: The interpretation of what is sensed.

Self-Test A: Multiple-Choice Questions

1. Eddie lies on his back in his crib and sees the mobile above his head but he is not able to raise himself up to reach it. This demonstrates the basic pattern of _____ development.
   a. cephalocaudal
   b. proximodistal
   c. encephalic
   d. primary

2. Two-month-old Stephanie uses her whole hand to grab for objects because she does not yet have good control of her fingers, suggesting which pattern of development?
   a. cephalocaudal
   b. proximodistal
   c. encephalic
   d. primary

3. The process of encasing axons with fat cells, which protects nerve cells and helps nerve impulses travel faster, is referred to as:
   a. neuronal growth.
   b. myelination.
   c. lipidation.
   d. insulation.

4. Which statement concerning infant brain development is NOT correct?
   a. Nearly twice as many synaptic connections are made as will ever be used.
   b. Blooming and pruning of synapses in the visual, auditory, and prefrontal cortex are critical for higher-level cognitive functioning.
   c. Blooming and pruning of synapses in the infant's brain takes place about the same time for all brain regions.
   d. The peak of overproduction of synapses in the prefrontal cortex takes place at about 1 year of age.

5. Charles Nelson is making strides in finding out more about the brain's development in infancy by using:
   a. PET scans.
   b. MRIs.
   c. electrodes.
   d. CT scans.

6. Briana is using the lobe of her cerebral cortex involved in voluntary movement and thinking, which is the _____ lobe.
   a. frontal
   b. occipital
   c. temporal
   d. parietal

7. Research on language processing in the brain has found that:
   a. virtually all language processing is carried out in the left hemisphere.
   b. speech and grammar are located in the right hemisphere in most people.
   c. language does not occur exclusively in the brain's left hemisphere.
   d. in normal people, tasks involving humor and metaphor are processed in the left hemisphere.

8. Which 5-year-old child is most likely to exhibit depressed brain activity?
   a. Olga, who lives in relative isolation in a Romanian orphanage.
   b. Tzvi, who spends most of his time, including nights, among his age peers on an Israeli kibbutz.
   c. Sara, whose mother is on medication for bipolar disorder.
   d. Angel, who lives on welfare with his mother and participates in a Head Start program.

9. Neuroscientists believe that _____ wires the brain.
   a. genetic heritage
   b. repeated experience
   c. constant stimulation
   d. a delicate balance of proteins and amino acids

10. How much sleep does the average newborn get each day?
    a. 8 to 10 hours
    b. 13 to 14 hours
    c. 16 to 17 hours
    d. 18 to 19 hours

11. Cross-cultural research demonstrates that infant sleep patterns around the world:
    a. are the same.
    b. differ for each culture.
    c. may relate to father-child interaction.
    d. have been steadily changing as humans evolve.

12. Which of the following has NOT been found with regard to REM sleep in infancy?
    a. Infants and adults exhibit similar patterns of REM sleep.
    b. Infants engage in more REM sleep than adults.
    c. REM sleep may provide infants with self-stimulation and promote brain development.
    d. About half of an infant's sleep is REM sleep.

13. All of the following were conclusions in the text about shared sleeping (infants sleeping in the same bed as their mothers), EXCEPT:
    a. some experts believe shared sleeping is beneficial to infants.
    b. the American Academy of Pediatrics Task Force on Infant Positioning and SIDS recommends against shared sleeping.
    c. the American Academy of Pediatrics Task Force on Infant Positioning and SIDS believes that bed sharing might lead to sudden infant death syndrome (SIDS).
    d. cross-cultural studies have found shared sleeping to be a much more common arrangement for mothers and newborns than having the infants sleep in their own beds.

14. Since 1992, when the American Academy of Pediatrics began recommending that infants sleep _____, the frequency of SIDS has decreased.
    a. on their stomachs
    b. on their backs
    c. on their sides
    d. with their mothers

15. LaShawna's mother is breast feeding her. We would expect LaShawna to experience all of the following benefits, EXCEPT:
    a. a lowered risk of childhood obesity.
    b. fewer allergies.
    c. improved mental health.
    d. reduced risk of cancer and SIDS.

16. Which mother should NOT breast feed her baby?
    a. Amanda, who has AIDS.
    b. Bertha, who is 21 years old.
    c. Chakra, who lives below the poverty level.
    d. Dara, who lives in Ghana.

17. Which of the following is NOT associated with malnutrition?
    a. marasmus
    b. kwashiorkor
    c. cognitive deficits
    d. late toilet training

18. Toilet training today, as compared with toilet training in previous generations is:
    a. being delayed until an older age.
    b. being started soon after the child's first birthday.
    c. more traumatic for children.
    d. being started at an earlier age.

19. The leading cause of fatal injury in infants over 1 year of age is:
    a. falling from high places, such as cribs.
    b. abuse by parents or other adults.
    c. automobile accidents, primarily due to improper restraint in the motor vehicle.
    d. asphyxiation by foreign material in the respiratory tract.

20. According to the _____, infants assemble motor skills for perceiving and acting.
    a. dynamic systems view
    b. new view of motor development
    c. genetic blueprint view
    d. traditional reflex view

21. Kenzi's mother strokes his cheek and Kenzi turns his head toward the side of his face that was stroked, exhibiting which reflex?
    a. stepping
    b. Babinski
    c. Moro
    d. rooting

22. According to Thelen (2000), _____ control is critical for engaging in adaptive activities.
    a. postural
    b. motor
    c. sensory
    d. perceptual

23. Assuming all of the following children are developing normally, which child would be the oldest?
    a. Adam, who stands with support
    b. Bernie, who walks using furniture as support
    c. Carlos, who can pull a toy attached to a string
    d. Dominic, who sits without support

24. _____ occurs when information interacts with sensory receptors.
    a. Sensation
    b. Perception
    c. Intermodal perception
    d. Perceptual-motor coupling

25. All objects have _____, or opportunities for interaction offered by objects that are necessary to perform activities.
    a. affordances
    b. options
    c. perceptions
    d. dynamics

26. Robert Fantz found that infants as young as 2 days old:
    a. focused on their mothers' eyes.
    b. distinguished contour.
    c. showed a preference for patterned stimuli over plain stimuli.
    d. perceived the oval shape of the head.

27. After seeing a toy tiger several times, Gadi no longer seemed interested in it, demonstrating:
    a. dishabituation.
    b. habituation.
    c. perceptual gap.
    d. tracking.

28. Benito recognizes that objects don't change shape even when viewed from different distances or different angles, demonstrating:
    a. size constancy.
    b. shape constancy.
    c. depth perception.
    d. habituation.

29. Infants on one side of a visual cliff refused to go to their mothers who were coaxing them from the other side, evidencing:
    a. depth perception.
    b. failure of visual acuity.
    c. inability to hear at a distance.
    d. inability to crawl.

30. Research on auditory perception has found that:
    a. a fetus can hear sounds during the last months of pregnancy.
    b. sound is one of the first senses to develop once the baby is born.
    c. infants cannot recognize their mothers' voices until the second or third week after birth.
    d. immediately after birth, infants hear soft sounds better than loud sounds.

Self-Test B: Matching

Match each of the following persons with the statement or theory that most closely reflects his or her perspective:

1. Charles Nelson
2. Ernesto Pollitt
3. T. Berry Brazelton
4. William James
5. Esther Thelen
6. Elizabeth Spelke
7. Robert Fantz
8. Eleanor Gibson
9. Mark Rosenzweig
10. Karen Adolph

a. Used looking chambers to see infants' visual preferences.
b. Called the newborn's perceptual world a "blooming, buzzing confusion."
c. Used the visual cliff to study infant depth perception.
d. Measured babies' brain activity to determine its role in memory development.
e. Young infants form visual expectations.
f. Pediatrician who observed development of infant sucking.
g. Early nutritional supplements have positive long-term effects on cognitive development.
h. Proponent of dynamic systems theory view of infant motor development.
i. Practice is important in learning to walk
j. Brains of animals reared in enriched environments developed better than brains of animals reared in standard or isolated conditions.

Self-Test C: True-False

T/F   1. The cephalocaudal pattern is the sequence in which growth starts at the center of the body and moves toward the extremities.

T/F   2. Lateralization is the specialization of function in either the left or right hemisphere of the brain.

T/F   3. REM sleep occurs more in early infancy than in childhood and adulthood.

T/F   4. Sleeping on the stomach is a risk factor for SIDS (sudden infant death syndrome).

T/F   5. Most doctors believe that there are no major advantages to breast feeding over bottle feeding.

T/F   6. The dynamic systems view sees motor development as the result of a genetic blueprint.

T/F   7. All of the baby's reflexes disappear several months following birth.

T/F   8. Sensation and perception are virtually the same phenomenon.

T/F   9. Infants exhibit depth perception by the age of 6 months.

T/F   10. The infant's sensory threshold for sounds is lower than that of adults.

Self-Test D: OLC

1. The _____ principle indicates that the pattern of growth proceeds from the head downward.

2. What evidence indicates that a fetus can hear?
   a. A fetus moves when a loud noise occurs.
   b. Newborns prefer their mother's voice to a stranger's voice.
   c. Hearing is more sensitive and better developed among newborns who have been experimentally stimulated before birth.
   d. Newborns prefer to hear stories that were read to them just before they were born.

3. T/F   The growing consensus is that bottle feeding is better for the baby's health during the first 6 months of life.

4. T/F   Neuroscientists believe that the brain's flexibility and resilience are developed through repeated experience.

Essay Questions

1. A good friend of yours just had a baby and, knowing you are taking this Child Development course, confides in you about her concerns. She says her baby sleeps "almost all the time" and doesn't seem to look at her when she feeds, rocks, or talks to the child. Because of this your friend is worried about her baby's hearing and vision and is concerned about whether the baby's nutritional needs are being adequately met. Her greatest concern comes from horror stories she has heard about SIDS. She's also told you that her baby seems to "thrash about" at things and doesn't seem coordinated.

   What would you tell her about sleep patterns that a normal baby experiences and the best sleeping position to reduce the risk of SIDS? What nutritional advice can you give her? How would you explain the development of motor skills as well as sensory and perceptual development, addressing issues of intermodal perception and perception-motor coupling and unification? What strategies might you suggest to your friend for helping her infant develop competently?

2. As you come upon two of your female friends in a heated discussion, you hear one of them say that American mothers are "so much more civilized" than mothers in other parts of the world. The two main issues they are arguing about are whether breast feeding or bottle feeding is better, and whether babies are better off sleeping with their parents or by themselves. As you approach, they ask you what you've learned in your Child Development class that can enlighten them.

Key to Self-Test A: Multiple Choice

1. a (LG1)   11. b (LG1)   21. d (LG2)
2. b (LG1)   12. a (LG1)   22. a (LG2)
3. b (LG1)   13. d (LG1)   23. c (LG2)
4. c (LG1)   14. b (LG1)   24. a (LG3)
5. c (LG1)   15. c (LG1)   25. a (LG3)
6. a (LG1)   16. a (LG1)   26. c (LG3)
7. c (LG1)   17. d (LG1)   27. b (LG3)
8. a (LG1)   18. a (LG1)   28. b (LG3)
9. b (LG1)   19. c (LG1)   29. a (LG3)
10. c (LG1)   20. a (LG2)   30. a (LG3)

Key to Self-Test B: Matching

1. d
2. g
3. f
4. b
5. h
6. e
7. a
8. c
9. j
10. i

Key to Self-Test C: True/False

1. False. The cephalocaudal pattern is the sequence in which growth proceeds from top to bottom; the proximodistal pattern starts at the center of the body and moves toward the extremities.
2. True
3. True
4. True
5. False. The consensus is that breast feeding is superior to bottle feeding.
6. False. In the dynamic systems view, motor development is far more complex than the result of a genetic blueprint.
7. False. Although many reflexes disappear as the infant's brain matures and voluntary control over behaviors develops, many reflexes (e.g., coughing, blinking, yawning) persist throughout life.
8. False. Sensation occurs when information interacts with sensory receptors; perception is the interpretation of sensation.
9. True
10. False. Immediately after birth, newborns can hear, but their sensory threshold is higher than that of adults.

Key to Self-Test D: OLC

1. cephalocaudal
2. d
3. False. The growing consensus is that breast feeding is better for the baby's health during the first 6 months of life.
4. True

Key to Essay Questions

1. An appropriate answer should include discussion of infant states, noting that the typical neonate will sleep about 17 hours a day, but may range from 10 to 21 hours a day. Advise her that sleeping on the back is the best position for reducing the risk of SIDS. Then discuss the notions of cephalocaudal and proximodistal development, noting that development proceeds from head down and from inside out, and that infants are first learning to coordinate gross motor skills before they can develop fine motor skills. In terms of your friend's concern about eye contact, tell her about the infant's visual limitations, then explain to her what we know about development of the other sensory modalities; here you should incorporate information about intermodal perception (how the sensory modalities are linked) and perception-motor coupling and unification (looking at how perception-motor development is integrated). Finally, you would want to make some suggestions for how your friend can maximize her baby's development and ensure that the baby is well, so this would include: (a) discussing her concerns with her pediatrician; (b) being flexible about the baby's own rhythms; (c) providing good nutrition and explaining infants' nutritional needs; (d) breast feed if possible; (e) toilet train in a warm, relaxed, supportive manner; (f) provide extensive opportunities to explore safe environments; and (g) don't push the infant's physical development or get uptight about physical norms.

2. First, dispel the ethnocentric notion that what we do in the United States is superior to what's done in other cultures; also, it's important to understand that even within our borders there is great variation. Next, you would want to address what you've learned about the advantages of breast feeding and

why it is strongly endorsed by the American Pediatric Association during the first year of life (e.g., it enhances appropriate weight gain while lowering the risk of childhood obesity; prevents or reduces diarrhea, respiratory infections, bacterial and urinary tract infections, and middle ear infections, etc.), but also discuss how it is not always appropriate or practical (e.g., physical difficulties) and how to ensure that a baby gets proper nutrition if not breast-fed. You should also point out the reasons why some mothers around the world choose not to breast feed and possible problems that may cause for their babies. One other issue to look at on this topic is a discussion of how long infants are breast-fed and any related consequences. Then move on to the issue of shared sleeping, considering the cultural factors involved, the benefits and risks involved in shared sleeping, and explain why the American Academy of Pediatrics Task Force on Infant Positioning and SIDS discourages shared sleeping.

Research Project 1: Cross-Cultural Infant Practices

Chapter 6 discusses many areas of cultural diversity with respect to practices such as breast feeding versus bottle feeding, when to wean a baby, shared sleeping, and variations in infant activity and motor development. The chapter also discusses recommendations by such organizations as the World Health Organization (WHO) and the American Academy of Pediatrics with regard to some of these topics. Together with some of your classmates, interview mothers from different ethnic, social, and cultural backgrounds to learn their attitudes and behaviors with regard to these infant practices. Also gather information about the children, such as age, height, weight, and health status. After you have collected this information chart it and analyze your data to determine if you see any particular patterns of child outcomes that correlate with the mothers' practices.

Mother's Ethnic Identification _____   Mother's Country of Origin _____

Child's Age (in days, weeks, months)   Child's Sex: Female [   ]   Male [   ]

Child's Height _____   Child's Weight _____

Child's Health Status (including any illnesses) _____

Other Relevant Information for Mother/Child _____

Infant practices	Mother's attitude	Mother's practice	When started/stopped
Breast feeding/ Bottle feeding			
Shared sleeping/ Nonshared sleeping			
Infant activity showing motor development			
Other			

1.   Did you notice any differences among the women in terms of their attitudes toward breast feeding or bottle feeding? Were their attitudes consistent with their actual practice?

2. Did you notice any differences among the women in terms of their attitudes toward shared sleeping or nonshared sleeping? Were their attitudes consistent with their actual practice?

3. What variations did you find in terms of whether mothers encouraged or discouraged the babies' activities? Did the mothers confine their babies in any way, including use of playpens, or did they encourage the babies to move about on their own?

4. Did you notice any relationship between the children's health status and such things as breast feeding versus bottle feeding, shared versus nonshared sleeping, or restriction/encouragement of activity?

5. How long did mothers breast feed or bottle feed? If their babies slept with them, until what age did the mothers believe this was appropriate? Were the fathers also involved in the shared sleeping?

6. What did you learn from the mothers that was not discussed in the text?

7. Based on what you have learned both from the text and from this research, what recommendations would you make about each of these infant practices? Why?

Research Project 2: Observing Infants' Reflexes and Sensory Abilities

After getting parental permission (or try to get permission to visit a neonatal unit in a local hospital), observe an infant for half an hour. Record the infant's age and your observations of the infant's use of reflexes and sensory modalities. If you know the child's parents, you may want to seek permission to test some of the reflexes, so long as this does not cause any distress for the infant. Compare your observations with what you would expect of a child this age from reading Chapter 6 and from researching other reflexes. Then answer the questions that follow.

Child's Age (in days or weeks) _____   Child's Sex   Female [ ]   Male [ ]

Sense	Observed	Expected	Expected Change Over Time
Visual (Sight)			
Auditory (Sound)			
Olfactory (Smell)			
Gustatory (Taste)			
Tactile (Touch)			
Integration of Senses			

Reflex	Observed	Expected	Expected Change Over Time
Blinking			
Grasping			
Rooting			
Sucking			
Moro			
Tonic Neck			
Babinski			
Plantar			

1. How did the infant demonstrate the presence of each of the senses?

2. In what way did you observe that the infant was able to integrate the different senses?

3. Were your observations of this infant's sensory development consistent with what you would expect from reading Chapter 6?

4. Which reflexes were you able to observe? Describe the infant's reflexive behaviors.

5. What additional reflexes did you observe that were not described in the chapter?

6. Were your observations of this infant's reflexes consistent with what you would expect from reading Chapter 6 and the outside sources you found?

7. What purpose do you think each reflex serves?

8. Note that some reflexes are permanent and others disappear after a certain period. Which reflexes remain, which disappear, and what might it mean if those that are expected to disappear don't disappear?

9. What have you learned about the infant's adaptive abilities from observing this child's use of sensory modalities, coordination of senses, and reflexive behaviors?

Personal Application 1: Reflecting on What You Learned

Consider what you read in Chapter 6, then answer the following questions:

1. What information in this chapter did you already know?
2. How can/do you use that information in your own life?
3. What information in this chapter was totally new to you?
4. How can you use that new information in your own life?
5. What information in this chapter was different from what you previously believed?
6. How was this information different?

7. How do you account for the differences between what you believed and what you learned in the chapter?
8. What is the most important thing you learned from reading this chapter?

Personal Application 2: Consider Your Own Development

Check with your parents to see what records, if any, they kept on your development. Consider each area of development discussed in Chapter 6, then use the following chart to complete your own developmental milestones, indicating if they were ahead of, behind, or in synchrony with the stated norms. Do you think your own rate of development affected your later life? If so, state how. If you cannot reconstruct your own early growth, look at your own child(ren) or other children with whom you have close contact (being sure to get parental consent if the children are not your own).

Self Aspect	Your Development	Norms in Chapter 6	Comments
Demonstrations of Cephalocaudal Pattern			
Demonstrations of Proximodistal Pattern			

Height:
     Age:
     Age:
     Age:			

Weight
     Age:
     Age:
     Age:			

Evidence of Brain Growth			

Gross Motor Skills
     Age:
     Age:
     Age:			

Fine Motor Skills
     Age:
     Age:
     Age:			

Sleeping Patterns			
Other (describe)			

Internet Projects

Check out the McGraw-Hill Web site for this text (www.mhhe.com/santrockc9). You'll find numerous activities there, in particular, information that will help you research the answers and complete the exercises in the "Taking It to the Net" section at the end of the textbook chapter. Please note that all Web site addresses in this Study Guide have been checked and were correct at the time of publication; however, Web sites may be discontinued or addresses may change, so when you search a given site it may no longer be viable. If that occurs, I apologize for the inconvenience and would appreciate you notifying me so I can make appropriate revisions in future editions of this Study Guide.

Internet Project 1: Sudden Infant Death Syndrome (SIDS)

SIDS is a mysterious problem that is the highest cause of infant death in the United States. Go to the SIDS Web site at http://sids-network.org to learn more about what SIDS is, risk factors for SIDS, how many children and families are affected, and what steps parents can take to minimize the risk of their children dying from SIDS.

Internet Project 2: Healthy Starts

The Caring for Children box in Chapter 6 discusses the Hawaii Family Support/Healthy Start Program. Explore the Internet to find more information about that program (you might try the Family Support Services of West Hawaii at http://www.fsswh.org/), and seek out other programs that offer similar support for high-risk families. Check out professional sites (e.g., medical [such as http://www.webmd.com], psychological [such as http://www.apa.org]) as well as general information sites (e.g., http://www.google.com, http://www.ask.com, etc.).

1. How many programs were you able to find?

2. Where are the programs located?

3. Who funds these programs?

4. What outcomes have these programs achieved?

5. What steps are taken to keep families in these programs?

6. Compare the professional and general information sites and state what differences you notice in terms of how the programs and the program outcomes are described.

7. Based on what you have learned about the Healthy Start Programs and the results that have been reported, how would you design an effective program to maximize the potential of children in at-risk families?

Additional Internet Resources

American Academy of Pediatrics: http://www.aap.org.

American Medical Association:http:// www.ama-assn.org.

APA site: http://www.apa.org—Offers a multitude of options for learning about pregnancy, childbirth options, and other topics covered in this chapter. Particularly, go to the "Public Publications" link and check out the "Database Info" and "Print and Media" offerings.

APS site: http://www.psychologicalscience.org.

The Child Development Web site: http://childstudy.net—Information on children's topics.

Children's Defense Fund (CDF): http://www.childrensdefense.org—The Web site for CDF, the organization headed by Marian Wright Edelman to promote child welfare (discussed in Chapter 1 of the text).

Healthfinder: http://healthfinder.gov, associated with www.health.gov, is a portal to the Web sites of a number of multi-agency health initiatives and activities of the U.S. Department of Health and Human Services and other federal departments and agencies.

Mayo Clinic's Health Site: http://www.mayoclinic.com.

Medscape: http://www.medscape.com/px/urlinfo—Free database of medical articles, plus access to medical dictionaries, drug databases, and breaking medical news.

Monell Chemical Senses Center: http://www.monell.org/researchoverview_h.htm—An overview of sensation and perception from "the world's first scientific institute for multidisciplinary research on taste, smell and chemosensory irritation."

Multimodoal Imaging of Perceptual Integration Processes of Humans and Monkeys, by Dr. Lars Muckli of the Max Planck Society: www.mpih-frankfurt.mpg.de/global/Np/Projects/muckli.htm— Discusses multimodal imaging, including how the research is conducted and what the researchers have found, and contains excellent graphic images.

National Institutes of Health: http://www.nih.gov—Starting point for getting into any subagency of NIH.

National Institute of Mental Health: http://www.nimh.nih.gov—Excellent resource for policy statements, NIMH research, grants; you might want to check out postpartum depression at this site.

New England Journal of Medicine: http://www.nejm.org—Abstracts to articles, full-text letters and commentaries.

New York University Infant Cognition Center: www.psych.nyu.edu/infant—NYU's Infant Cognition Center's site presenting current research studies on how babies think. Contact information is provided for parents who are interested in having their children participate in the studies.

Psychological Resources: Hanover College: A Tutorial on Basic Neural Processes: http://psych.hanover.edu/Krantz/neurotut.html; at http://psych.hanover.edu/Krantz/sen_tut.html—you will find a tutorial on sensation and perception.

Scientific American: http://www.sciam.com—General scientific resource.

SIDS Network: http://sids-network.org—Provides information about SIDS, including risk factors, support groups, information on who is affected by SIDS, and ways parents can minimize the risk of their children dying from SIDS.

Society for Research in Child Development (SRCD): http://www.srcd.org—The Web site for SRCD, an organization whose purposes are to promote multidisciplinary research in the field of human development, to foster the exchange of information among scientists and other professionals of various disciplines, and to encourage applications of research findings.

Types of Neurons can be found at http://faculty.washington.edu/chudler/cells.html—You will learn about many different types of neurons, their parts, and how to put a neuron together, and you will find review tests.

Web MD: www.webmd.com—Offers a wide variety of information for the medical profession and for consumers.

Zero to Three: www.zerotothree.org—A site for parents and professionals. Zero to Three is a nonprofit organization that focuses on promoting the healthy development of babies and toddlers.

CHAPTER 7: COGNITIVE DEVELOPMENT IN INFANCY

Learning Goals

By the time you have completed this chapter, you should be able to reach the following goals:

1. Summarize Piaget's theory of infant development.

2. Describe how infants learn and remember.

3. Discuss the assessment of intelligence in infancy.

4. Characterize early environmental influences on cognitive development.

5. Describe the nature of language and how it develops in infancy.

Explain Piaget's concepts of *schemes* and his two components of *adaptation*.	Describe Piaget's substage of *tertiary circular reactions, novelty, and curiosity*.
List the six substages of the *sensorimotor* stage.	Explain Piaget's substage of *internalization of schemes*.
Describe *simple reflexes* as they relate to the sensorimotor stage.	What is *object permanence*? When does it develop?
Describe Piaget's substage of *first habits and primary circular reactions*. What are *primary circular reactions*?	Describe how Baillargeon and her colleagues use *violation of expectations* to assess object permanence.
Describe Piaget's substage of *secondary circular reactions*.	Explain the role of *attention* in cognitive development. How are *habituation* and *dishabituation* linked to attention?
Explain Piaget's substage of *coordination of secondary circular reactions*.	How does *deferred imitation* relate to *memory*? Differentiate between *implicit memory* and *explicit memory*.

Tertiary circular reactions, novelty, and curiosity: Piaget's fifth sensorimotor substage; develops between 12 and 18 months; infants become intrigued by the variety of properties that objects possess and by the many things they can make happen to objects; infant purposely explores new possibilities with objects.	***Schemes***: In Piaget's theory, actions or mental representations that organize knowledge. The two basic concepts involved in adaptation are ***assimilation***, incorporation of new information into existing knowledge (schemes), and ***accommodation***, adjusting schemes to fit new information and experiences.
Internalization of schemes: Piaget's sixth sensorimotor substage, develops between 18 and 24 months; the infant's mental functioning shifts from a purely sensorimotor plane to a symbolic plane; infant also develops the ability to use primitive symbols (i.e., an internalized sensory image or word that represents an event).	***Sensorimotor stage***: Birth to about age 2; infants construct an understanding of the world by coordinating sensory experiences with motoric actions. Substages: (1) simple reflexes; (2) first habits and primary circular reactions; (3) secondary circular reactions; (4) coordination of secondary circular reactions; (5) tertiary circular reactions; and (6) internalization of schemes.
Object permanence: The Piagetian term for the infant's ability to understand that objects and events continue to exist even when they cannot directly be seen, heard, or touched. One of the infant's most important accomplishments.	***Simple reflexes***: Piaget's first sensorimotor substage; corresponds to the first month after birth; the basic means of coordinating sensation and action is through reflexive behaviors, such as rooting and sucking, which are present at birth.
Violation of expectations: A research method used by Baillergeon to assess object permanence. An infant sees an event happen as it normally would, then if the event is changed in a way that violates what the infant expects to see, the infant looks at the event longer, indicating that the infant is surprised by what occurred.	***First habits and primary circular reaction***: Piaget's second sensorimotor substage, develops between 1 and 4 months; reflexes evolve into adaptive schemes that are more refined and coordinated. ***Primary circular reactions***: Schemes based on the infant's attempt to reproduce an interesting or pleasurable event that initially occurred by chance.
Attention: focusing of mental resources; it improves cognitive processing on many tasks. Researchers study ***habituation*** (decreased responsiveness to a stimulus after repeated presentations) and ***dishabituation*** (recovery of a habituated response after a change in stimulation) to determine infants' sensory abilities; to assess memory; to measure maturity, well-being, and brain damage.	***Secondary circular reactions***: Piaget's third sensorimotor substage, develops between 4 and 8 months; infant becomes more object-oriented or focused on the world, moving beyond preoccupation with the self in sensorimotor interactions.
Deferred imitation: Imitation that occurs after a time delay of hours or days (thus indicating that the infant has memory for a previous event). ***Memory***: a central feature of cognitive development that involves retention of information over time. ***Implicit memory***: Perceptual-motor memory involved in conditioning tasks (e.g., skills); e***xplicit memory***: conscious ability to recall the past (occurs in the second half of the 1st year).	***Coordination of secondary circular reactions***: Piaget's fourth sensorimotor substage; develops between 8 and 12 months; significant changes involve coordination of schemes and intentionality; infant combines and recombines previously learned schemes in a coordinated way.

Explain the *developmental quotient (DQ)*.	What is the relationship between *aphasia* and language?
Describe the *Bayley Scales of Infant Development* and how they are used.	Differentiate between *Broca's area* and *Wernicke's area*.
Define the term *language*. Explain the concept of *infinite generativity* as it relates to language.	What is the *language acquisition device (LAD)*? Who has suggested its existence?
Describe the five systems of rules involved in the organization of language.	What is *child-directed speech*?
When does the *vocabulary spurt* occur? Contrast *overextension* with *underextension.*	Explain the language acquisition strategies of *recasting*, *expanding*, and *labeling*.
Describe *telegraphic speech*.	Describe some ways that parents can facilitate the language development of their infants and toddlers.

Aphasia: A language disorder, resulting from brain damage, that involves a loss of the ability to use words.	*Developmental quotient (DQ)*: An overall developmental score that combines subscores in motor, language, adaptive, and personal-social domains in Arnold Gesell's assessment of infants (a clinical assessment).
Broca's area: an area of the brain's left frontal lobe that directs the muscle movements involved in speech production. *Wernicke's area*: An area of the brain's left hemisphere that is involved in language comprehension.	*The Bayley Scales of Infant Development*: (developed by Nancy Bayley, 1969) Widely used to assess infant development; three components: mental scale, motor scale, and infant behavior profile (used to predict later development).
Language acquisition device (LAD): Chomsky's theoretical concept of a biological endowment that enables the child to detect certain language categories, such as phonology, syntax, and semantics.	*Language*: A form of communication, whether spoken, written, or signed, that is based on a system of symbols. *Infinite generativity*: An individual's ability to generate an endless number of meaningful sentences using a finite set of words and rules.
Childt-directed speech: The type of speech often displayed by parents and other adults to talk to babies in a higher pitch than normal and with simple words and sentences.	The five systems of language rules: *phonology*: the sound system of the language; *morphology*: units of meaning involved in word formation; *syntax*: the way words are combined to form acceptable phrases and sentences; *semantics*: the meanings of words and sentences; and *pragmatics*: the appropriate use of language in context.
Recasting: rephrasing a statement the child has made, perhaps turning it into a question. *Expanding*: restating what a child says in linguistically sophisticated form. *Labeling*: identifying the names of objects.	The *vocabulary spurt*, the rapid increase in vocabulary, occurs between average age of 18 months (about 50 words) and 2 years (about 200 words). *Overextension* is the tendency to apply a word to objects that are not related to or appropriate for the word's meaning; *underextension* is the tendency to apply a word too narrowly.
For infants and toddlers, be an active conversational partner and use a language style you are comfortable with (but consider ways to expand toddler's language abilities); for infants, talk as if the infant understands what you are saying; for toddlers, remember to listen and adjust to child's idiosyncrasies. Avoid sexual stereotypes; resist normative comparisons.	*Telegraphic speech*: The use of short and precise words without grammatical markers (e.g., articles, auxiliary verbs, other connectives) to communicate; it characterizes young children's two- or three-word combinations.

Self-Test A: Multiple-Choice Questions

1. Jean Piaget believed that children's minds develop as children:
   a. get reinforcement from their environment.
   b. create new neural pathways.
   c. actively construct their cognitive worlds.
   d. resolve unconscious conflicts.

2. In a Piagetian model, a(n) _____ is a cognitive structure that helps individuals organize and understand their experiences.
   a. memory
   b. image
   c. cognition
   d. scheme

3. Ahmed sees a cow and calls it a goat. His mother tells him that cows are much bigger than goats and their milk is not as sweet. Ahmed learns to differentiate between cows and goats through the process of:
   a. schematic adaptation.
   b. assimilation.
   c. accommodation.
   d. disequilibrium.

4. According to Piaget, during the first sensorimotor substage, infants' behaviors are:
   a. reflexive.
   b. maladaptive.
   c. unchanging.
   d. reinforced.

5. By chance, Abigail shook her rattle. She then began to repeat this action of shaking her rattle. As a normal infant, Abigail is in which substage?
   a. reflexive
   b. first habits and primary circular reactions
   c. secondary circular reactions
   d. coordination of secondary circular reactions

6. Laurent has problems retrieving a ball that rolled out of reach, so he uses a Tinkertoy stick to hit it. He is in which substage?
   a. primary circular reactions
   b. secondary circular reactions
   c. coordination of secondary circular reactions
   d. tertiary circular reactions

7. When Andy was 5 months old, he was playing with a toy rabbit that fell behind the sofa. Because he could no longer see the rabbit, he did not search for it. Now that he is 9 months old he does look for it, reflecting the presence of:
   a. schemata.
   b. self-differentiation.
   c. assimilation.
   d. object permanence.

8. In a study by Baillergeon et al., infants saw a toy car roll down an inclined track, then later saw a mouse placed on the track and the car rolled down the track, apparently not being blocked by the mouse (which the infants didn't know had been removed from the track). The infants showed surprise because:
   a. their expectations had been violated.
   b. of the AB error.
   c. they had not yet acquired object permanence.
   d. their vision was still poor.

9. Matsuyo is 7 months old and knows that the size of a moving object determines how far it will move a stationary object with which it collides, suggesting an understanding of:
   a. causality.
   b. object permanence.
   c. habituation.
   d. dishabituation.

10. Recent research on infants' perceptual and conceptual development suggests that:
    a. infants have less sophisticated perceptual abilities than Piaget suggested.
    b. infants' perceptual abilities develop much earlier than Piaget envisioned.
    c. Piaget was more specific than today's researchers in infant development.
    d. infants are far less competent than Piaget suggested.

11. Carolyn Rovee-Collier has consistently demonstrated:
    a. young infants' inability to learn from operant conditioning.
    b. how infants can retain information through operant conditioning.
    c. young infants' inability to learn from classical conditioning.
    d. how infants can retain information through classical conditioning.

12. Shawna has been shown the flashing face of a chimpanzee seven times. At first she was very interested in the face, now she doesn't look at it, demonstrating that _____ has taken place.
    a. dishabituation
    b. object permanence
    c. transference
    d. habituation

13. Research by Andrew Meltzoff showing the infant's ability to imitate adult facial expressions shortly after birth demonstrates that:
    a. imitation has a biological base.
    b. imitative abilities are learned quickly.
    c. infants have a full range of emotional expression at birth.
    d. imitation is a form of emotional expression.

14. Developmental researchers believe that _____ memory does not emerge until the second half of the first year.
    a. implicit
    b. explicit
    c. tacit
    d. short term

15. Mary tells her coworkers that she remembers events that happened when she was a year old. This is:
    a. likely, because many adults can remember events from the first year or two of life.
    b. unlikely, because most adults cannot remember anything from the first three years of their life.
    c. an indication of a serious memory problem called *infantile amnesia*.
    d. an indicator that she was sexually molested as an infant.

16. Unlike Gesell's scales, the Bayley Scales of Infant Development were developed to assess infant behavior and to:
    a. provide clinical information.
    b. evaluate language development.
    c. predict later development.
    d. provide information about neurological problems.

17. The Fagan Test of Infant Intelligence:
    a. estimates intelligence by comparing the amount of time a baby looks at a new object and the amount of time spent looking at a familiar object.
    b. assesses infants' overall development in terms of motor, language, adaptive, and personal-social domains.
    c. has been successful at measuring infant intelligence in industrialized nations, but not in third-world countries.
    d. was the first measure of infant intelligence.

18. Current information concerning the ability to predict intelligence later in life from assessments in infancy suggests that:
    a. the Fagan and Bayley Scales have been useful in predicting later intelligence.
    b. intelligence in adolescence cannot be predicted from infant assessments.
    c. assessments using information-processing tasks suggest greater continuity between infant and childhood intelligence than previously believed.
    d. assessments using information-processing tasks suggest less continuity between infant and childhood intelligence than previously believed.

19. Research has found that nutrition has an important impact on _____ development.
    a. physical
    b. cognitive
    c. both physical and cognitive
    d. neither physical nor cognitive

20. The Abecedarian Intervention program resulted in all of the following, EXCEPT:
    a. higher IQ scores were evident for children in the program by age 3.
    b. the greatest IQ gains were for children whose mothers had high IQ scores (over 130).
    c. the effects of the program were long-lasting.
    d. over time children in the program were less likely than peers not in the program to be held back a year in school.

21. Language is most accurately defined as a system of _____ that allows for communication with others.
    a. images
    b. symbols
    c. vocalizations
    d. words

22. Mrs. Mandrake gives her class a list of 50 words and tells them to use all of those words, but no others, to write a poem. Each child's poem is unique, demonstrating a characteristic of human language called:
    a. phonology.
    b. morphology.
    c. infinite generativity.
    d. semantic application.

23. _____ involves the ways words are combined to form acceptable phrases and sentences.
    a. Syntax
    b. Semantics
    c. Pragmatics
    d. Morphology

24. Which of the following early communications develops latest?
    a. crying
    b. babbling
    c. gestures
    d. cooing

25. Jessica is 8 months old. We would expect all of the following from her EXCEPT:
    a. she is able to perceive changes in sounds from her "own" language.
    b. she demonstrates an ability to find boundaries between words in her "own" language.
    c. she is beginning to use gestures, such as waving "bye-bye."
    d. she is able to recognize changes in sounds that don't exist in her "own" language.

26. Eran has just said his first words. We would expect that these words:
    a. are the same today as children's first words were 50 years ago.
    b. are more likely related to people than to objects than were the first words of children 50 years ago.
    c. are more likely related to objects than to people than were the first words of children 50 years ago.
    d. are more complex today than children's words were 50 years ago.

27. Zoe calls every man she sees "DaDa." This demonstrates a concept called:
    a. overproduction.
    b. the holophrase hypothesis.
    c. underextension.
    d. overextension.

28. The strongest evidence for the biological basis of language is that:
    a. a language acquisition device (LAD) has been located in the brain's temporal lobe.
    b. language represents chains of responses and imitation.
    c. children all over the world reach language milestones at about the same time and in the same order.
    d. children from middle-income professional and welfare backgrounds develop normally in terms of language.

29. Damage to _____ would result in the patient babbling words in a meaningless way.
   a. Broca's area
   b. Wernicke's area
   c. the right frontal lobe
   d. the corpus callosum

30. Sue talks her baby using a high pitch and simple words and sentences. It is likely that:
   a. her baby will be attentive and engaged in communication with her mother.
   b. Sue talks to everyone that way.
   c. her baby will become upset and begin to cry.
   d. Sue has emotional problems that will create communication problems for her baby.

Self-Test B: Matching

Match each of the following persons with the statement or theory that most closely reflects his or her perspective:

1. Arnold Gesell
2. Carolyn Rovee-Collier
3. Nancy Bayley
4. Andrew Meltzoff
5. Patricia Kuhl
6. Jean Piaget
7. Jean Mandler
8. Ernesto Pollitt
9. Renée Baillargeon
10. Naomi Baron

a. Devised a widely used infant intelligence test to assess infant behavior and predict later development.
b. Contributed to cognitive theory by observing his three children.
c. Studied imitation and deferred imitation by infants.
d. Argued that explicit memory does not occur until the second half of first year.
e. Found that early nutritional supplements have positive long-term consequences for cognitive development.
f. Provides parents with techniques to promote children's language development.
g. Believed infants as young as 4 months expect objects to be substantial and permanent.
h. Demonstrated memory in 2-1/2 month-old infants.
i. Developed a clinical measure to assess potential abnormality in infants.
j. Demonstrated that after 6 months of age infants get better at perceiving changes in sounds in their "own" language, and lose the ability to recognize changes in sounds in other languages.

Self-Test C: True-False

T/F   1. In Piaget's theory, children construct their own cognitive worlds.

T/F   2. Research studies based on Piaget's theory have found that children develop at a slower rate than Piaget had proposed.

T/F   3. Assessment of habituation has assisted researchers in measuring infants' maturity and well-being.

T/F   4. Infants as young as 2 to 3 months of age display explicit memory.

T/F   5. The most widely used developmental scale used with infants today is the one created by Gessell.

T/F   6.   The Bayley and Fagan tests of infant intelligence are good predictors of intelligence later in life.

T/F   7.   Nutritional supplements given to malnourished infants improve their cognitive development.

T/F   8.   Intervention programs that target infants are more effective if they are short-term and focus on only a few areas of concern.

T/F   9.   Most human languages lack infinite generativity.

T/F   10.   The behavioral view of language development has been supported by extensive research.

Self-Test D: OLC

1. Damage to _____ would result in the patient babbling words in a meaningless way.

2. A child who learns the word "car" and then calls all moving vehicles on the road "cars," including motorcycles and trucks, is engaging in the process of
   a. accommodation.
   b. assimilation.
   c. first habits and primary circular reactions.
   d. simple reflexes.

3. T/F   According to Piaget, accommodation occurs when children adjust their schemes to fit new information and experiences.

4. T/F   Morphology involves the way words are combined to form acceptable phrases and sentences.

Essay Questions

1. The head of a local business organization has asked you to talk to members of his organization concerning early childhood intervention programs. He advises you that many members of the group are upset with a recent local movement to help "underprivileged children," believing that it's really up to their parents to get jobs and support their kids rather than relying on society—and tax payers— to foot the bill. What insights would you offer with regard to the effects of malnutrition and poverty not only for the children who are affected, but also society in general? How would you encourage them to support early intervention programs?

2. Your 15-month-old nephew has started using two-word sentences. His father is overjoyed with what a genius his son is, and he shares his delight with you every time the two of you speak. While he constantly lets you know that this is clearly a matter of genetics, he also wants to know what he can do to encourage his child's language development. Explain the process of language development to him, including the stages of language development and explanations of the biological and behavioral theories involved, and discuss with him the research on the influence of both genetics and environment with regard to language development. On the basis of what you know, do you agree with the boy's father that his language skills are advanced? Or do you believe they are either normal or delayed? Give your reasons.

Key to Self-Test A: Multiple Choice

1. c (LG1)	11. b (LG2)	21. b (LG5)
2. d (LG1)	12. d (LG2)	22. c (LG5)
3. c (LG1)	13. a (LG2)	23. a (LG5)
4. a (LG1)	14. b (LG2)	24. c (LG5)
5. c (LG1)	15. b (LG2)	25. d (LG5)
6. c (LG1)	16. c (LG3)	26. a (LG5)
7. d (LG1)	17. a (LG3)	27. d (LG5)
8. a (LG1)	18. c (LG3)	28. c (LG5)
9. a (LG1)	19. c (LG4)	29. b (LG5)
10. b (LG1)	20. b (LG4)	30. a (LG5)

Key to Self-Test B: Matching

1. i
2. h
3. a
4. c
5. j
6. b
7. d
8. e
9. g
10. f

Key to Self-Test C: True/False

1. True
2. False. Researchers who have built on Piaget's theory have found that many abilities develop earlier than Piaget proposed.
3. True
4. False. Infants as young as 2 to 3 months of age display implicit, not explicit, memory.
5. False. The Bayley scales and the Fagan Test of Infant Intelligence are the most widely used developmental scales today, although Gessell's scale is still used by pediatricians.
6. False. Although the Bayley and Fagan tests are not highly correlated with IQ scores in later childhood and adolescence, the attentional processes of habituation and dishabituation are.
7. True
8. False. The most effective intervention programs for infants are long term, time-intensive, provide direct educational benefits, and are comprehensive and multidimensional.
9. False. Infinite generativity is a landmark of human speech (i.e., we have the ability to produce an endless number of meaningful sentences using a finite set of words and rules).
10. False. The behavioral view that children acquire language as a result of reinforcement has not been supported.

Key to Self-Test D: OLC

1. Wernicke's area
2. b
3. True
4. False. Morphology refers to the units of meaning involved in word formation; syntax refers to the way that words are combined to form acceptable phrases and sentences.

Key to Essay Questions

1. First, address the issue of the effects of poor nutrition and poverty on cognitive development, and how that translates into a person's later ability to contribute to society. Then describe some of the early intervention programs from the text (e.g., research on nutrition and cognitive development by Pollitt et al. and the Abecedarian Intervention program) and the effects of these programs on children's cognitive development and follow with your own thoughts on how that would benefit

society. Finally, discuss what elements have been found to lead to the most effective interventions (e.g., long-lasting programs that are time-intensive, provide educational benefits for children and parents, and are comprehensive and multidimensional).

2. This question requires you to explain each stage of language development discussed in this chapter, beginning with receptive language (understanding words at about 6 to 9 months of age), the one-word stage (which begins at approximately 12 months), etc. Present the biological influences, such as biological prewiring as suggested by Noam Chomsky (i.e., the language acquisition device) and the evidence for a critical period for learning language. Also discuss the evidence for environmental influences (e.g., the use of infant-directed speech and the strategies such as recasting that adults use with children). The research of Hart and Risley that compares children from middle-class professional families with children from welfare families should help this father understand the importance of communicating with his son. Finally, it would appear that your nephew is, indeed, advanced in his language skills, since the two-word stage doesn't typically begin until 18 to 24 months.

Research Project 1: Observing Imitation

Something I particularly enjoy doing (as a developmental psychologist) is observing babies when I'm standing in a line somewhere, such as the grocery store. The next time you find yourself standing behind an infant, observe the child to see what you notice that would (or would not) be consistent with what you've learned in this chapter. Then smile at the baby and see what kind of response you get—does the baby smile back, turn away, ignore you, cry? Sometimes, though, you'll notice a baby is crying, and what I've found often stops the crying is to make a big "O" with your mouth as if you are sympathizing with the child and acknowledging the child's distress. Whenever I do this, I find the child will stop crying and look at me in wide-eyed interest. Try opening and shutting your mouth to see if the child will imitate you. You might also try wiggling your nose or your ears. Although people would clearly think you're weird if you did this in some other context, they generally understand when they see the baby, so they'll either ignore you or be amused. Typically the parent(s) will acknowledge your presence, and if they do, you might say you are taking this class and ask the baby's age. (Obviously, if the parent(s) seems annoyed or asks you to stop, do stop immediately.) Based on your observations, answer the questions that follow:

1. What have you noticed about the child's perceptual abilities?
2. Are they what you would expect for a child of this age (if the parent doesn't tell you how old the child is, you might be able to make an "educated" guess)?
3. Did the child do anything that surprised you?
4. What did you learn from observing this interaction?

Research Project 2: Charting Cognitive Development in Infancy

Describe the components of cognitive development through the first 2 years of life, stating what you would expect to observe based on what you've read in the text. Then observe children during this life stage and record your observations (unless you are watching unobtrusively, be sure to get permission from parents and, if possible, the children). (You could create a similar chart to observe language development.) Finally, answer the questions that follow.

Developmental Issue	Age Range	Expected Behavior(s)	Observed Behavior(s)
Simple reflexes			
Primary circular reactions			
Secondary circular reactions			
Coordination of secondary circular reactions			
Tertiary circular reactions			
Internalization of schemes			
Perceptual development			
Conceptual development			
Habituation/Dishabituation			
Imitation			
Deferred imitation			
Memory			

1. What did you notice when you compared what you would expect to see from reading the chapter with what you actually did see?
2. Did you observe anything that particularly surprised you with respect to what you expected after reading the chapter? Explain.
3. What observations were consistent with Piaget's theory?
4. What observations were inconsistent with Piaget's theory?
5. Based on your observations, which theories and research studies appeared to be supported?
6. What other comments do you have concerning these observations?

Personal Application 1: Reflecting on What You Learned

Consider what you read in Chapter 7, then answer the following questions:

1. What information in this chapter did you already know?
2. How can/do you use that information in your own life?
3. What information in this chapter was totally new to you?
4. How can you use that new information in your own life?
5. What information in this chapter was different from what you previously believed?
6. How was this information different?
7. How do you account for the differences between what you believed and what you learned in the chapter?
8. What is the most important thing you learned from reading this chapter?

Personal Application Project 2: Consider Your Own Development

This may be difficult, but if you can, give it a try. Now that you have learned about infantile amnesia (look back at the chapter if you don't remember what that is), you might understand why you can't remember back to your early life, so you will have to rely on input from older adults who were around at the time you were a baby. Ask your relatives about your developmental milestones during the first 2 years of your life. Be sure to include cognitive milestones (such as Piaget's six substages, if possible), imitation, and language development. Based on these recollections, indicate how consistent your early development was with what the theorists would predict.

Developmental Milestone	Your Development	Comments
Piaget's sensorimotor substages (describe)		
Other cognitive milestones (describe)		
Language development (describe)		
Other (describe)		

Internet Projects

Check out the McGraw-Hill Web site for this text (www.mhhe.com/santrockc9). You'll find numerous activities there, in particular, information that will help you research the answers and complete the exercises in the "Taking It to the Net" section at the end of the textbook chapter. Please note that all Web site addresses in this Study Guide have been checked and were correct at the time of publication; however, Web sites may be discontinued or addresses may change, so when you search a given site it may no longer be viable. If that occurs, I apologize for the inconvenience and would appreciate you notifying me so I can make appropriate revisions in future editions of this Study Guide.

Internet Project 1: The Long-Term Effects of Early Deprivation in Infancy

The textbook discusses the effects of early deprivation on children's cognitive development and the benefits of early intervention programs. Do an Internet search for early childhood intervention programs, starting at http://www.apa.org, the site of the American Psychological Association. At that site, type in "early childhood intervention programs" and other terms from this chapter (e.g., Abecedarian) to read about research that has been conducted and recommendations that have been made. Then check out the Web site for the Consultative Groups on Early Childhood Care and Development at http://www.ecdgroup.com. Link to "site map," then link to "Resources" and check out several of the numerous articles available about research around the world.

1. How does what you find in these articles support what you learned from reading Chapter 7?
2. What new information did you learn?
3. If you were to design an early intervention program, what would it look like? How would it be similar to and different from some of the programs you've read about in the textbook?
4. Consider your attitudes of early intervention before reading Chapter 7, then assess whether these attitudes have changed now that you have more information. If they have changed, describe the changes; if not, why do you think they have remained constant?
5. With the information you now have, how would you respond to someone who believes that governmental and nongovernmental agencies should not be putting money into early intervention programs?

Note that a prolific researcher and writer on the effects of early life experience on brain development is University of Southern California Professor Adrian Raine—you can find information about him and some of his work at the USC site, http://www.usc.edu/dept/LAS/psychology/people/raine.html. You can read the abstract of his article "Effects of environmental enrichment at ages 3–years on schizotypal personality and antisocial behavior at ages 17 and 23 years" at http://ajp.psychiatryonline.org/cgi/content/abstract/160/9/1627. After reading the abstract, what do you believe to be some benefits of providing nutritional support to at-risk children?

Internet Project 2: Stimulating Cognitive and Linguistic Development

The text offers several studies that demonstrate the importance of interactions between the baby and others (parents, siblings, other adults, other children) for maximum development. (One thing to watch out for is to avoid overstimulation—take your cue from the baby.) http://babyparenting.about.com/od/childdevelopment/a/babytalk.htm is a good site with many ideas plus suggestions for appropriate books. Do a search for "early learning" and check out the information and activities that can help the child's cognitive development. One of the useful sites there is "Precursors to Reading": http://childparenting.about.com/cs/k6education/a/prereading.htm. Also check out the Zero to Three site, http://www.zerotothree.org, and look particularly at the "Magic of Everyday Moments" link in the "Parents" section.

1. How does the information on these sites augment what you learned from the text?
2. Was there anything that particularly surprised you?
3. What information did you already know? What was new to you?
4. How will this information help you interact effectively with young children?
5. How will this information help you interact effectively with parents of young children?
6. What concerns might there be about overstimulating children? How would you address those concerns?
7. If you were to design a program that provided the optimal experience for children to encourage their cognitive (and linguistic) development, while at the same time helping them learn to *enjoy* learning, what would that program look like?

Additional Internet Resources

APA site: http://www.apa.org—Offers a multitude of options for learning about pregnancy, childbirth options, and other topics covered in this chapter. Particularly, go to the "Public Publications" link and check out the "Print and Media" offerings.

APS site: http://www.psychologicalscience.org

The Child Development Web site: http://childstudy.net—Provides information on children's topics encouraging social activism.

Children's Defense Fund (CDF): http://www.childrensdefense.org—The Web site for CDF, the organization headed by Marian Wright Edelman to promote child welfare (discussed in Chapter 1 of the text).

Child Development Institute Web site offers a useful chart of language development at http://childdevelopmentinfo.com/development/language_development.shtml. First peruse the Lanauge Development chart, then explore the entire site for a wealth of information on child development topics.

Children's Nutrition Research Center (CNRC) at Baylor College of Medicine: http://www.bcm.tmc.edu/cnrc provides useful information about how good nutrition is critical to healthy development.

Kidsource: http://www.kidsource.com/NICHCY/speech.html—Discusses the various types of speech and language problems that children may develop.

Medscape: http://www.medscape.com/px/urlinfo—Free database of medical articles, plus access to medical dictionaries, drug databases, and breaking medical news

National Health Information Center: http://www.health.gov/nhic/ is a national information referral center that provides information organizations that can answer health questions.

National Institute of Mental Health: http://www.nimh.nih.gov—Excellent resource for policy statements, NIMH research, grants; you might want to check out postpartum depression at this site.

New England Journal of Medicine: http://www.nejm.org—Abstracts to articles, full text on letters, and commentaries.

Scientific American: http://www.sciam.com—General scientific resource.

Society for Research in Child Development (SRCD): http://www.srcd.org—The Web site for SRCD, an organization whose purposes are to promote multidisciplinary research in the field of human development, to foster the exchange of information among scientists and other professionals of various disciplines, and to encourage applications of research findings.

Web MD: http://www.webmd.com—Offers a wide variety of information for the medical profession and for consumers—type in a search term (e.g., "infant nutrition" or "children's health") and check out the Web MD Physicians Recommend and the WebMD Search Results.

Zero to Three: http://www.zerotothree.org—A site for parents and professionals. Zero to Three is a nonprofit organization that focuses on promoting the healthy development of babies and toddlers.

CHAPTER 8: SOCIOEMOTIONAL DEVELOPMENT IN INFANCY

CHAPTER OUTLINE

HOW DO EMOTIONS AND PERSONALITY DEVELOP IN INFANCY?

    Emotional Development
    Temperament
    Personality Development

HOW DOES ATTACHMENT DEVELOP IN INFANCY?

    Theories of Attachment
    Individual Differences and the Strange Situation
    The Significance of Attachment
    Caregiving Styles and Attachment Classification

HOW DO SOCIAL CONTEXTS INFLUENCE SOCIOEMOTIONAL DEVELOPMENT IN INFANCY?

    The Family
    Child Care

REACH YOUR LEARNING GOALS

1. **HOW DO EMOTIONS AND PERSONALITY DEVELOP IN INFANCY?**

Emotional Development	Personality Development

   Temperament

2. **HOW DOES ATTACHMENT DEVELOP IN INFANCY?**

Theories of Attachment	The Significance of Attachment
Individual Differences and The Strange Situation	Caregiving Styles and Attachment Classification

3. **HOW DO SOCIAL CONTEXTS INFLUENCE SOCIOEMOTIONAL DEVELOPMENT IN INFANCY?**

The Family	Child Care

Learning Goals

By the time you have completed this chapter, you should be able to reach the following goals:

1. Discuss emotional and personality development in infancy.

2. Describe how attachment develops in infancy.

3. Explain how social contexts influence the infant's socioemotional development.

How is *emotion* defined?	What is *stranger anxiety*? When does it develop and what influences it?
Differentiate between *primary emotions* and *self-conscious emotions*.	What is *separation protest*? How common is it and when does it develop?
Describe the baby's *basic cry*.	Describe the development of *social referencing*.
Describe the baby's *anger cry*.	What is involved in *emotional regulation*?
Describe the baby's *pain cry*.	What is temperament? Differentiate the three types of temperament described by Chess and Thomas.
Contrast the baby's *reflexive smile* with the baby's *social smile*.	How does Kagan classify temperament? What are the classifications of temperament proposed by Rothbart and Bates (1998)?

Stranger anxiety: Involves the infant showing a fear and wariness of strangers; it is the most frequent expression of an infant's fear and needs to appear in the second half of the first year of life, emerging gradually; influenced by social context and the stranger's characteristics.	***Emotion***: Feeling or affect that occurs when people are in a state or interaction important to them, especially to their well-being. Can be positive, such as joy, or negative, such as anger.
Separation protest: Infant distress at being separated from the caregiver; most babies show a fear of being separated from their caregiver at some point in infancy; it can appear as early as 5 months in some cultures, more typically 8 to 9 months, and tends to peak about 15 months, then it decreases.	***Primary emotions***: Emotions present in humans and animals, including surprise, interest, joy, anger, sadness, fear, and disgust; appear by age 6 months. ***Self-conscious emotions***: Emotions that require cognition, especially consciousness; include empathy, jealousy, embarrassment, pride, shame, and guilt; first appear by middle of second through middle of third year of life.
Social referencing: "Reading" emotional cues in others to help determine how to act in a particular situation; helps infants interpret ambiguous situations; they will look to others (especially mother) for cues about how to react or behave in a situation; dramatically improves in second year of life with increased (14–22 months) tendency to "check" with caregiver before acting.	***Basic cry***: A rhythmic pattern consisting of a cry, a briefer silence, a shorter inspiratory whistle that is higher pitched than the main cry, then a brief rest before the next cry. (Note that crying is the newborns' most important means of communicating with their world.)
Emotional regulation: Effectively managing arousal to adapt and reach a goal; gradually develops from infancy. It allows the child to inhibit or minimize the intensity and duration of emotional reactions.	***Anger cry***: A cry similar to the basic cry, with more excess air forced through the vocal cords;
Temperament: An individual's behavioral style and characteristic emotional response. ***Easy child***: generally in a positive mood, regular routines in infancy, adapts easily (40%); ***difficult child***: reacts negatively, cries often, irregular routines, slow to adapt (10%); ***slow-to-warm-up child***: low activity level/adaptability/intensity, somewhat negative (15%). But, 35% of children do not fit any of the three patterns.	***Pain cry***: Stimulated by high-intensity stimuli; sudden appearance of an initial loud cry without preliminary moaning followed by an extended period of breath holding.
Kagan differentiates between shy, subdued, timid children and scoiable, extroverted, bold children. ***Rothbart and Bates: Extraversion/surgency:*** "positive anticipation, impulsivity, activity level, sensation seeking"; ***negative affectivity:*** involves being easily distressed; ***effortful control (self-regulation):*** ability to keep arousal from getting too high and have strategies to soothe themselves.	***Reflexive smile***: Appears during the first month after birth, usually during irregular patterns of sleep, it is a smile that does not occur in response to external stimuli. ***Social smile***: Occurs in response to an external stimulus—in early development, typically in response to a face; begins to occur about 2–3 months; some researchers believe infants grin in response to voices as early as 3 weeks.

How does *goodness of fit* relate to children's temperament?	Compare the three types of insecure attachments described by Ainsworth.
What is the first of Erikson's eight stages of development? What is the age range for this stage? What is the infant's primary task during this stage?	How does *reciprocal socialization* work?
What is the second of Erikson's eight stages of development? What is the age range for this stage? What is the child's primary task during this stage?	Explain the concept of *scaffolding*.
What is *attachment*? Differentiate among Freud's, Erikson's, and Bowlby's views of attachment.	Describe how the family works as a reciprocal social system.
Describe the *Strange Situation* and what it tests. Which researcher designed the Strange Situation?	Describe the various types of child care.
What is meant by the term *secure attachment*? What types of behaviors would suggest a child is securely attached?	What are the components of quality child care?

Insecure avoidant babies avoid the caregiver. *Insecure resistant babies* may cling to caregiver, then resist by fighting against the closeness (e.g., by kicking or pushing away). *Insecure disorganized babies* show insecurity by being disorganized and disoriented (dazed, confused, fearful).	*Goodness of fit*: The match between a child's temperament and the environmental demands with which the child must cope; some temperament characteristics are more challenging for parents than others and may lead to the emergence of avoidant or coercive parental responses.
Reciprocal socialization: The view that socialization is bidirectional—children socialize parents just as parents socialize children; the successive actions of the partners are coordinated through mutual synchrony or matching a partner's actions.	*Trust versus mistrust*: Erikson's first stage, occurring in the first year of life, in which infants experience the world as either secure and comfortable or insecure and uncomfortable; infants learn trust when cared for in a consistent, warm manner; develop mistrust if not well fed or kept consistently warm.
Scaffolding: Parental behavior that supports children's efforts, allowing them to be more skillful than they would be if they relied only on their own abilities; parents time interactions so the infant experiences turn-taking with the parents.	*Autonomy versus shame and doubt*: Erikson's second stage (1–3 years); child either develops self-determination and pride or is overcontrolled and experiences shame and doubt; builds on development of mental and motor abilities, including control of muscles (e.g., for toilet training); development of autonomy during toddler years gives adolescents courage to be independent, develop their identity, and be able to guide their future.
As a social system: The family has subsystems of generation, gender, and role; each family member is a participant in several subsystems; marital relations, parenting, and infant behavior and development can have both direct and indirect effects on each other.	*Attachment*: A close emotional bond between two people. *Freud*: Infants become attached to the person or object that provides oral satisfaction. *Erikson*: Related to development of trust in the first year. *Bowlby*: Newborns are biologically equipped to elicit attachment behavior from primary caregivers to keep the caregiver nearby and increase the infant's chances of survival.
Child care may include (but is not limited to) the following: a center housing large groups of children with elaborate facilities; commercial operations; nonprofit centers run by churches, civic groups, or employers; in private homes by child care professionals or mothers wanting to earn extra income (or one of the child's relatives); some facilities offer trained professionals, others have little or no training.	*Strange Situation*: Ainsworth's observational measure of infant attachment to the caregiver that requires the infant to move through a series of introductions, separations, and reunions with caregiver and an adult stranger in a prescribed order.
Quality child care: Caregivers enjoy children, understand and record their development; adult-to-child ratio depends on children's age; adequate number of activities/equipment to foster growth and development, including language and understanding of child's world; support needs of family, involved in community; protect health of children, staff and parents; safe and spacious environment.	*Secure attachment*: Infants use their caregiver as a secure base from which to explore their environment; secure attachment in first year provides important foundation of later psychological development (Ainsworth); infant moves freely away from mother, but keeps visually connected; responds positively to being picked up by others; freely moves to play.

Self-Test A: Multiple Choice

1. Emotion is:
   a. a combination of sensations and perceptions.
   b. a behavior that occurs when people are in a state or interaction important to them.
   c. an affect that occurs when people are in a state or interaction important to them.
   d. the ability to manage arousal.

2. Which of the following statements is NOT an implication of the functionalist view of emotions?
   a. Emotions are relational.
   b. Emotions are internal phenomena.
   c. Parents' facial expressions and tone of voice influence children's behavior.
   d. Emotions are linked with an individual's goals.

3. Which of the following emotions develops before the others?
   a. guilt
   b. pride
   c. surprise
   d. shame

4. The most important mechanism newborns have for communicating with their world is:
   a. emotions.
   b. facial expressions.
   c. crying.
   d. smiling.

5. Which cry is a rhythmic pattern consisting of a cry, followed by a briefer silence, then a shorter inspiratory whistle that is higher in pitch than the main cry, then a brief rest before the next cry?
   a. basic
   b. anger
   c. pain
   d. colicky

6. The _____ smile appears in response to an external stimulus.
   a. social
   b. internal
   c. reflexive
   d. universal

7. Nishi is a year old. Which situation is most likely to cause her distress?
   a. sitting on her mother's lap
   b. meeting a stranger in a research laboratory
   c. meeting an adult she does not know in her home
   d. meeting a child she does not know in her home

8. One-year-old Taisha begins to scream and cry when her parents leave her with a babysitter, while Taisha's older brother and sister run to get a game they enjoy playing with this sitter. Taisha's behavior:
   a. is normal for her age.
   b. suggests the babysitter is abusing the child.
   c. needs discipline.
   d. suggests she should see a therapist.

9. Who is most likely to look at her mother to understand how to act in a given situation?
   a. 6-month-old Angelica
   b. 9-month-old Belinda
   c. 12-month-old Carrie
   d. 15-month-old Danielle

10. Temperament is best defined as:
    a. the way an individual reacts to a special person in the environment.
    b. an individual's behavioral style and characteristic way of emotional response.
    c. the emotions experienced by infants and children.
    d. the reaction displayed by a parent when a child engages in an unwanted activity.

11. Which child has the most commonly observed temperament?
    a. Ernest, who is generally in a positive mood, has regular routines, and adapts easily to new experiences.
    b. Danielle, who reacts negatively and cries frequently, has irregular daily routines, and is slow to accept change.
    c. Sylvia, who has a low activity level, is somewhat negative, and exhibits a low intensity of mood.
    d. Norman, who is easily distressed and often frets and cries.

12. The revised classifications of temperament proposed by Rothbart and Bates include all of the following, EXCEPT:
    a. extraversion/surgency.
    b. negative affectivity.
    c. emotionality.
    d. effortful control.

13. Research on how parenting meshes with children's temperaments suggests that:
    a. we are now able to define what is involved in "good parenting."
    b. parents should refrain from structuring their child's environment.
    c. researchers have not yet developed any effective programs for dealing with the "difficult child."
    d. parents need to be sensitive to their infant's signals and needs.

14. Erikson believed that infants learn _____ when they are cared for in a consistent, warm manner.
    a. trust
    b. autonomy
    c. independence
    d. attachment

15. Jeremy, a normal child, is beginning to develop a sense that he has a separate existence from the other people in his life, or a sense of self-recognition. How old is he?
    a. 6 months
    b. 12 months
    c. 18 months
    d. 24 months

16. According to Erik Erikson, children will develop an excessive sense of shame and a sense of doubt about their abilities under all of the following circumstances, EXCEPT when:
    a. impatient parents do things children can do for themselves.
    b. children are consistently overprotected.
    c. accidents the children have had or caused are criticized.
    d. children are allowed to express their emotions.

17. _____ is a close emotional connection between two people.
    a. Bonding
    b. Attachment
    c. Closeness
    d. Security

18. Harry Harlow wanted to test Freud's assumption that infants become attached to the person who provides oral satisfaction. What Harlow found was that:
    a. Freud was correct.
    b. contact comfort is more important than oral satisfaction.
    c. food is the most critical element in forming attachments.
    d. attachment is best formed if the caregivers give comfort to their crying children.

19. Erik Erikson believed the _____ stage is the most relevant for the formation of attachment.
    a. anal
    b. phallic
    c. trust versus mistrust
    d. autonomy versus shame and doubt

20. According to Bowlby, the long-term effect for the infant of forming an attachment with the parents is to:
    a. keep the primary caregiver nearby.
    b. provide comfort.
    c. increase chances of survival.
    d. develop a more secure sense of self.

21. Ariel is a securely attached child. We would expect that her primary caregivers did all of the following EXCEPT:
    a. were sensitive and responsive to Ariel's signals.
    b. exhibited love and concern for Ariel's welfare.
    c. consistently responded to Ariel while attending to child care routines.
    d. reinforced attachment behaviors.

22. Laura was physically abused and neglected when she was a baby. We would expect Laura to develop which attachment style?
    a. secure
    b. insecure disorganized
    c. insecure avoidant
    d. insecure resistant

23. Reciprocal socialization is best defined in which of the following ways?
    a. Children are products of their parents' socialization techniques.
    b. Parents are products of their children's socialization techniques.
    c. Socialization is bidirectional.
    d. The interactions that children have with people other than their parents determine how they will be socialized.

24. _____ plays an important role in reciprocal socialization.
    a. Mutual synchrony
    b. Consistency
    c. Trust
    d. Attachment

25. Veronica and Archie love playing peek-a-boo, pat-a-cake, and so-big with their baby. They time their interactions so their baby experiences turn-taking with them. These games are a demonstration of a form of reciprocal socialization called:
    a. bidirectionality.
    b. scaffolding.
    c. social interaction.
    d. bonding.

26. Fathers are more likely to be involved in caregiving when all of the following occur EXCEPT:
    a. when the children are girls.
    b. when fathers work fewer hours and mothers work more hours.
    c. when both parents are relatively young.
    d. when mothers report greater marital intimacy.

27. Which of the following countries has the most extensive family leave policy?
    a. the United States
    b. Sweden
    c. Australia
    d. New Zealand

28. Child care for American children:
    a. is primarily provided by large day care centers.
    b. is least often provided in private homes.
    c. is run by nonprofit organizations.
    d. varies extensively.

29. A longitudinal study by the National Institute of Child Health and Human Development (NICHHD) assessed the child care experiences of children and their development and found all of the following, EXCEPT:
    a. infants from low-income families were more likely to receive low-quality child care than their higher-income counterparts.
    b. child care did not adversely affect the security of infants' attachments to their mothers.
    c. the quality of child care was linked with fewer child problems.
    d. children reared in the exclusive care of their mothers had higher cognitive abilities.

30. The text suggests that each of the following is important for helping infants develop socioemotional competencies EXCEPT:
    a. understanding and respecting the infant's temperament.
    b. a two-parent family.
    c. selecting competent child care.
    d. adapting to the infant's developmental changes.

Self-Test B: Matching

Match each of the following persons with the statement or theory that most closely reflects his or her perspective:

1. Sheila Kammerman
2. Jacob Gewirtz
3. Mary Ainsworth
4. John Bowlby
5. Margaret Mahler
6. Jerome Kagan
7. Harry Harlow
8. Mary Rothbart
9. Erik Erikson
10. Alexander Chess/ Stella Thomas

a. Classified temperament based on affect, approach, negative affectivity, and control.
b. In first year of life infants experience the world as secure and comfortable or insecure and uncomfortable.
c. Children are evolutionarily equipped to stay on a positive developmental course.
d. Described easy, difficult, and slow-to-warm-up temperaments in infants.
e. Tested Freud's theory of attachment via oral gratification using monkeys.
f. Extensively researched parental leave policies around the world.
g. Devised the Strange Situation to measure attachment in children.
h. Said children go through processes of separation then individuation.
i. British psychiatrist who stated attachment has a biological basis.
j. Found that caregivers' quick, soothing response to crying increased subsequent crying.

Self-Test C: True-False

T/F   1. Emotions are influenced more by biology than by experience.

T/F   2. Primary emotions are experienced by both human and nonhuman animals.

T/F   3. Developmentalists now agree that babies should be soothed when they cry.

T/F   4. Children inherit a physiology that biases them to have a particular type of temperament.

T/F   5. According to Erikson, the child's first year is characterized by the crisis of trust versus mistrust.

T/F   6. Bowlby believed that attachment is instinctively triggered by the caregiver and infant.

T/F   7. Life-span research suggests that early attachment is not strongly related to later development.

T/F   8. Caregivers of avoidant babies tend to be inconsistently available to their babies and are not very affectionate.

T/F   9. Mothers tend to be more playful than fathers in interactions with their children.

T/F   10. A study by the NICHD found that low-income families receive the lowest quality of child care.

Self-Test D: OLC

1. Studies of reciprocal socialization during infancy reveal that _____ plays an important role in socialization.

2. Which of the following is a primary emotion?
   a. anger
   b. empathy
   c. embarrassment
   d. guilt

3. T/F   Stranger anxiety and separation protest are phenomena that appear to be unique to U.S. infants.

4. T/F   Paternal care of infants involves more play than maternal care.

Essay Questions

1. One of your cousins just had a baby and wants to know how she will teach him emotional control. She's heard that some psychologists say you should just let a baby cry so he doesn't get spoiled, and others say you should be sure the child is soothed so he develops the ability to trust. She is also confused about her role in teaching him appropriate social skills. What will you tell her?

2. The local PTA has asked you to talk to their parents and teachers about working with young children. They have specifically asked you to address the idea of attachment—what it is, the research supporting the notion of attachment, the different forms of attachment, and how to help a child develop secure attachment—and the different types of temperament, including how to deal effectively with children according to their temperamental styles. What will you tell these parents and teachers?

Key to Self-Test A: Multiple Choice

1. c (LG1)	11. a (LG1)	21. d (LG2)
2. b (LG1)	12. c (LG1)	22. b (LG2)
3. c (LG1)	13. d (LG1)	23. c (LG3)
4. c (LG1)	14. a (LG1)	24. a (LG3)
5. a (LG1)	15. c (LG1)	25. b (LG3)
6. a (LG1)	16. d (LG1)	26. a (LG3)
7. b (LG1)	17 b (LG2)	27. b (LG3)
8. a (LG1)	18. b (LG2)	28. d (LG3)
9. d (LG1)	19. c (LG2)	29. d (LG3)
10. b (LG1)	20. c (LG2)	30. b (LG3)

Key to Self-Test B: Matching

1. f
2. j
3. g
4. i
5. h
6. c
7. e
8. a
9. b
10. d

Key to Self-Test C: True/False

1. False. Emotions are influenced more or less equally by biological foundations and experience.
2. True
3. False. There continues to be controversy about whether babies should be soothed when they cry, although increasingly experts recommend responding in a caring way in the first year.
4. True
5. True
6. True
7. False. Security of attachment reflects a positive parent–infant relationship and provides a foundation to support healthy socioemotional development in the years that follow.
8. False. Caregivers of avoidant babies tend to be unavailable or rejecting; caregivers of resistant babies tend to be inconsistently available and are not very affectionate and show little synchrony when interacting with them.
9. False. Mothers tend to be the nurturing caregivers and fathers tend to have more playful interactions with their children.
10. True

Key to Self-Test D: OLC

1. mutual gaze
2. a
3. False. Stranger anxiety and separation protest have been observed in babies in different cultures around the world.
4. True

Key to Essay Questions

1. The first issue to address here is what psychologists say about responding to a baby's cries, which also requires understanding the different types of crying and what crying represents. In that regard, begin by explaining that crying is the infant's way of communicating with others, and describe the three different types of cries (basic, anger, and pain) and indicate which needs immediate attention, then explore both sides of the question of the benefits and concerns about responding every time an infant cries and how the "experts" disagree on this topic. Next, address the interaction between infants and caregivers (you might want to bring in the reflexive and social smiles) and explain how infants use social referencing to learn how to respond in various social situations, discuss reciprocal socialization (noting that your cousin's son will socialize her even as she socializes him), and tell her how to use scaffolding effectively. Finally, explore how, during the first year of life, infants learn to inhibit the intensity and duration of their emotional reactions, including how they comfort themselves, how they can be comforted by their caregivers, and the influence of contextual cues such as fatigue, hunger, etc. Be sure to underscore for your cousin those behaviors that are developmentally normal (such as sucking hands or thumbs and crying).
2. Here you would define attachment, then look at the various research studies that have explored attachment, including, among others, the research of Harry and Margaret Harlow with the rhesus monkeys, John Bowlby's ethological perspective and the survival quality of attachment, and Ainsworth's Strange Situation research. Talk about the different types of attachment that Ainsworth described and discuss ways to promote secure attachment so children will feel safe to explore new environments and take on new challenges (be sure to include Erikson's stage of trust versus mistrust in your discussion), and consider the long-term effects of secure versus insecure attachment. Then look at the work by Chess and Thomas on temperament, discussing the three types of temperament that they describe (note that only 65% of children are clearly able to be designated into one of the

three types), as well as Kagan's perspective and the factors that Rothbart and Bates suggest (e.g., positive affect and approach). Finally, using the guidelines in the chapter, provide some strategies for the parents and teachers to use to work most effectively with children's different temperaments.

Research Project 1: Observing Developmental Periods

Bearing in mind the three temperaments described by Thomas and Chess (i.e., easy, difficult, slow-to-warm-up) and the three temperament classifications of affect, approach, and control suggested by Rothbart and Bates, observe six different infants and, using the following chart, determine into which category(ies) each child fits. Indicate each child's sex and age in months, and state the specific behaviors that justify this categorization.

	Child 1 Sex:__ Age:__	Child 2 Sex:__ Age:__	Child 3 Sex:__ Age:__	Child 4 Sex:__ Age:__	Child 5 Sex:__ Age:__	Child 6 Sex:__ Age:__
Temperament Style						
Affect						
Approach						
Control						
Behaviors observed to justify classification						

1. How easy was it to classify each child?
2. What effect do you believe the child's age or sex had on that child's behavior?
3. If you were able to observe the child interacting with parents or other adults, describe the nature of the interactions and what effect you believe that had on the child's behavior.
4. In terms of classification, which system (Chess & Thomas's or Rothbart & Bates's) works best for you? Explain.
5. Describe what you would include in your own system for classifying temperament.
6. Based on your observations, what advice would you give to parents to maximize the positive and minimize the negative aspects of their children's temperaments?

Research Project 2: Parental Leave and Child Care

In a group with other students in your class, prepare a chart that compares parental leave policies around the world, different types of child care facilities, and what the research indicates are the effects that parental leave and various forms of child care have on the developing child. After comparing and contrasting each of these variables, write a paper that presents a policy statement concerning what you believe would be the best possible situation in the United States to ensure optimal development of our next generation. You may wish to go a step further and write a letter based on your findings to your elected officials in Washington and in your home state. You would then want to report back to the class whether you received any response to your letter, what the response was, and how it relates to the information in this chapter.

Personal Application 1: Reflecting on What You Learned

Consider what you read in Chapter 8, then answer the following questions:
1. What information in this chapter did you already know?
2. How can/do you use that information in your own life?
3. What information in this chapter was totally new to you?
4. How can you use that new information in your own life?
5. What information in this chapter was different from what you previously believed?
6. How was this information different?
7. How do you account for the differences between what you believed and what you learned in the chapter?
8. What is the most important thing you learned from reading this chapter?

Personal Application 2: Comparing Temperaments

A common question among siblings is, "Did we really grow up in the same family?" This puzzling dilemma stems from each child's unique temperament (as well as nonshared environment discussed in Chapter 3), which in turn affects the child's experiences and perceptions. Observe your own family (or, if you have no siblings, look at your parents and their siblings, or your friends who have siblings) and consider the temperament of each child in the family (if it's your parents, for purposes of this exercise, consider them as children of their family). Using the following chart, indicate the temperament type and the different characteristics of each individual included. Feel free to add siblings as needed.

	Temperament Type	Positive Affect/ Approach	Negative Affectivity	Effortful Control
Self				
Sibling 1				
Sibling 2				
Sibling 3				
Sibling 4				

1. How similar are you (or are your parents or your friends) to the siblings listed?
2. Do you have similar or dissimilar temperaments? In what ways are you similar or dissimilar?
3. Do your dissimilarities complement each other or create conflict?
4. How can you use this information to improve your relationships with your siblings?
5. Were you or any of your siblings difficult to categorize? (Note that not everyone is easily described using the Chess and Thomas labels, so feel free to use Kagan's or Rothbart & Bates's.)
6. What do you think would be the best way to categorize a child's temperament? Describe your "labels" and the characteristics each would have.
7. What have you learned about yourself and your family by looking at temperament?

Internet Projects

Check out the McGraw-Hill Web site for this text (www.mhhe.com/santrockc9). You'll find numerous activities there, in particular, information that will help you research the answers and complete the exercises in the "Taking It to the Net" section at the end of the textbook chapter. Please note that all Web site addresses in this Study Guide have been checked and were correct at the time of publication; however, Web sites may be discontinued or addresses may change, so when you search a given site it may no longer be viable. If that occurs, I apologize for the inconvenience and would appreciate you notifying me so I can make appropriate revisions in future editions of this Study Guide.

Internet Project 1: Child Care Guidelines

Go to http://nccic.org, which is the Web site for the National Child Care Information Center. This center, which is supported by a contract from the U.S. Department of Health and Human Services, provides information and resources to promote the delivery of high-quality child care services to children and families. Scroll down to the link Tribal Child Care Technical Assistance Center, then link to Minimum Standards for Tribal Child Care Centers and pull up the document at that site. (You'll need Adobe to get the document, but if you don't have it you can go to the necessary links and get it for free—it's extremely useful for downloading and/or printing documents online.) After reviewing the guidelines set out in this document, compare them with the characteristics of high-quality child care that are outlined in the text. How do they compare? What differences do you find? If you were to design your own child care facility, what would you take from each of these sets of guidelines?

Internet Project 2: How Important Is Temperament?

Go to http://www.temperament.com, the Web site for Temperament.com, and scroll down to the link for "Things to Do at This Web Site," then link "Things to Learn About," then to "Practical Importance of Temperament." After reading the article, indicate:

1. What did you learn from the article that wasn't in the text?
2. In what ways is understanding temperament important in your own personal life?
3. How is understanding temperament a valuable tool for parents and teachers?
4. In what ways can a child's temperament traits be used to enhance that child's life?
5. We often think of certain traits that a child has as harmful (particularly for the "difficult" child). How can these traits be used to help the child develop in a healthy direction?
6. How can you use this information in your personal and professional life?

Additional Internet Resources

The Administration for Children and Families (Department of Health and Human Services): http://www.acf.dhhs.gov—Offers links and information concerning child care, child welfare, and agencies to assist children, parents, and families.

Attachment Disorder Site: http://www.attachmentdisorder.net /—Lots of information and links about attachment, attachment disorder, resources, support groups, and other useful information.

Cascade Center for Family Growth: http://www.attach-bond.com/links.html —Offers links for understanding attachment issues and for assistance to parents and children to develop healthy attachment, and addresses issues of both healthy attachment and attachment disorders.

Child Abuse Prevention Network: http://child-abuse.com/—Worldwide network for professionals in the field of child abuse and neglect.

The Child Development Web site: http://childstudy.net—Provides information on children's topics.

Children Now: http://www.childrennow.org—Focuses on improving conditions for children who are poor and at risk and offers free pamphlets for parents to talk to their children about difficult topics.

Children's Defense Fund (CDF): http://www.childrensdefense.org—The Web site for CDF, the organization headed by Marian Wright Edelman to promote child welfare (discussed in Chapter 1 of the text).

The Consultative Group on Early Childhood Care and Development: http://www.ecdgroup.com

Mayo Clinic's Health Site: http://www.mayoclinic.com

Medscape: http://www.medscape.com/px/urlinfo—Free database of medical articles, plus access to medical dictionaries, drug databases, and breaking medical news.

National Institutes of Health: http://www.nih.gov—Starting point for getting into any subagency of NIH.

National Institute of Mental Health: http://www.nimh.nih.gov—Excellent resource for policy statements, NIMH research, grants.

Prevent Child Abuse America: http://www.childabuse.org

Program for Infant/Toddler Caregivers Web site: http://www.pitc.org/cs/pitclib/view/pitc_res_wkshp/20 is presented by the State of California and provides a good overview of temperament plus many articles, handouts, and a downloadable PowerPoint presentation. (If you have trouble getting there with this URL, go through the home page at www.pitc.org/index.csp then go to Library, Resource Detail, Session Training Usage Detail to "Temperament: A Practical Approach to Meeting Individuals Needs").

Scientific American: http://www.sciam.com—General scientific resource

Society for Research in Child Development (SRCD): http://www.srcd.org—The Web site for SRCD, an organization whose purposes are to promote multidisciplinary research in the field of human development, to foster the exchange of information among scientists and other professionals of various disciplines, and to encourage applications of research findings.

Web MD: http://www.webmd.com—Offers a wide variety of information for the medical profession and for consumers.

Zero to Three: http://www.zerotothree.com—A site for parents and professionals. Zero to Three is a nonprofit organization that focuses on promoting the healthy development of babies and toddlers.

CHAPTER 9: PHYSICAL DEVELOPMENT IN EARLY CHILDHOOD

CHAPTER OUTLINE

HOW DOES A YOUNG CHILD'S BODY GROW AND CHANGE?

Height and Weight
The Brain
Vision

HOW DO YOUNG CHILDREN'S MOTOR SKILLS DEVELOP?

Gross and Fine Motor Skills
Young Children's Artistic Drawings
Handedness

WHAT ARE SOME IMPORTANT ASPECTS OF YOUNG CHILDREN'S HEALTH?

Sleep and Sleep Problems
Nutrition
Health, Safety, and Illness

REACH YOUR LEARNING GOALS

1. **HOW DOES A YOUNG CHILD'S BODY GROW AND CHANGE?**

Height and Weight   Vision

The Brain

2. **HOW DO YOUNG CHILDREN'S MOTOR SKILLS DEVELOP?**

Gross and Fine Motor Skills   Handedness

Young Children's Artistic Drawings

3. **WHAT ARE SOME IMPORTANT ASPECTS OF YOUNG CHILDREN'S HEALTH?**

Sleep and Sleep Problems   Health, Safety, and Illness

Nutrition

Learning Goals

By the time you have completed this chapter, you should be able to reach the following goals:

1. Discuss body growth and change in early childhood.

2. Describe changes in motor development in early childhood.

3. Characterize the health of young children.

Describe growth rate
in early childhood.

Describe two common vision problems in early
childhood and how they are treated.

What are the two most important
contributors to children's height differences
in early childhood?
What other factors have been noted
that affect growth rate?

Describe the changes in
gross motor skills
during early childhood.

Why are some children
unusually short?

Describe the changes in
fine motor skills
during early childhood.

Describe
growth hormone deficiency.
How many children in the
United States does it affect?
How is it treated?

What is the
Denver Developmental Screening Test?
How is it administered?

Explain the process of
myelination.
Why do some developmentalists
believe it is important?

How is art relevant to children's development?
Explain Kellogg's notion of the
"20 basic scribbles."

Describe the changes that occur
in visual perception during early childhood.
What signs suggest a child might
be having vision problems?

Explain Kellogg's "*placement stage*"
with respect to children's
drawings.

Functional amblyopia: "Lazy eye"; results from not using one eye enough to avoid the discomfort of double vision produced by imbalanced eye muscles; treated by patching the stronger eye for several months, wearing glasses, eye exercises, and occasionally surgery. *Strabismus*: Misalignment of the eyes in which they do not point at the same object together; treated with contact lenses, vision therapy to train eyes to be straight, exercises, computerized stimulation techniques.	The growth rate in early childhood continues to slow down. The average child grows 2-1/2 inches in height and gains between 5 to 7 lbs. a year; as the preschooler grows older, the percentage of increase in height and weight decreases with each additional year. Girls are only slightly smaller and lighter than boys during this period.
Gross motor skill changes: 3-year-olds can run, hop, jump, throw underhanded, catch large balls; by age 4 they are more adventurous and can scramble over low jungle gyms, climb up and down stairs with one foot on each step, bounce and catch ball; even more adventurous by age 5 they can throw a ball, kick a rolling ball, skip on alternating feet and skip rope, roller skate, ride two-wheel bike with training wheels; improved perceptual-motor skills allow children to copy others' movements.	The two most important contributors to height differences in early childhood are ethnic origin and nutrition. Other factors that affect growth are: urban or rural environment, SES, birth order, and mother's smoking habits during pregnancy.
Fine motor skill changes: Grasping and precision increase; by age 3 cut paper, paste with pointer finger, build 3-block bridge/8-block tower, dress/undress dolls, pour water from pitcher without spilling; by age 4 string and lace shoelace, string beads, copy figure X, open/place clothespins, pour from containers, print first name; by age 5 fold paper in halves and quarters, trace hand, draw geometric figures and letters, use crayons properly.	Reasons why some children are unusually short include: congenital factors (genetic or prenatal problems), growth hormone deficiency, a physical problem that develops in childhood (e.g., malnutrition, chronic infections), or an emotional difficulty.
Denver Developmental Screening Test: a simple, inexpensive, fast method of diagnosing developmental delay in children from birth through 6 years of age; it is individually administered and includes separate assessments of gross and fine motor kills, as well as language and personal-social ability.	*Growth hormone deficiency*: The absence or deficiency of growth hormone produced by the pituitary gland to stimulate the body to grow; occurs during infancy or later in childhood and affects 10,000 to 15,000 children in the U.S. It is treated with regular injections of growth hormone over a period of several years.
Art: Provides unique insights into children's perceptual worlds—what they are attending to, how space and distance are viewed, how they experience patterns and forms. Kellogg: Every form of graphic art contains the lines found in children's artwork, the *20 basic scribbles*, including vertical, horizontal, diagonal, circular, curving, waving, or zigzag lines and dots.	*Myelination*: The process in which nerve cells are covered and insulated with a layer of fat cells, which increases the speed of the information traveling through the nervous system. Some developmentalists argue myelination is important in the maturation of many abilities (e.g., hand-eye coordination).
The placement stage: Kellogg's term for 2- to 3-year-olds' drawings, drawn on a a page in placement patterns (Kellogg looks at placement on the page).	*Visual changes*: Toward the end of early childhood, eye muscles are adequately developed to allow efficient movement across a series of letters; by first grade, most children are no longer farsighted; they can focus their eyes and sustain attention; depth perception matures. *Signs of vision problems* include appearance of the eyes (e.g., crusted eyelids) and evidence of discomfort.

Explain Kellogg's *shape stage* with respect to children's drawings.	Define *somnambulism*. What is its prevalence? How should caregivers deal with somnambulistic children?
Explain Kellogg's *design stage* with respect to children's drawings.	Define *basal metabolism rate (BMR)* and its relation to nutritional needs in early childhood.
Explain Kellogg's *pictorial stage* with respect to children's drawings.	What are caregivers' special concerns with regard to fat and sugar in young children's diets? What are some problems associated with excess sugar? What should appropriate nutrition include?
When does hand preference develop? What role does handedness play in linguistic and other abilities?	Describe one of the most common nutritional problems seen in early childhood. What causes this problem? Who is most at risk for malnutrition?
What are *transitional objects*? What is the current developmental philosophy regarding their use?	What are the main causes of death in children ages 1 through 4 years in the United States? What preventative methods can help reduce children's unintentional injuries? What other health factors are of particular concern?
Differentiate between *nightmares* and *night terrors*. How serious are they considered to be?	State the main causes of children's death in the world today? How can they be treated effectively? What role does oral rehydration therapy (ORT) play in this regard?

Somnambulism: (sleepwalking) occurs during deepest stage of sleep; about 15% of children sleepwalk at least once; 1–5% do it regularly; most outgrow it without professional help; it is not abnormal, but parents should wake the children to keep them from hurting themselves; also, make the house as safe as possible.	**Shape stage**: Kellogg's term for 3-year-olds' drawings, consisting of diagrams in six different shapes: circles, squares or rectangles, triangles, crosses, Xs, and forms.
Basal metabolism rate (BMR) is the minimum amount of energy a person uses in a resting state; an average preschool child requires 1,700 calories per day and energy requirements for individual children are determined using BMR; energy needs are affected by physical activity, basal metabolism, and efficiency of energy use.	**Design stage**: Kellogg's term for 3- to 4-year-olds' drawings in which young children mix two basic shapes into a more complex design; occurs quickly after the shape stage.
Caregivers' special concerns: Appropriate amount of fat and sugar in children's diets. Sugar consumption is associated with dental cavities and obesity. **Appropriate nutrition**: Well-balanced diets that include fats, carbohydrates, protein, vitamins, and minerals; not hamburgers, fries, shakes, and candy bars.	**Pictorial stage**: Kellogg's term for 4- to 5-year-olds' drawing that consist of objects adults can recognize.
Iron deficiency anemia: A common nutritional problem in early childhood is iron-deficiency anemia, which causes chronic fatigue and results from inadequate amounts of quality meats and dark green vegetables; young children from low-income families are most likely to develop iron-deficiency anemia; approximately 11 million preschool children in the U.S. are malnourished.	**Handedness**: (whether left or right hand is dominant) Strong likelihood of genetic inheritance; may begin in utero; while many preschoolers use both hands, by 2 years 10% are left-handed; left-handers more likely to have reading problems, but are more common among mathematicians, musicians, architects, and artists; have unusually good visuospatial skills; do well on SATs.
Primary causes of death: Unintentional accidents (motor vehicle accidents, drowning, falls, poisoning); congenital malformations, deformations, chromosomal abnormalities; cancer; homicide (typically firearm-related); heart disease; influenza, and pneumonia. **Prevention:** Use car seats, reduce access to firearms, make homes/playgrounds safer. **Other concerns:** Poverty, second-hand smoke, lead exposure.	**Transitional objects**: Objects that are repeatedly used by children as bedtime companions; they are usually soft and cuddly, and most developmentalists view them as representing a transition from being a dependent person to being a more independent one; it is normal for children to use them.
Causes of childhood death in the world: Dehydration caused by diarrhea, measles, tetanus, whooping cough, acute respiratory infections, undernutrition, HIV/AIDS. **Treatment for diarrhea includes** giving large volumes of water and liquids (ORT); treatments for other health concerns include immunization and education; reduction in poverty, and improvements in nutrition, sanitation, and health services.	**Nightmares**: Frightening dreams that awaken the sleeper, more often toward morning. **Night terrors**: Sudden arousal from sleep and intense fear, usually accompanied by physiological reactions (e.g., rapid heart rate and breathing, screams, perspiration, physical movement), usually not remembered. Children who have nightmares have higher levels of anxiety than other children; night terrors worry caregivers but usually are not serious.

Self-Test A: Multiple Choice

1. The growth rate in early childhood:
   a. speeds up.
   b. finally begins to slow down.
   c. continues to slow down.
   d. is about the same as in infancy.

2. Preschoolers tend to be _____ their bodies.
   a. embarrassed about
   b. unconcerned with
   c. fascinated with
   d. shy about

3. Two important factors that can produce individual differences in height are:
   a. ethnic origin and nutrition.
   b. genetic predisposition and early behavior.
   c. central nervous system functioning and reduction of fat intake.
   d. standard of living and cost of living.

4. Which of the following statements is NOT correct with regard to growth hormone deficiency?
   a. It may occur during infancy or later in childhood.
   b. Children who are not treated grow only to about 4 feet in height.
   c. It can be treated with regular injections of growth hormone.
   d. Abused or neglected children may not secrete adequate growth hormone.

5. Kaneisha is typical of other 5-year-old children. Thus we would expect her brain to have reached about _____ of its adult size.
   a. one-half
   b. two-thirds
   c. three-quarters
   d. nine-tenths

6. Which parts of the body grow fastest during the preschool years?
   a. brain and head
   b. arms and legs
   c. fingers and toes
   d. trunk and legs

7. _____ is a process in which the nerve cells are covered and insulated with a layer of fat cells, which protects neurons and increases the speed at which information travels through the nervous system.
   a. Lipid enhancement
   b. Myelination
   c. Neurotransmission
   d. Neural development

8. Recent research using brain scans has found that from ages 3 to 15:
   a. the overall size of the brain shows dramatic growth spurts.
   b. there are dramatic changes in local patterns within the brain.
   c. there are dramatic changes in brain size from age 3 to 6, then a slowing of growth thereafter.
   d. many diseases that are manifested later in life can be seen early on.

9. Sam is 5 years old. We would expect the most rapid growth in his brain to be in the:
   a. frontal lobe areas.
   b. temporal lobe areas.
   c. parietal lobes.
   d. occipital lobe.

10. The brain is organized according to _____, which are networks made up of many neurons that have certain functions.
    a. functional circuits
    b. cortical circuits
    c. neural circuits
    d. cortical pathways

11. Fareda has just begun first grade. We would expect that she:
    a. can focus her eyes and sustain her attention.
    b. watches and imitates other children.
    c. is farsighted.
    d. colors within the lines.

12. Teri is wearing a patch over her left eye and is doing eye exercises because she has double vision caused by imbalanced eye muscles. She tells her classmates she has a "lazy eye," but in technical terms, Teri has:
    a. presbyopia.
    b. strabismus.
    c. myopia.
    d. functional amblyopia.

13. When Dr. Leslie examines children's eyes, she knows that each of the following suggests possible vision problems EXCEPT:
    a. looking cross-eyed while fooling around.
    b. rubbing the eyes.
    c. avoiding bright light.
    d. keeping their eyes closed much of the time.

14. Ariadne is 4 years old. In comparison with children who are 3, we would expect Ariadne to:
    a. be more careful when engaging in rough-and-tumble play.
    b. fall more often.
    c. frighten her mother by climbing on tall objects.
    d. be more adventurous.

15. Catherine Poest and her colleagues suggest that a good way to promote development of young children's gross motor skills is to encourage:
    a. somersaults.
    b. beam walking.
    c. organized team sports.
    d. group calisthenics.

16. Which child is least likely to be interested in building block towers?
    a. 3-year-old Jennie
    b. 3-1/2-year-old Jarrod
    c. 4-year-old Jerome
    d. 5-year-old Jennifer

17. Angel was given the Denver Developmental Screening Test, which assesses all of the following, EXCEPT:
    a. language and personal-social ability.
    b. fine motor skills.
    c. gross motor skills.
    d. intelligence.

18. Junior comes home from school and excitedly shows you his newly acquired artistic skills, a series of circles, X's, and squares. Junior is in Kellogg's _____ stage.
    a. placement
    b. shape
    c. design
    d. pictorial

19. Which of the following would NOT be consistent with Golomb's view of child art?
    a. Children use forms economically.
    b. Children's art is primitive.
    c. Talent, motivation, familial support, and cultural values are reflected in children's art.
    d. Child art is related to children's sociocultural contexts.

20. Left-handedness is associated with:
    a. early maturation of motor skills.
    b. unusually good visuospatial skills.
    c. cognitive and perceptual deficits.
    d. delinquent tendencies.

21. Cash walks in his sleep. His parents should:
    a. avoid waking him during these episodes.
    b. take him to a psychotherapist.
    c. wake him while he sleepwalks to avoid harm.
    d. ignore it, because he will outgrow this problem.

22. What a child eats during the early childhood period affects all of the following, EXCEPT:
    a. skeletal growth.
    b. body shape.
    c. susceptibility to disease.
    d. basal metabolism rate.

23. Research assessing children's eating patterns suggests all of the following EXCEPT:
    a. most children have poor diets.
    b. children's diets improve as they get older.
    c. young children do not like eating vegetables.
    d. parental persistence can increase children's healthy eating.

24. Ms. Ebersole is a nutritionist. She is most likely to suggest that children:
    a. eat more protein.
    b. avoid fats.
    c. reduce their carbohydrate intake.
    d. avoid sugar.

25. Which of the following is NOT associated with obesity in children?
    a. insufficient activity.
    b. low self-esteem.
    c. a need for rapid weight loss.
    d. increased health problems.

26. One of the most common nutritional problems in early childhood for children from low-income families is:
    a. iron deficiency anemia.
    b. anorexia.
    c. marasmus.
    d. dehydration.

27. The leading cause of death in children 1 through 4 years of age in the United States is:
    a. diarrhea.
    b. lead poisoning.
    c. accidents.
    d. homicide.

28. Ellen and her three siblings are poor. Their single mother relies on welfare to support her family. These children are more likely than other children to be exposed to which environmental toxin?
    a. lead
    b. radiation
    c. tobacco smoke
    d. pesticides

29. A leading cause of childhood death in impoverished countries is:
    a. dehydration caused by diarrhea.
    b. oral rehydration.
    c. small pox.
    d. tetanus.

30. Young children's physical development can be supported by:
    a. providing them with opportunities to be active and explore their world.
    b. giving them ample opportunities to engage in art without constraining what they draw.
    c. making sure that they have regular medical checkups including vision testing, immunizations, and dental care.
    d. All of these are important.

Self-Test B: Matching

Match each of the following with the statement or theory that fits best:

1. Catherine Poest	a. Found that children's artistic productions are orderly, meaningful, and structured.
2. Rhoda Kellogg	b. A pediatric nurse who promotes positive parent–child experiences.
3. Teresa Amabile	c. Developed programs to encourage young children's gross motor skills.
4. Barbara Deloin	d. Underscores the importance of motivation in children's creativity.
5. Denver Developmental Screening Test	e. Recommends that children be screened for lead contamination.
6. Claire Golomb	f. Recommended that parents of chronically ill children balance the illness with other family needs and use active coping efforts.
7. American Heart Association	g. Has been effective in improving maternal and child health in nine states and the District of Columbia.
8. Special Supplemental Food Program for Women, Infants, and Children	h. Recommends that the daily limit for calories from fat should be about 35%.
9. Barbara Melamed	i. Child art flourishes in sociocultural contexts where tools are made available and the activity is valued.
10. Centers for Disease Control	j. A simple, inexpensive, fast method to diagnose developmental delay in children from birth through age 6.

Self-Test C: True-False

T/F   1. By age 5, the brain has reached its adult size.

T/F   2. From 3 to 6 years of age the most rapid brain growth occurs in the temporal and parietal lobes.

T/F   3. Functional amblyopia is often treated by wearing an eye patch.

T/F   4. Rough-and-tumble play is normal during early childhood.

T/F   5. The Denver Developmental Screening Test is widely used to measure development of gross and fine motor skills.

T/F   6. Golomb believes that sociocultural contexts are irrelevant to children's art.

T/F   7. Being left-handed has been found to have a negative impact on a child's cognitive development.

T/F   8. Most young children sleep through the night.

T/F   9. Children's diets should exclude fats.

T/F   10. The leading cause of death in children 1 to 4 years of age is accidents.

Self-Test D: OLC

1. Four-year-old Jose screams in the middle of the night, wakes up covered in perspiration, with his heart racing. In the morning he has no memory of what occurred. Jose has had a _____.

2. Recent research using brain scans has found that from ages 3 to 15
   a. the overall size of the brain shows dramatic growth.
   b. there are dramatic changes in local patterns within the brain.
   c. there are dramatic changes in brain size from age 3 to 6, then a slowing of growth thereafter.
   d. many diseases that are manifested later in life can be seen early on.

3. T/F   Being overweight is linked with lower self-esteem in children.

4. T/F   Motor vehicle accidents are the leading cause of death in young children.

Essay Questions

1. A woman you know tells you that she is aware of the major obesity epidemic in the United States, so when she has children she is going to keep them on a low-fat diet. She also confides in you that she thinks parents of chronically ill children have actually created their children's illnesses and she would never change her lifestyle to accommodate a sick child's needs because she thinks that only reinforces the problem. How can you enlighten her?

2. Your favorite elementary school teacher has kept track of you all these years and remembers what an excellent student you were. He knows that you are taking this class in child development and has asked you to talk to the parents at their next PTA (Parent-Teacher Association) meeting. The parents have specifically asked to have you discuss the "normal" development of preschoolers. They have also asked about sleep problems and ways to foster healthy development for their children. What will you tell them?

Key to Self-Test A: Multiple Choice

1. c (LG1)	11. a (LG1)	21. c (LG3)
2. c (LG1)	12. d (LG1)	22. d (LG3)
3. a (LG1)	13. a (LG1)	23. b (LG3)
4. b (LG1)	14. d (LG2)	24. d (LG3)
5. d (LG1)	15. b (LG2)	25. c (LG3)
6. a (LG1)	16. d (LG2)	26. a (LG3)
7. b (LG1)	17. d (LG2)	27. c (LG3)
8. b (LG1)	18. b (LG2)	28. a (LG3)
9. a (LG1)	19. b (LG2)	29. a (LG3)
10. c (LG1)	20. b (LG2)	30. d (LG3)

Key to Self-Test B: Matching

1. c
2. a
3. d
4. b
5. j
6. i
7. h
8. g
9. f
10. e

Key to Self-Test C: True/False

1. False. By age 5, the brain has reached nine-tenths its adult size.
2. False. From 3 to 6 years of age the most rapid growth is in the frontal lobes; from age 6 to puberty the most substantial growth is in the temporal and parietal lobes.
3. True
4. True
5. True
6. False. Golomb believes that the sociocultural contexts of children's art is important and that such factors as talent, motivation, familial support, and cultural values influence the development of children's art.
7. False. Although left-handers have more reading problems, they often show up in higher than expected numbers as mathematicians, musicians, architects, and artists, probably because they have unusually good visuospatial skills.
8. True
9. False. Children's diets should contain well-balanced proportions of fats, carbohydrates, protein, vitamins, and minerals.
10. True

Key to Self-Test D: OLC

1. night terror
2. b
3. True
4. True

Key to Essay Questions

1. First, you would acknowledge that she is correct about the problem with obesity in the United States and discuss some of the reasons for and research about this problem (e.g., eating away from home more often, increases in consumption of non-nutritional foods, high-fat/high-salt/high-sugar diets, etc.) and some of the trends as children get older, noting daily eating routines for children aged 3, 4, and 5. Then, delineate some of the recommendations for developing healthy eating habits, noting that fat is an important part of everyone's diet, young and old alike. Also explore the connection between obesity and self-esteem and ways to address that problem with children, both prevention and treatment. While you're on the subject of nutrition, you might want to address issues of malnutrition, noting who is most at risk, what some of the consequences of malnutrition are, and how to deal with it effectively. Next, address her attitudes toward chronically ill children and the need to understand that although parents who are positively oriented toward health rather than illness are more likely to promote positive health behaviors, some children still develop health problems unrelated to anything the parents do. Consequently, the parents need to develop effective strategies, as outlined by Melamed (e.g., balance the illness with other family needs; maintain clear family boundaries; develop communication boundaries; etc.).

2. Discuss the various aspects of brain growth and development, as well as gross and fine motor development for children ages 3 through 5, providing examples of both "normal" behaviors (e.g., increased maturation of depth perception, a 3-year-old can catch a large ball) and problems they should watch for (e.g., "lazy eye"). You might want to show them samples of the different stages of drawing as described by Kellogg, but also include Golomb's view that children's art is reflective of

sociocultural factors in their environment. Then move into the different sleep problems, such as nightmares, night terrors, and somnambulism and offer suggestions for how to deal with these issues. Then go into children's nutritional needs and "normal" eating routines, pointing out concerns about too much/too little fat, problems of children being overweight, and suggestions for encouraging proper nutrition and activity level. Finally, be sure to discuss the health, safety, and illness issues for children in this age range, pointing out, for example, the importance of properly using car seats and seatbelts, why parents should not smoke around children, the risk factors of poverty, and other issues you feel are important from the chapter.

Research Project 1: To Sleep, per Chance to Dream

Chart the three sleep problems discussed in Chapter 9 (note that sleep talking is not considered abnormal), then see what others you can learn about. Describe their characteristics, the problems they can create for children and their parents, and what the text suggests in terms of how to deal with them.

Sleep Disorder	Characteristics	Problems Caused for Child	Problems Caused for Parents	Suggested Way to Handle It	Other Relevant Information
Nightmares					
Night Terrors					
Sleepwalking					
Sleep Talking					
Enuresis					
Other					

1. What relationship is there between these sleep activities and other behaviors?
2. What have you learned about development from looking at these problems from this perspective?
3. Based on what you have learned, what is the best advice you can think of for parents of young children?

Research Project 2: Is Left-Handedness Really Sinister?

It is common to see left-handedness associated with difficulties, both in language (e.g., the French word for "left" is "gauche," which is translated into English as "awkward"; the word "sinister," which is associated with evil or misfortune, derives from the Latin "sinistre," which means "on the left side") and in everyday life (very few scissors are made for the left-handed person). If that isn't bad enough, some research indicates that left-handed people don't live as long as right-handed people (see, e.g., Coren, S., & Halpern, D. F. [1991]. "Left-handedness: A marker for decreased survival fitness," *Psychological Bulletin*, *109*(1), 90–106). Consider the information contained in the text about being left-handed, then review the literature (psychological, medical, sports, arts—you might also want to check out an interesting Web site on primate handedness and brain lateralization research: http://www.indiana.edu/~primate/index.html) to see what you can find about being left-handed and important issues of living (e.g., longevity, creativity). Consider also how you can apply this information in a meaningful way to left-handed individuals you know.

Personal Application 1: Reflecting on What You Learned

Consider what you read in Chapter 9, then answer the following questions:

1. What information in this chapter did you already know?
2. How can/do you use that information in your own life?
3. What information in this chapter was totally new to you?
4. How can you use that new information in your own life?
5. What information in this chapter was different from what you previously believed?
6. How was this information different?
7. How do you account for the differences between what you believed and what you learned in the chapter?
8. What is the most important thing you learned from reading this chapter?

Personal Application 2: Consider Your Own Development

Consider the story in the beginning of the chapter about Teresa Amabile and her experiences in school that frustrated her creativity. Reflect on your own early years in school and think about what experiences you had that hindered your creative talents and what experiences nurtured them. What long-term effects can you attribute to each of these factors? How can you use this information to foster young children's creativity?

Internet Projects

Check out the McGraw-Hill Web site for this text (www.mhhe.com/santrockc9). You'll find numerous activities there, in particular, information that will help you research the answers and complete the exercises in the "Taking It to the Net" section at the end of the textbook chapter. Please note that all Web site addresses in this Study Guide have been checked and were correct at the time of publication; however, Web sites may be discontinued or addresses may change, so when you search a given site it may no longer be viable. If that occurs, I apologize for the inconvenience and would appreciate you notifying me so I can make appropriate revisions in future editions of this Study Guide.

Internet Project 1: Homelessness and Children

The chapter addresses some issues of poverty in childhood, particularly in the sections on illness and health and early education. Go to the Web site for National Coalition for the Homeless, which is located at http://www.nationalhomeless.org/. Scroll down to the Site Map, and first scroll down through the "Facts About Homelessness," looking particularly at some of the links for children ("Homeless Families with Children," "Homeless Youth"); then go to the next section, "Legislation and Policy," and check out "Child & Youth Health" and "Homelessness" under the Health Issues link. How does that information augment what you learned in the chapter? How widespread is homelessness generally (and how is homelessness defined); how prevalent is homelessness among our children? What are some of the causes of homelessness, what are some of the consequences for the children involved, and what policy issues are being promoted? What are the societal consequences of having *any* children being homeless (considering such things as children's health and how that affects our society, and the ability of homeless children to get an education and how that affects our society)? Combining what you have learned from the chapter with information you gather from this Web site (and any other sources), design a program that you believe would help these children, explaining how it would also help our nation.

Internet Project 2: Children's Health

The Web site http://www.intelihealth.com/IH/ihtIH/WSIHW000/408/408.html, a subsidiary of Aetna U.S. Healthcare, presents information from sources such as Harvard Medical School and the Pennsylvania School of Dental Medicine. Go to the site under "Your Health," and click on "Children's Health." Look at the various sections, such as news articles, features, and "Ask the Expert." In the news and features sections, check out the types of articles presented. Then, reflecting on Chapter 9, think about what questions come to mind that either weren't answered in the text or that were generated by what you read. Then go ahead and "Ask the Expert" that question. Feel free to do a search for any other topic that seems relevant.

1. What articles did you find at this Web site?
2. How did these articles relate to what you read in Chapter 9?
3. Was the information consistent with what you read? Explain.
4. What question came to mind that you decided to "Ask the Expert"?
5. What answer did you get back? Was it helpful?
6. What other topics did you decide to check out at this Web site?
7. How credible do you believe the information is from this site?

Additional Internet Resources

The Administration for Children and Families (Department of Health and Human Services): http://www.acf.dhhs.gov—Offers links and information concerning child care, child welfare, and agencies to assist children, parents, and families.

American Academy of Pediatrics: http://www.aap.org

APS site: http://www.psychologicalscience.org

The Child Development Web site: http://childstudy.net—Provides information on children's topics and encourages social activism.

Children Now: http://www.childrennow.org—Uses research and mass communications to provide information about children's issues; provides many useful links.

Children's Defense Fund (CDF): http://www.childrensdefense.org—The Web site for CDF, the organization headed by Marian Wright Edelman to promote child welfare (discussed in Chapter 1 of the text).

Drkoop.com: http://www.drkoop.com—a Web site full of information on medical topics and links to many others that provide information and links on a wide range of health issues, psychological and physiological.

International Food Information Council Foundation: http://www.ific.org/—Provides current information about food safety and nutrition information—check out the link to children and adolescents.

Keep Kids Healthy: http://www.keepkidshealthy.com/—Provides a wealth of information on such topics as safety, parenting tips, nutrition, first aid, childhood illnesses, and any other topic on childhood health you can think of; you may also subscribe to their free newsletter.

Society for Research in Child Development (SRCD): http://www.srcd.org—The Web site for SRCD, promotes multidisciplinary research in the field of human development, fosters the exchange of information among scientists and other professionals of various disciplines, and encourages applications of research findings.

UNICEF-HIV/AIDS: http://www.unicef.org/aids/—Explore how HIV and AIDS affect children around the world and how UNICEF is attacking the problem.

The World of Handedness: http://jackie.freeshell.org/woh/lefty.htm—A fun site on handedness created by a natural lefty with lots of creativity.

Zero to Three: http://www.zerotothree.com—A site for parents and professionals. Zero to Three is a nonprofit organization that focuses on promoting the healthy development of babies and toddlers.

CHAPTER 10: COGNITIVE DEVELOPMENT IN EARLY CHILDHOOD

CHAPTER OUTLINE

WHAT COGNITIVE CHANGES OCCUR IN EARLY CHILDHOOD?

Piaget's Preoperational Stage
Vygotsky's Theory of Development
Evaluating and Comparing Piaget's and
    Vygotsky's Theories
Information Processing
The Young Child's Theory of Mind

HOW DO YOUNG CHILDREN DEVELOP LANGUAGE?

Understanding Phonology and Morphology
Understanding Syntax
Advances in Semantics
Advances in Pragmatics

WHAT ARE SOME IMPORTANT FEATURES OF EARLY CHILDHOOD EDUCATION?

The Child-Centered Kindergarten
Developmentally Appropriate Practice
Literacy and Early Childhood Education
Early Childhood Education for Children from
    Low-Income Families
Issues in Early Childhood Education

REACH YOUR LEARNING GOALS

1. **WHAT COGNITIVE CHANGES OCCUR IN EARLY CHILDHOOD?**

Piaget's Preoperational Stage	Evaluating and Comparing Piaget's and Vygotsky's Theories	Information Processing
Vygotsky's Theory of Development		The Young Child's Theory of Mind

2. **HOW DO YOUNG CHILDREN DEVELOP LANGUAGE?**

Understanding Phonology and Morphology	Advances in Semantics
Understanding Syntax	Advances in Pragmatics

3. **WHAT ARE SOME IMPORTANT FEATURES OF EARLY CHILDHOOD EDUCATION?**

The Child-Centered Kindergarten	Literacy and Early Childhood Education	Issues in Early Childhood Education
Developmentally Appropriate Practice	Early Childhood Education for Children from Low-Income Families	

Learning Goals

By the time you have completed this chapter, you should be able to reach the following goals:

1. Discuss the cognitive changes that occur in early childhood.

2. Describe language development in early childhood.

3. Characterize early childhood education.

Describe the **Reggio Emilia** approach to early childhood education.

Describe the **intuitive thought** substage of the preoperational stage.

In terms of Piaget's theory of cognitive development, explain his concept of **operations**.

Define **centration** and explain its limitations.

What is Piaget's second stage of development? What are the two substages of this stage?

What is **conservation**? Describe the different types of conservation tasks.

Describe the **symbolic function** substage of the preoperational stage.

What are the major criticisms of Piaget's theory?

Define the term **egocentrism** and explain how Piaget tested it.

What is Vygotsky's **zone of proximal development (ZPD)**?

What is **animism**? Give some examples.

Explain how **scaffolding** is linked to the idea of ZPD.

Intuitive thought substage: Second preoperational substage, approximately ages 4 to 7; children begin to use primitive reasoning and want answers to all sorts of questions; they seem sure about their knowledge, but don't know how they know what they know.	***Reggio Emilia Approach***: An approach to early childhood education developed in the northern Italian city of Reggio Emilia that views young children as competent and having rights (especially to a good education), encourages them to learn by investigating and exploring topics that interest them, and uses a wide range of stimulating media and materials.
Centration: Focusing or centering attention on one characteristic to the exclusion of all others; most clearly evidenced by the preoperational child's inability to conserve (e.g., a tall, thin glass may be believed to have more water than a short, wide glass because the child pays attention only to the dimension of height rather than both height and width).	***Operations***: Internalized sets of actions that allow the child to do mentally what was done physically before.
Conservation: A belief in the permanence of certain attributes of objects or situations despite superficial changes. Some dimensions of conservation: number, matter, length, volume, area.	***The preoperational stage***: Stretching from approximately 2 to 7 years of age, it is a time when stable concepts are formed, mental reasoning (thoughts) emerges, egocentrism begins strongly then weakens, and magical beliefs are constructed. Substages: ***symbolic function*** and ***intuitive thought***.
Some criticisms of Piaget's theory: He tended to underestimate when conservation skills emerge; many of the tasks used to assess cognitive development may not be sensitive to the child's cognitive abilities.	***Symbolic function substage***: Roughly ages 2 to 4; the child is able mentally to represent an object that is not present; engages in symbolic thought (scribbled drawings representing people and objects, use of language, pretend play).
Zone of proximal development (ZPD): Vygotsky's term for tasks too difficult for children to master alone but that can be learned with the guidance and assistance of adults or other children who are more skilled at the task.	***Egocentrism***: The inability to distinguish between one's own perspective and someone else's. It is a salient feature of preoperational thought. Piaget and Inhelder used the three-mountain task to test children's egocentrism.
Scaffolding: Vygotsky's term for changing the level of support over the course of the teaching session with a more skilled person (a teacher or advanced peer) adjusting guidance to fit the student's (child's) current performance level.	***Animism***: The belief that inanimate objects have "lifelike" qualities and are capable of action (e.g., the moon is following me; the tree pushed the leaf off and made it fall; I'm mad at the sidewalk because it made me fall down; my other dolls' feelings will be hurt if I can only choose one).

What are the ways that Vygotsky's ideas can be incorporated into education?	What developmental changes in linguistic rule systems occur in early childhood? What other advances are seen in their use of language?
Define the *social constructivist approach*.	What is the *Montessori approach* to education?
What are some of the ways that Piaget's views differ from those of Vygotsky?	Explain the concept of the *child-centered kindergarten*.
What changes take place in the attention processes in early childhood? Discuss *selective attention* and the impact of *salience* on attention.	Describe some developmentally appropriate and developmentally inappropriate practices in early childhood education.
What is *short-term memory*? What are its limitations in early childhood? What is *long-term memory*?	What is the purpose of *Project Head Start* and *Project Follow Through*?
Describe the young child's *theory of mind*. What are the components of awareness that Flavell, Miller, and Miller (2001) noted are part of the child's developing notion of mind?	What effects have generally been found for children who attend preschool or kindergarten?

Changes in linguistic rule systems and use of language: children begin using plurals and possessive forms of nouns (e.g., dogs and dog's); put appropriate endings on verbs (e.g., add "ed" for past tense and "ing" for present progressive); use prepositions, articles, and forms of the verb "to be" (e.g., I went to the store); this is evidenced in their overgeneralization (e.g., "foots" instead of "feet"); learn and apply rules of syntax; advances in semantics and pragmatics.	***Vygotsky and education***: Use the child's zone of proximal development in teaching; use more skilled peers as teachers; monitor and encourage children's use of private speech; effectively assess the child's ZPD; place instruction in a meaningful context; transform the classroom with Vygotskian ideas (e.g., children read then interpret story; small groups).
Child-centered kindergarten: Education involves the whole child and includes concern for the child's physical, cognitive, and social development; instruction is organized around the child's needs, interests, and learning styles; emphasis is on the *process* of learning rather than *what* is learned.	***Social constructivist approach***: Emphasizes the social contexts of learning and that knowledge is mutually built and constructed.
Montessori approach: Children are allowed considerable freedom and spontaneity in choosing activities; they are allowed to move from one activity to another as they desire; teacher acts as a facilitator rather than a director of learning (patterned after educational philosophy of Maria Montessori, Italian physician/educator).	***Vygotsky and Piaget:*** Both constructivists (children actively construct their knowledge and understanding); ***Vygotksy***: emphasized social context of learning; knowledge mutually built and constructed through social interaction with others; ***Piaget***: children construct knowledge by transforming, organizing, and reorganizing previous knowledge.
Developmentally appropriate: Based on knowledge of the typical development of children within an age span (age appropriateness) and the uniqueness of the child (individual appropriateness). ***Developmentally inappropriate***: Ignores the concrete, hands-on approach to learning; direct teaching through abstract, paper-and-pencil activities presented to large groups of young children.	***Changes in child's attention processes***: Switch in habituation/dishabituation to increase in attention; research looks at ***selective attention***, focusing on a specific experience while ignoring others; strong influence of ***salient*** over relevant features of a task until age 6 or 7 when children begin to attend more efficiently to relevant aspects, reflecting a shift to cognitive control of attention with decreased impulsivity.
Project Head Start: Compensatory education program designed to provide children from low-income families the opportunity to acquire skills and experiences important for academic success. ***Project Follow Through***: Different types of educational programs devised to determine which Head Start programs were most effective; enriched programs were carried through the first few years of elementary school.	***Short-term memory (STM)***: Information retained 15–30 seconds without rehearsal; 2- to 3-year-olds hold about 2 digits in STM; by 7, they hold about 5; between 7 and 13 it's up to 8 1/2 digits; older children process information more quickly. ***Long-term memory (LTM)***: A relatively permanent type of memory that holds huge amounts of information for a long period of time.
Effects of early education: More interaction with peers (positive and negative); less cooperative with/responsive to adults than home-reared children; more socially competent and mature: confident, extroverted, assertive, self-sufficient, independent, verbally expressive, knowledgeable about the social world, comfortable in social/stressful situations, better adjusted when in school; less social competence: less polite, less compliant, louder, and more aggressive and bossy.	***Theory of mind***: Refers to awareness of one's own mental processes and the mental processes of others. ***Flavell, Miller, and Miller***: Children's theory of mind changes over childhood: ages 2–3 they begin to understand perceptions, desires, and emotions; ages 4–5 they understand the mind can represent objects and events accurately/inaccurately (e.g., false beliefs).

Self-Test A: Multiple Choice

1. The Reggio Emilia approach to education assumes that children:
   a. need structured programs.
   b. are competent and have rights.
   c. are little scientists.
   d. need to keep switching activities to stay interested.

2. Fumiko is in the preoperational stage of cognitive development. As a consequence, we would expect to see all of the following develop EXCEPT:
   a. formation of stable concepts.
   b. emergence of mental reasoning.
   c. demonstration of conservation.
   d. construction of magical beliefs.

3. Fundamental to Piaget's theory of cognitive development are _____, internalized sets of actions that allow the child to do mentally what before he or she did physically.
   a. logistics
   b. schemata
   c. operations
   d. behaviors

4. Arwen invites her father to a tea party and pours him an imaginary cup of tea. As she pick up her cup, she says, "Daddy, taste the tea. It's SO good." This suggests Arwen is at what stage of development?
   a. symbolic function substage
   b. intuitive thought substage
   c. primary circular reaction substage
   d. sensorimotor stage

5. Piaget and Inhelder's three mountains task was used to assess:
   a. animism.
   b. egocentrism.
   c. centration.
   d. conservation.

6. When Frodo fell, his mother said, "Oh! I bet you hurt the sidewalk more than it hurt you." Frodo took her seriously, thinking the sidewalk felt more pain than he did. This demonstrates:
   a. animism.
   b. egocentrism.
   c. centration.
   d. conservation.

7. Five-year-old Aisha tells you there is more water in a tall, thin glass than in a short, wide glass. You ask how she knows that and she says, "Because I do!" This response would indicate that Aisha is in the:
   a. symbolic function substage.
   b. formal operational stage.
   c. concrete operational stage.
   d. intuitive thought substage.

8. Five-year-old Monsoor watched as you took two round balls of clay that were the same size and rolled one of them into a long "snake," without taking away any clay. If you ask Monsoor, "Are these the same size or is one bigger?" he will most likely tell you:
   a. the snake is bigger.
   b. they are the same size.
   c. he can't tell.
   d. the round ball was bigger, now the snake is bigger.

9. Children in the preoperational stage have difficulties with conservation tasks because of a characteristic called:
   a. centration.
   b. decentration.
   c. seriation.
   d. reversibility.

10. Rochel Gelman believes that children are more likely to conserve when:
    a. they are told what to do.
    b. their attention to relevant aspects of the tasks is improved.
    c. they teach the task to another child.
    d. they can understand why researchers are testing them.

11. Which of the following questions is least likely to be asked by a 5-year-old child?
    a. "What makes you grow up?"
    b. "How much is two plus two?"
    c. "Where does the moon go when it's light outside?"
    d. "Why do leaves fall?"

12. Lev Vygotsky believed children develop through:
    a. social interaction.
    b. their actions and interactions with the physical world.
    c. a natural process of maturation.
    d. reinforcement and punishment.

13. The range of tasks that are too difficult for a child to master alone but that can be learned with guidance and assistance of adults or more skilled peers is called:
    a. the zone of proximal development.
    b. intelligence range.
    c. cognitive competence.
    d. the task range.

14. Mrs. Begay is teaching her granddaughter to weave by watching the girl create her own patterns. When the granddaughter begins to get confused and ask what she should do, Mrs. Begay guides her thinking and actions to help her granddaughter figure it out. Vygostky would call this:
    a. guiding.
    b. zoning.
    c. scaffolding.
    d. entraining.

15. Which of the following reflects Lev Vygotsky's beliefs about language and thought?
    a. Children who engage in high levels of private speech are usually socially incompetent.
    b. Children use internal speech earlier than they use external speech.
    c. All mental functions have external or social origins.
    d. Language and thought initially develop together and then become independent.

16. With regard to private speech, researchers have found all of the following EXCEPT:
    a. self-talk is egocentric and reflects immaturity.
    b. private speech plays a positive role in children's development.
    c. children use private speech more when tasks are difficult.
    d. children who use private speech are more attentive than children who do not use private speech.

17. Ms. Nahmanson believes that Vygotsky provides the best structure for early education. She would therefore be most likely to:
    a. monitor and encourage her students' use of private speech.
    b. incorporate educational programs on television into her curriculum.
    c. read to her students from a state approved book list, then discuss what was read.
    d. use computers to teach math concepts.

18. In comparing Piaget and Vygotsky, although there are differences between them, both emphasize:
    a. social interaction.
    b. the child as a little scientist.
    c. construction of knowledge by transforming, organizing, and reorganizing previous knowledge.
    d. that teachers serve as facilitators and guides, rather than as directors and molders of learning.

19. Trish is in preschool. We could expect that she will:
    a. ignore unimportant but distracting details of a task.
    b. pay attention to relevant elements of a task.
    c. pay attention to salient elements of a task.
    d. shift her attention quickly from one thing to another.

20. Sanjay, who is 7 years old, has a better memory than Tamara, who is 5. This is most likely because Sanjay's speed and efficiency are better, but also because he is more likely than Tamar to:
    a. focus on salient information.
    b. use rehearsal.
    c. use private speech.
    d. focus on external cues.

21. Brandon is 3 years old. We would expect that he is not yet able to understand:
    a. perceptions.
    b. desires.
    c. emotions.
    d. false beliefs.

22. Four-year-old Xavier says to his father, "Look Papa, I doed it!" This indicates that:
    a. Xavier is behind in his language development.
    b. Xavier has been overly influenced by friends who are not in preschool.
    c. Xavier's parents are teaching him inappropriate grammar.
    d. Xavier has learned to use the rule that you add "ed" to make the past tense.

23. When young Luke asks, "Am I a Jedi?" he shows the mastery of complex rules for how words should be ordered referred to as:
    a. syntax.
    b. semantics.
    c. morphology.
    d. phonology.

24. Amadala attends a school that is concerned with physical, cognitive, and socioemotional development, and the process, not the "what," of learning. Amadala attends a:
    a. Head Start program.
    b. Montessori school.
    c. child-centered kindergarten.
    d. Reggio Emilia program.

25. Which of the following is NOT an aspect of a developmentally appropriate classroom?
    a. hands-on activities.
    b. physical, cognitive, and socioemotional experiences.
    c. children select activities from those prepared by the teacher.
    d. direct instruction emphasizing use of workbooks.

26. Preschool literacy programs should include all of the following EXCEPT:
    a. instruction based on what children do not yet know about oral language, reading, and writing.
    b. encouragement of children's early writing attempts without concern for proper formation of letters or conventional spelling.
    c. children's feelings of success and pride in their early reading and writing exercises.
    d. integration of reading into the broad communication process.

27. Project Head Start was designed to:
    a. determine the feasibility of starting formal education at an earlier age.
    b. assess the advantages and disadvantages of preschool educational programs.
    c. give parents an educational day care center.
    d. provide low-income children with skills to help them succeed at school.

28. David Elkind says preschool education:
    a. is critical for the young child's socialization.
    b. is necessary for most children because most parents don't have the competence, time, and resources to ensure that their children are sufficiently educated.
    c. should not begin until a child is socially mature.
    d. can produce excessive stress and anxiety.

29. Researchers have found that compared with children in highly academic programs, young children who attend early childhood education programs with a low academic orientation:
    a. experience no harmful effects.
    b. are more likely to experience test anxiety.
    c. are less creative.
    d. have a less positive attitude toward school.

30. Research on delaying children's entry into first grade in the hope that the extra year will provide a child with a competitive advantage has found:
    a. there are short-term advantages for these children.
    b. there are long-term advantages for these children.
    c. there are both short-term and long-term advantages for these children.
    d. there are long-term disadvantages for these children.

Self-Test B: Matching

Match each of the following persons with the statement or theory that most closely reflects his or her perspective:

1. Jean Berko
2. Lev Vygotsky
3. Diane Burts
4. Jean Piaget
5. Rochel Gelman
6. Maria Montessori
7. David Elkind
8. Barbara Rogoff
9. Friedrich Froebel
10. Zhe Chen and Robert Siegler

a. Believed early childhood education should be part of public education on its own terms.
b. Used fictional words to test children's understanding of language rules.
c. Developed the concept of guided participation, which involves arranging and structuring a child's participation in activities.
d. Believed that language and thought, initially independent, eventually merge.
e. Revolutionized teaching by allowing children freedom and spontaneity.
f. Stated that developmentally inappropriate classrooms promote children's stress-related behaviors.
g. Noted that young children's conservation improves when attending to relevant aspects of tasks.
h. Believed that preoperational thought moves from primitive to sophisticated use of symbols.
i. Found that children as young as 2 years of age can learn strategies.
j. This researcher's concern for quality education for young children led to the founding of the kindergarten.

Self-Test C: True-False

T/F   1. According to Piaget, between the ages of approximately 2 and 7 children transition from primitive to more sophisticated use of symbols.

T/F   2. Children in the intuitive substage of preoperations tend to know what they know while being unaware of HOW they know it ("I know it because I know it").

T/F   3. Piaget's theory is social constructivist while Vygotsky's is cognitive constructivist.

T/F   4. Young children are more likely to focus on what's relevant rather than on what's salient.

T/F   5. Children understand concepts such as lies and deception as early as 2-1/2 years of age.

T/F   6. Support for the universality of language development is seen in the use—and overgeneralization—of rules.

T/F   7. Around age 4, children demonstrate sensitivity to the needs of others in conversation.

T/F   8. The Montessori approach involves education of the whole child with emphases on individual variation, the process of learning, and play.

T/F   9. High-quality early childhood education programs improve the competence of young children from low-income backgrounds.

T/F   10. Children placed in preschool and/or kindergarten are generally more compliant with adults than children who remain at home until they begin first grade.

Self-Test D: OLC

1. T/F   When first asking young children a question beginning "Do you remember…" and asking them about something that did not happen, they will typically say that they DO remember because they want to please the interviewer.

2. Adult professionals viewed 14-week follow-up videos of children who eventually came to believe something happened, even though initially the children knew the event had not happened. The professionals:
   a. could tell that the children's memories had been altered.
   b. were fooled by the children's sincerity about believing the event actually happened.
   c. became angry when they saw how the children had been manipulated.
   d. noticed subtle differences between children whose memories had been manipulated and children who were obviously just trying to please the interviewers.

3. T/F   Ceci's research in manipulating children's memories demonstrates that children resist such manipulation.

Essay Questions

1. You are stuck in the middle of an argument among your three best friends concerning cognitive development during early childhood. One of them thinks that Piaget had the best explanations of how children develop; the second believes Vygotsky had the most plausible theory; and the third says that Gelman and information processing offer the best explanations, not to mention criticisms of (especially) Piaget's theory. Discuss all three of these theories and state which you think makes the most sense and why.

2. As you join two of your friends for coffee you find them in a heated debate about the effects of early education on children. One believes that children who do not begin their formal education until they enter first grade are at a distinct disadvantage that will have a cumulatively negative effect on their ability to learn; the other says that children who begin their education early turn into noncompliant monsters. They turn to you for your input. What do you tell them about the positive and negative impacts of early childhood education?

Key to Self-Test A: Multiple Choice

1. b (LG1)   11. b (LG1)   21. d (LG1)
2. c (LG1)   12. a (LG1)   22. d (LG2)
3. c (LG1)   13. a (LG1)   23. a (LG2)
4. a (LG1)   14. c (LG1)   24. c (LG3)
5. b (LG1)   15. c (LG1)   25. d (LG3)
6. a (LG1)   16. a (LG1)   26. a (LG3)
7. d (LG1)   17. a (LG1)   27. d (LG3)
8. a (LG1)   18. d (LG1)   28. b (LG3)
9. a (LG1)   19. c (LG1)   29. a (LG3)
10. b (LG1)   20. b (LG1)   30. d (LG3)

Key to Self-Test B: Matching

1. b
2. d
3. f
4. h
5. g
6. e
7. a
8. c
9. j
10. i

Key to Self-Test C: True/False

1. True
2. True
3. False. Vygotsky's theory is social constructivist, and Piaget's is cognitive constructivist.
4. False. Younger children focus more on the salient than on the relevant dimensions of a task.
5. False. Children do not begin to understand that the mind can represent objects and events (accurately or) inaccurately until age 4 or 5.
6. True
7. True
8. False. The Montessori approach emphasizes children's spontaneity and freedom in choosing activities, while the child-centered kindergarten involves education of the whole child with emphases on individual variation, the process of learning, and play.
9. True
10. False. Although there are many benefits to children attending preschool and/or kindergarten, particularly in terms of peer socialization, they do tend to be less cooperative and responsive to adults than home-reared children.

Key to Self-Test D: OLC

1. False. Initially the children were adamant about not remembering events that did not occur.
2. b
3. False. Eventually the children came to believe that the event happened, even though it didn't.

Key to Essay Questions

1. To answer this question you will need to explain the three cognitive approaches that describe development at this point in time (i.e., Piaget, Vygotsky, and information processing). This will involve a discussion of the various facets of the two substages (symbolic function and intuitive thought) of the preoperational stage (e.g., animism, egocentrism), how Piaget arrived at his ideas, and how they have been supported; then address the criticisms of Piaget's findings (e.g., problems with his research designs, the fact that children demonstrate certain abilities earlier than he suggested); then contrast Piaget's theory with that of Vygotsky, which states that development is embedded within the sociocultural context (be sure to discuss the zone of proximal development and scaffolding); then compare those theories with the information-processing approach concerning attention, memory, and children's theory of mind. After presenting these three perspectives, state which makes most sense to you (or whether all three are needed together), and explain the rationale for your choice.

2. First, since socialization seems to be an issue here, begin with both the positive and negative effects of early education on children, including interactions with peers, lower cooperation with/ responsiveness to adults, and both the increased and decreased areas of social competence. Then discuss how early education can increase cognitive competence, but be careful to caution against academic pressure. Be sure to delineate between developmentally appropriate practices that are based on age-appropriate and individual appropriate awareness, giving some examples (e.g., curriculum provides experience in all developmental areas, children select many of their own activities from among a variety teachers offer) and developmentally inappropriate practices that ignore the concrete, hands-on approach to learning. Compare some of the types of early education offered, contrasting the Reggio Emilia program, the Montessori approach, and the child-centered kindergarten. Also, it's important to include a discussion of what Project Head Start and Project Follow Through are, how they include children and parents, what constitutes a good program (e.g., encouraging adequate preparation for learning, varied activities, parental involvement) and how these programs have helped low-income children bridge the cognitive gap when entering the public school system. You may also want to address why David Elkind believes that early childhood education should become a part of public education on its own terms.

Research Project 1: Designing a Developmentally Appropriate Preschool Curriculum

Considering everything you have learned in this chapter concerning developmentally appropriate and inappropriate practices, avoiding sexist education, and creating an atmosphere that will optimize children's learning abilities while minimizing stress, design a developmentally appropriate preschool curriculum. Also, be sure to read about the Perry Preschool program in Ypsilanti, Michigan and the research on the benefits of early educational and health enrichment on the island of Mauritius by Adrian Raine and his colleagues that are discussed in this chapter. What educational and noneducational elements to you think are particularly important? Which will you specifically include? What will you specifically omit? Describe your "dream" preschool, explaining the kinds of personnel, activities, curriculum, and physical environment you would want, and why you think these would be important. Which theories would you consider to be most relevant when designing this curriculum? How are they important and how would they be incorporated into your design?

Research Project 2: Early Language Development

This project will help you understand language development. First, get permission from the parents of several children ages 2 to 6 (being sure to ask the children themselves if they are willing to help you with this project—if a child is reluctant to participate, find another child). Using the chart below as a template, record examples of the elements of language discussed in Chapter 10, including phonology (e.g., rhymes, poems, silly sounds); morphological rules, noting examples of overgeneralization with regard to plurals (e.g., "foots" or "footsies" instead of feet) and tenses (e.g., "doed" instead of "did"); syntax (e.g., correct word order for simple sentences, wh-questions, and complex sentences); semantics (i.e., using words correctly/incorrectly in terms of their meaning); and pragmatics (e.g., use of displacement to refer to imaginary people and things, use of articles "a/an" and "the," whether form of speech changes when speaking to people of different ages). Record the words/sentences spoken by each child and indicate which element of language is illustrated.

Child's Age:_____
Child's Sex:_____

Element of Language	What Was Said	Description of How the Example Illustrates Language Development
Phonology: rhyme/poem		
Phonology: other sounds		
Morphology: plurals		
Morphology: tense		
Syntax		
Semantics		
Pragmatics		

1. According to the text, what would you expect to find in terms of each child's language development? Were your findings consistent with these expectations?
2. What elements of language did you notice with each child? Were these consistent with what you read in the text? If so, explain how; if not, explain how they were not consistent.
3. What examples did you observe that made you more aware of how children develop language? Did you notice speaking patterns or other aspects of language that you were unaware of before making these observations?

4. What similarities did you notice among the children in the way they performed? What differences did you notice?

4. Based on your observations of these children, how has your understanding of children and of language development changed? If it has not changed, explain why not.

Personal Application 1: Reflecting on What You Learned

Consider what you read in Chapter 10, then answer the following questions:

1. What information in this chapter did you already know?
2. How can/do you use that information in your own life?
3. What information in this chapter was totally new to you?
4. How can you use that new information in your own life?
5. What information in this chapter was different from what you previously believed?
6. How was this information different?
7. How do you account for the differences between what you believed and what you learned in the chapter?
8. What is the most important thing you learned from reading this chapter?

Personal Application 2: Consider Your Own Development

Check with your parents or other caregivers from your early childhood to see what records, if any, they kept on your development. Consider each area of development discussed in Chapter 10, then use the following chart to complete your developmental milestones and the different aspects of each of the three primary theories discussed (Piaget's, Vygotsky's, and information processing), indicating whether it is relevant to your development and which is the best fit for each aspect of development you explore. If you cannot reconstruct your early growth, look at your child(ren) or other children with whom you have close contact (be sure to get parental consent if the children are not your own and be sure to get consent from the children themselves).

Fill in the chart on the next page , then reflect on your findings and answer the following questions:

1. In the comments section, indicate if you were ahead of, behind, or in synchrony with the stated norms.
2. Do you think your own rate of development affected your later life? If so, state how.
3. What can you say about the "fit" of each of these theories of cognitive development? Is one "better" than the others, do they overlap?
4. If you were to develop a theory of cognitive development, what would it look like?

Aspect of Your Development	Piaget	Vygotsky	Information Processing	Comments
Symbolic function substage (egocentrism, animism, language and thought processes, drawing, etc.)				
Intuitive function substage (classification, conservation, asking questions)				
Zone of Proximal Development				
Scaffolding				
Attention (control of attention, salient vs. relevant dimensions, planfulness, adjusting attention, knowledge of attention)				
Memory **Short-term memory** **Long-term memory** **Accuracy of memory**				
Theory of Mind **Awareness of mind** **Cognitive connections to the world** **Detecting accuracies/ inaccuracies**				
Language Development **Use of phonological and morphological rules**				
Other (describe)				

Internet Projects

Check out the McGraw-Hill Web site for this text (www.mhhe.com/santrockc9). You'll find numerous activities there, in particular, information that will help you research the answers and complete the exercises in the "Taking It to the Net" section at the end of the textbook chapter. Please note that all Web site addresses in this Study Guide have been checked and were correct at the time of publication; however, Web sites may be discontinued or addresses may change, so when you search a given site it may no longer be viable. If that occurs, I apologize for the inconvenience and would appreciate you notifying me so I can make appropriate revisions in future editions of this Study Guide.

Internet Project 1: Children's Memory

A lot of research is currently underway concerning children's memory. Consider the various reasons that memory is such an important topic in childhood (you can gather some from the text, e.g., ways that we learn; the role of memory in IQ testing; susceptibility to suggestion, which can have a major impact on a child's testimony in court; and the impact of various psychotherapeutic techniques). Can you think of other ways that knowing about the development of memory in childhood is important? Check out two sites in particular to look at research that is currently being done to understand children's memory and its impact on children's well-being: http://www.unc.edu/depts/childmem (note that several of the articles relate to children's memory in regard to medical procedures) and http://www.luc.edu/psychology/research/cms/. Compare the two sites (both relate to the Children's Memory Study) to see which is easier to navigate, which is more enjoyable, how they complement each other, and how they differ. What have you learned about areas of research and the importance of understanding the development of memory in early childhood? Among the articles you might want to read for more in-depth understanding of children's memory development is the article "Memory Development or the Development of Memory" by Catherine Haden and Peter A. Ornstein.

Internet Project 2: Intel Inside

The last sections of Chapter 10 explore various types of education for the preschool-age child. As you read about the different types of educational settings, consider how you would develop the optimal educational experience discussed in Research Project 1. Then go to the Web site for Intel Innovation in Education, http://www97.intel.com/education/index.asp, to see what resources it offers for children and adults (including teachers), how that company envisions incorporating technology into early education, and what you think is the primary objective of its Web site. Explore the entire site and then determine how you would go about working with Intel to improve early educational programs in your area. Are there certain federal guidelines to consider? Are there institutional issues involved? What steps would be necessary and, after reviewing the site, what do you think would be the advantages and disadvantages of pursuing this?

Two other sites to check out that directly relate to information in Chapter 10 are http://www.naeyc.org, the Web site for the National Association for the Education of Young Children (NAEYC), and http://www.ccinfoline.8k.com/reggio_emilia.htm, where you can learn about the Reggio Emilia approach to learning (and can link to many other resources on child development).

Additional Internet Resources

Adrian Raine, the Robert G. Wright Professor of Psychology at the University of Southern California, has spent many years exploring the connections between genetics and early childhood experiences (including nutrition) with later developmental outcomes. Check out some of these Web sites to learn more about Professor Raine and his research: http://www.newstarget.com/002527.html, http://www.futurepundit.com/archives/002454.html, http://news.bbc.co.uk/1/hi/programmes/if/4102371.stm (this one is an interview with Professor Raine), and http://www.healthyplace.com/communities/thought_disorders/schizo/news/research_psychosis.asp.

American Academy of Pediatrics: http://www.aap.org

American Medical Association: www.ama-assn.org

APA site: www.apa.org—Offers a multitude of options for learning about topics covered in this chapter. Particularly, go to the "Public Publications" link and check out the "Print and Media" offerings.

APS site: http://www.psychologicalscience.org

The Child Development Website: http://childstudy.net—Provides information on children's topics.

The Consultative Group on Early Childhood Care and Development: http://www.ecdgroup.com

Drkoop.com: http://www.drkoop.com—Full of information on medical topics and links to many other Web sites that provide information and links on a wide range of health issues, both psychological and physiological.

Early Childhood and Parenting Collaborative Information Technology Group, offers a broad array of content and information technology services to the early childhood community, including information on education (e.g., Reggio Emilia) at http://ecap.crc.uiuc.edu/info/.

The Educator's Reference Desk (previously AskERIC): http://www.eduref.org—Leads to numerous documents related to early childhood education—anyone involved in education or developmental psychology would be wise to bookmark this site for ease of reference.

Healthfinder: http://healthfinder.gov

Mayo Clinic's Health Site: http://www.mayoclinic.com

Medscape: http://www.medscape.com—Free database of medical articles, plus access to medical dictionaries, drug databases, and breaking medical news.

Memoryzine: http://www.memoryzine.com—A rich source for information about memory throughout the life span from Practical Memory Institute. Particularly, check out "Memory Health Notes" and read some of the fascinating articles that are available on memory research.

National Institutes of Health: http://www.nih.gov—Starting point for getting into any subagency of NIH.

National Institute of Mental Health: http://www.nimh.nih.gov—Excellent resource for policy statements, NIMH research, grants.

New England Journal of Medicine: http://www.nejm.org—Abstracts to articles, full text on letters and commentaries.

New York University Infant Cognition Center: http://www.psych.nyu.edu/infant—NYU's Infant Cognition Center's site presents current research studies on how babies think. Contact information is provided for parents who are interested in having their children participate in the studies.

Project Zero: http://pzweb.harvard.edu—Harvard's Project Zero conducts longitudinal research in adults' and children's learning processes.

Scientific American: http://www.sciam.com—General scientific resource.
Web MD: http://www.webmd.com—Offers a wide variety of information for the medical profession and for consumers.

CHAPTER 11: SOCIOEMOTIONAL DEVELOPMENT IN EARLY CHILDHOOD

CHAPTER OUTLINE

WHAT CHARACTERIZES YOUNG CHILDREN'S SOCIOEMOTIONAL DEVELOPMENT?

The Self
Emotional Development
Moral Development
Gender

WHAT ROLES DO FAMILIES PLAY IN YOUNG CHILDREN'S DEVELOPMENT?

Parenting
Sibling Relationships and Birth Order
The Changing Family in a Changing Society

HOW ARE PEER RELATIONS, PLAY, AND TELEVISION INVOLVED IN YOUNG CHILDREN'S DEVELOPMENT?

Peer Relations
Play
Television

REACH YOUR LEARNING GOALS

1. **WHAT CHARACTERIZES CHILDREN'S SOCIOEMOTIONAL DEVELOPMENT?**

   The Self   Moral Development

   Emotional   Gender
   Development

2. **WHAT ROLES DO FAMILIES PLAY IN YOUNG CHILDREN'S DEVELOPMENT?**

   Parenting   The Changing
                            Family in a
                            Changing Society

   Sibling
   Relationships and
   Birth Order

3. **HOW ARE PEER RELATIONS, PLAY, AND TELEVISION INVOLVED IN YOUNG CHILDREN'S DEVELOPMENT?**

   Peer   Television
   Relations

   Play

Learning Goals

By the time you have completed this chapter, you should be able to reach the following goals:

1. Discuss emotional and personality development in young children.

2. Explain how families can influence young children's development.

3. Describe the role of peers, play, and television in young children's development.

What is Erikson's third stage of development? How does that relate to a sense of self?	What is *empathy* and how does it relate to moral development?
Describe the concept of *self-understanding*. Where and when does it begin?	Differentiate between *gender*, *gender roles*, and *gender typing*.
Differentiate between *emotion-coaching* and *emotion-dismissing* parents.	What are the main classes of male and female hormones?
What is *moral development*?	Describe Eagly's *social role theory* with respect to social influences on gender development.
Describe Piaget's two stages of moral development.	Explain Freud's *psychoanalytic theory of gender development*.
Explain the notion of *immanent justice*.	Contrast the *social cognitive theory of gender* and the *cognitive developmental theory of gender development*.

Empathy: Reacting to another's feelings with an emotional response similar to the other's; has emotional and cognitive aspects (the ability to discern another's inner psychological states, i.e., perspective taking). For effective moral action, children need to learn how to identify a wide range of emotional states in others and anticipate what kinds of action will improve another's emotional state.	***Initiative v. guilt:*** Erikson's third psychosocial stage occurs in early childhood; children have become convinced they are a person of their own and attempt to discover what type of person they will become; they enthusiastically begin new activities but feel guilt when their effort results in failure or criticism; they intensely identify with their parents.
Gender: The social and psychological dimensions of being male or female (***sex***=biological aspects). ***Gender role:*** A set of expectations that prescribe how females and males should act, think, and feel. ***Gender typing:*** The process by which children acquire the thoughts, feelings, and behaviors considered appropriate for their gender in a particular culture.	***Self-understanding:*** The child's cognitive representation of self, the substance and content of the child's self-conceptions; begins with self-recognition around age 18 months.
Estrogens: A main class of sex hormones that primarily influence development of female sexual characteristics and help regulate the menstrual cycle (estradiol is an important estrogen). ***Androgens:*** A main class of sex hormones that primarily influence development of male genitals and secondary sex characteristics (testosterone is an important androgen).	***Emotion-coaching parents*** monitor their children's emotions, view their children's negative emotions as opportunities for teaching, help them label emotions, and coach them in dealing effectively with emotions. The children are able to self-soothe and regulate their emotions, and have fewer behavior problems. ***Emotion-dismissing parents*** deny, ignore, or change their children's negative emotions.
Social role theory: Eagly's theory that psychological gender differences are caused by the contrasting social roles of women and men; in most cultures around the world, women have less power and status than men and control fewer resources; as women adapted to these roles they showed more cooperative, less dominant profiles than men.	***Moral development:*** concerns rules and conventions about what people should do in their interactions with other people.
Psychoanalytic theory of gender: Freud's view that preschool children develop a sexual attraction to opposite-sex parent; which is renounced at age 5 or 6 because of anxious feelings; subsequently the child identifies with same-sex parent, unconsciously adopting that parent's characteristics.	***Heteronomous:*** Piaget's first stage of moral development, from about age 4 to 7; justice and rules seen as unchangeable properties of the world, removed from personal control. ***Autonomous:*** Piaget's second stage, from about age 10 and older; child becomes aware that rules and laws are created by people; in judging actions, consider the actor's intentions and consequences.
Social cognitive theory: Gender development occurs through observation and imitation of gender behavior, and through rewards/punishments for gender-appropriate/inappropriate behavior. ***Cognitive developmental theory:*** Gender typing occurs after children think of themselves as boys/girls; once they consistently conceive of themselves as male/female, they prefer activities, objects, and attitudes consistent with the label.	***Immanent justice:*** In heteronomous thinking, the concept that if a rule is broken, punishment will be meted out immediately.

Define the terms
schema and *gender schema*.
What does gender schema theory
say about gender development?

What are the guidelines developed by Galinsky
and David for communicating with young
children about divorce?

Describe Baumrind's two styles
of parenting that involve
placing limits on children.
What type of child behavior is
typically associated with each?

Explain the term *peer*.
What functions do
peer groups serve?

Describe Baumrind's two styles
of undemanding/uncontrolling parenting.
What type of child behavior is
typically associated with each?

What is *play*?
What functions does play serve?
How does *play therapy* benefit
children?

How does the term *child abuse*
differ from the term
child maltreatment?

List Parten's six categories
of children's play.

Describe the common
developmental consequences
of child maltreatment.

Compare *sensorimotor play* with
practice play.

How can coparenting practices
undermine children's well being and
how can good coparenting benefit
developmental outcomes?

Describe *pretense/symbolic play*.
When does it typically occur and what
is its primary function?
Contrast *social play* and *games*, indicating
how social play is related to games.

Galinsky and David suggest: explain the separation; explain that the separation is not the child's fault; explain that it may take time to feel better; keep the door open for further discussion; provide as much continuity as possible; and provide support for your children and yourself.	***Schema***: Cognitive structure/network of associations that organize/guide perception. ***Gender schema***: Organizes the world in terms of male/female. ***Gender schema theory***: Gender typing emerges as children gradually develop gender schemas of what is gender-appropriate and gender-inappropriate in their culture.
Peers: Children of about the same age or maturity level. Peer groups provide a source of information and comparison about the world outside the family; important for normal socioemotional development.	***Authoritarian***: rRstrictive, punitive; child is taught to follow directions, respect work and effort; firm limits and controls on the child; little verbal exchange; associated with children's social incompetence. ***Authoritative***: Limits and controls but encourages independence; warm and nurturant; much verbal give and take; associated with children's social competence.
Play: Pleasurable activity engaged in for its own sake; essential to child's health; some ***functions***: increase affiliation with peers, release tension, advance cognitive development, increase social interaction; practice roles that will be assumed later in life; ***play therapy***: lets children work off frustrations while therapists analyze their conflicts and coping methods.	***Neglectful***: The parent is uninvolved in the child's life; associated with children's social incompetence, especially lack of self-control. ***Indulgent***: parents are highly involved with children, but place few demands or controls on them; associated with social incompetence, especially lack of self-control.
Parten's categories of play: unoccupied (not engaging in play); solitary (play alone and independently); onlooker (watch other children play); parallel (play separately from others, but with similar toys or in a similar manner); associative (social interaction with little or no organization); cooperative (involves social interaction with a sense of group identity and organized activity)	***Child abuse:*** Term used by public and professionals, refers to abuse and neglect. ***Child maltreatment:*** Developmentalists use the term to reduce emotional impact of "abuse"; addresses multifaceted nature to include physical abuse, child neglect, sexual abuse, and emotional abuse (psychological/verbal abuse/mental injury).
Sensorimotor play: Behavior engaged in by infants to derive pleasure from exercising their sensorimotor schemes. ***Practice play***: Involves repetition of behavior when new skills are being learned, or physical/mental mastery and coordination of skills are required for games or sports; practice play can be engaged in throughout life.	***Developmental consequences of maltreatment*** include poor emotion regulation, attachment problems, problems in peer relations, difficulty adapting to school; psychological problems (e.g., anxiety, personality problems, depression, suicide attempts, conduct disorder, substance abuse), increased violence toward others; and difficulties initiating and modulating positive and negative affect.
Pretense/symbolic play: Occurs when the child transforms the physical environment into a symbol; occurs between 9 and 30 months, although make-believe appears about 18 months, peaks at 4–5 years, then declines. ***Social play***: Involves social interaction with peers. ***Games***: Activities engaged in for pleasure; include rules, often involving competition.	***Poor coordination*** between parents, undermining the other parent, lack of cooperation and warmth, and disconnection by one parent are risk factors for children's problems; ***parental cooperation*** and warmth are linked with children's prosocial behavior and competence in peer relations.

Self-Test A: Multiple Choice

1. Young children often hear an inner voice called "conscience" that involves all of the following EXCEPT:
   a. self-observation.
   b. self-guidance.
   c. self-punishment.
   d. self-confidence.

3. Olivia's parents openly value her participation in family conversations. They answer her questions, help her join in, or simply enjoy her fantasies and imagination. According to Erik Erikson, Olivia's parents are encouraging her:
   a. initiative.
   b. conscience.
   c. identification.
   d. self-concept.

3. The rudimentary beginning of self-understanding begins with _____, which occurs when the child is about _____.
   a. self-observation; 1 year old.
   b. conscience; 18 months of age.
   d. self-recognition; 18 months of age.
   e. self-concept; 2 years old.

4. Children show an increased ability to reflect on emotions by age:
   a. 18 to 24 months.
   b. 2 to 3 years.
   c. 4 to 5 years.
   d. 6 to 7 years.

5. What should Kim and Joon do if they want to help their children regulate their emotions effectively and reduce the potential that their children will develop behavior problems?
   a. View their children's negative emotions as opportunities for teaching.
   b. Tell their children to turn their negative emotions into positive feelings.
   c. Tell their children not to "feel that way" when they express negative emotions.
   d. Not listen when their children wish to express negative emotions.

6. Chen is at the level of autonomous morality, so we would expect him to judge behavior based on the:
   a. consequences of behavior.
   b. intentions of someone who breaks a rule.
   c. way a specific behavior makes him feel.
   d. rewards moral behavior will bring.

7. "Oh, oh!," says Jane. "Dick broke his arm when he fell off the swing, so he MUST have done something bad to deserve getting hurt like that." Jane's comment suggests Piaget's notion of:
   a. immanent justice.
   b. autonomy.
   c. the just world phenomenon.
   d. behavioral consequences.

8. According to social cognitive theorists, the ability to resist temptation is closely tied to the development of:
   a. empathic behavior.
   b. spontaneity.
   c. abstract reasoning.
   d. self-control.

9. Which cognitive ability is essential to the capacity for empathy?
   a. conservation
   b. logical reasoning
   c. decentration
   d. perspective taking

10. Zinab knows that as a girl there are certain ways she should act, think, and feel. She has developed an understanding of gender:
    a. typing.
    b. roles.
    c. stereotypes.
    d. scripts.

11. Sex hormones that primarily influence the development of female sex characteristics are _____; those that promote male characteristics are _____.
    a. estrogens/androgens
    b. testosterones/estrogens
    c. androgens/testosterones
    d. androgens/estrogens

12. All of the following are criticisms of the evolutionary view of gender development EXCEPT:
a. its hypotheses are backed by speculations about prehistory.
b. it places too much emphasis on environmental factors.
c. people are not locked into behavior that was adaptive in the evolutionary past.
d. the view pays little attention to cultural and individual variations in gender differences.

13. Dr. Perrott adopts social role theory with respect to gender development. He believes that:
a. our gender roles are learned by imitating the important people around us.
b. the roles of men and women differ as a result of evolutionary processes.
c. gender differences result from the contrasting roles of women and men in society.
d. gender roles are biologically determined.

14. With respect to gender-role development, psychoanalytic and social cognitive theories agree that:
a. gender differences are due to social experiences.
b. rewards directly shape gender-role development.
c. children actively acquire gender roles.
d. anatomy is destiny.

15. The research examining peer influences on gender development suggests all of the following EXCEPT:
a. by age 3, children show a preference for spending time with same-sex playmates.
b. by age 5, girls show a preference for larger groups than boys.
c. boys are more likely than girls to engage in competitive activities.
d. boys are more likely than girls to participate in organized group games.

16. When Del showed up at kindergarten with a barrette in his hair, Andrew got upset because he thought if Del wore a barrette he was a girl, not a boy. Andrew has not yet developed:
a. gender constancy.
b. gender schema.
c. sexual identification.
d. gender typing.

17. Charles is typically cheerful, self-controlled, self-reliant, achievement-oriented, has friendly peer relations, cooperates with adults, and copes well with stress. It is likely that Charles' parents use which parenting style?
a. authoritarian
b. authoritative
c. neglectful
d. indulgent

18. Mr. Williams was talking to Ms. Jones on the phone and they got disconnected. When he called Ms. Jones back, he explained that his daughter had cut the phone cord. Ms. Jones asked, "Didn't you see her with the scissors?" to which Mr. Williams replied, "Oh, we don't like to put limits on our children—they need to experience life to the fullest." It sounds like Mr. Williams is a/an _____ parent.
a. authoritarian
b. authoritative
c. neglectful
d. indulgent

19. Reasons to avoid spanking or similar punishments with children include all of the following EXCEPT:
a. there is no immediate effect on stopping the unwanted behavior.
b. children are likely to imitate their parents' aggressive, out-of-control behavior.
c. although children MAY learn what not to do, they don't learn what they should do instead.
d. punishment can be abusive.

20. According to the text, which circumstance is most likely to result in abuse?
    a. A raging, uncontrolled father physically abuses his child.
    b. An overwhelmed single mother in poverty neglects her child.
    c. An alcoholic socialite emotionally rejects her child.
    d. Authoritarian parents demand strict obedience to their rules.

21. Mallory is a survivor of child maltreatment. If she is like other adults who were maltreated, we would expect her to exhibit all of the following behaviors EXCEPT:
    a. empathy for other maltreated children.
    b. increased violence toward others.
    c. a high risk for substance abuse.
    d. greater likelihood of anxiety and depression.

22. Which child is most likely to show difficulties in social adjustment?
    a. Carrie, whose mother and stepfather are receiving marital counseling
    b. Linda, whose parents have a problem coordinating parenting responsibilities because her father works 80 hours a week
    c. Chucky, whose parents work hard at trying to help him develop prosocial behavior
    d. Damien, whose parents cooperate with each other in trying to teach him moral behavior and attitudes

23. Parents are likely to treat their firstborns differently from their later-born children in that they:
    a. have higher expectations for later-born children.
    b. put more pressure on the firstborn for achievement and responsibility.
    c. interfere less with the firstborn's activities.
    d. "baby" the firstborn more than later-born children.

24. Which conclusion has NOT been found with regard to the effects of maternal employment on children's development?
    a. Working mothers are likely to overinvest their energies in their children, thereby discouraging the children's independence.
    b. Work outside the home can produce positive or negative effects on parenting.
    c. Children whose mothers work more than 30 hours a week during the first 9 months of the child's life have poorer cognitive outcomes.
    d. Negative effects of working mothers can be lessened when mothers are sensitive to their children and the children receive high-quality child care.

25. Which is a good recommendation when parents are getting divorced?
    a. Do not explain the separation because no matter what you say, the children are likely to believe it's somehow their fault.
    b. Explain that it may take time to feel better.
    c. Help children understand the divorce by being honest about your ex-spouse's shortcomings as well as your own.
    d. Make a "clean break" by starting fresh and getting rid of as many reminders of the marriage as possible.

26. It is more common for low-income families than middle- or upper-income families to:
    a. use verbal praise.
    b. encourage questions.
    c. use reasoning.
    d. use physical punishment.

27. An important function of peer groups is to:
    a. foster love and understanding that children may not otherwise get.
    b. act as a surrogate for the parents.
    c. teach the importance of friendship.
    d. provide information and comparison about the world outside the family.

28. Daniel Berlyne saw play as:
    a. satisfying our need for pleasure.
    b. satisfying our exploratory drive.
    c. a way that children test out gender roles.
    d. a way to survive childhood.

29. Which conclusion about the effects of television on children is NOT correct?
    a. Television can have a negative influence on children's development.
    b. Television can have a positive influence on children's development.
    c. Exposure to television violence can cause increased aggression in children.
    d. Exposure to television violence has not been found to increase aggression in children.

30. Research suggests that children who view educational television programming in preschool are noted to have all of the following adolescent outcomes EXCEPT:
    a. decreased creativity.
    b. higher grades.
    c. reading more books.
    d. placing a higher value on achievement.

Self-Test B: Matching

Match each of the following persons with the statement or theory that most closely reflects his or her perspective:

1. Lawrence Kohlberg
2. Anna Freud
3. Daniel Berlyne
4. Mildred Parten
5. Lois Hoffman
6. Diana Baumrind
7. Alice Eagly
8. Erik Erikson development.
9. Aimee Leifer development.
10. Harry Stack Sullivan peers.

a. Believed play satisfies an exploratory drive in each of us.
b. Analyzed and characterized children's play.
c. Stated that maternal employment is part of modern life.
d. Described the crisis of early childhood as one of initiative versus guilt.
e. Believed that gender differences result from the contrasting roles of women and men.
f. Thought gender constancy depends on cognition and develops in concert with the development of conservation and categorization skills.
g. Psychiatrist who showed that peers are important for social
h. Believed that parenting style is related to children's socioemotional
i. Thought that children learn reciprocity through interaction with their
j. Demonstrated that television is associated with prosocial behavior in young children.

Self-Test C: True-False

T/F   1. Erikson described the period of early childhood as a time for balancing feelings of trust with mistrust.

T/F   2. By 4 to 5 years of age, children understand that a single event can elicit different emotions in different people.

T/F   3. According to Freud, young children conform to societal standards to avoid guilt.

T/F 4. Androgens primarily influence the development of female physical sex characteristics and help regulate the menstrual cycle.

T/F 5. Cognitive developmental theory states that gender typing emerges as children gradually develop gender schemas of what is gender-appropriate and gender-inappropriate in their culture.

T/F 6. Many psychologists believe that physical punishment is not a good way to discipline children.

T/F 7. A common but unfortunate theme in today's society is the idea that parenting can be done quickly.

T/F 8. Most developmental psychologists agree that both parents working full-time outside the home has negative long-term effects on children.

T/F 9. Peers provide a source of information and comparison about the world outside the family.

T/F 10. Television can have both negative and positive influences on children's development.

Self-Test D: OLC

1. Preschoolers most often describe themselves in terms of their _____.

2. In terms of parental influences on their children's gender development,
   a. fathers are more consistently given responsibility for physical care.
   b. mothers are more likely to engage in playful interaction.
   c. mothers are more likely to be given responsibility for ensuring that their children conform to cultural norms.
   d. fathers are more involved in socializing their sons than their daughters.

3. T/F "Because I said so—that's why" is something a parent with an authoritative style would say.

4. T/F Both indulgent and neglectful parenting styles may cause children to have poor self-control.

Essay Questions

1. As you join some friends for coffee they are in a heated debate about morality in the world today. Each agrees that we are in deep trouble, but they don't agree on causes or solutions. Knowing you are taking this class in child development, they turn to you for some insight. They ask you to explain how moral behavior is learned generally, and how they will be able to teach their own children to think and act in a way that will benefit the world and not just themselves. What guidance can you offer?

2. Your next-door neighbor comes to you for advice. She confides in you that her husband has been repeatedly unfaithful and she has recently learned that he is having unprotected sex with multiple partners. His behavior has been "erratic" in that she never knows if or when he'll be home, he does not participate in the children's school and extracurricular activities, and the two of them spend most

of their time together either arguing or in icy silence. She has suggested they see a marriage counselor, but he says he is perfectly happy with the way things are. She tells you she is considering leaving him and asks you what the effect might be on her children if she divorces him. She has heard that even in the worst of relationships, it is better for the couple to stay together "for the sake of the children." Short of giving her legal advice (other than "see an attorney to learn what you can do and what your rights are"), what can you tell her about the effects of divorce on children and how she can minimize the trauma to her children in the event of a divorce?

Key to Self-Test A: Multiple Choice

1. d (LG1)	11. a (LG2)	21. a (LG3)
2. a (LG1)	12. b (LG2)	22. b (LG3)
3. c (LG1)	13. c (LG2)	23. b (LG3)
4. c (LG1)	14. a (LG2)	24. a (LG3)
5. a (LG1)	15. b (LG2)	25. b (LG3)
6. b (LG1)	16. a (LG2)	26. d (LG3)
7. a (LG1)	17. b (LG3)	27. d (LG3)
8. d (LG1)	18. d (LG3)	28. b (LG3)
9. d (LG1)	19. a (LG3)	29. d (LG3)
10. b (LG2)	20. b (LG3)	30. a (LG3)

Key to Self-Test B: Matching

1. f
2. g
3. a
4. b
5. c
6. h
7. e
8. d
9. j
10. i

Key to Self-Test C: True/False

1. False. Erikson described the period of early childhood as one of initiative versus guilt; trust versus mistrust is the crisis of the first year of life.
2. True
3. True
4. False. Androgens primarily promote the development of male genitals and secondary sex characteristics; the female counterpart is estrogens.
5. False. That's the definition of gender schema theory; the cognitive developmental theory of gender states that children's gender typing occurs after they think of themselves as boys and girls.
6. True
7. True
8. False. Overall, there is no indication that both parents working full-time outside the home has negative long-term effects on children.
9. True
10. True

Key to Self-Test D: OLC

1. material attributes
2. d
3. False. The statement is more likely to come from an authoritarian parent; authoritative parents allow give-and-take with their children.
4. True

Key to Essay Questions

1. First you need to outline the theories of moral development presented by Piaget (explaining the movement from heteronomous morality and the notion of immanent justice to the more mature autonomous morality). Then contrast the behavioral and social cognitive theories of how moral behavior develops (e.g., reinforcement, punishment, and imitation and situational influences, and development of self-control). You will also need to discuss Freud's view that the superego develops with resolution of the Oedipus conflict and identification with the same-sex parent and the role of guilt in getting children to conform to societal standards. Finally, discuss the importance of parenting in helping children develop empathy and perspective taking, noting how authoritative parenting is more likely than the other three parenting styles (i.e., authoritarian, indulgent, and neglecting-rejecting) to teach children to make independent decisions and become socially responsible.

2. Here you will need to discuss what the text has presented about how children adjust to divorce (although more children from divorced families have adjustment problems than children from nondivorced families, most children competently cope with their parents' divorce); the factors involved in children's risk and vulnerability (e.g., adjustment before divorce, temperament, gender, age); and change in socioeconomic status. Since she specifically asked whether they should "stay together for the sake of the children," you will need to address the research in that regard. It would also be particularly important to discuss with her the guidelines for communicating with young children about divorce (e.g., explaining the separation, explaining that it is not the children's fault, etc.).

Research Project 1: Parental Guidelines for Children's Television Viewing

Apply the concepts discussed in Chapter 11 to devise guidelines that would assist parents in using television as a positive influence on their children's lives. Consider the different roles that television plays, the types of influence that it has on children, the characteristics of children who are attracted to specific types of programs, how the amount of television watching may affect children, and how parents can most effectively use television as a positive factor for their children's socioemotional development. Suggest possible guidelines and how parents might interact with their children to discuss what their children view on television.

Research Project 2: Sibling Birth Order

The text provides interesting findings about the effects of birth order on later development, but notes that these effects may be "overdramatized and overemphasized." Using the following chart as a starting point, track as many of your friends and relatives as you practically can, indicating each person's birth order (e.g., only child, firstborn of six, second of four, etc.), sex, their personal characteristics (per those indicated in the text or otherwise), their job title/position, and other information that you believe is relevant. Then answer the questions that follow. (For sake of confidentiality, be sure to use each respondent's initials only, not their actual names.)

Person (Initials Only)	Birth Order	Sex	Characteristics	Job Title/ Position	Other

1. Looking at your data overall, and understanding that there will be individual differences, were your observations consistent with what you might expect from the research described? Explain your response.
2. What patterns did you notice when comparing persons of similar birth order in terms of the material discussed in this chapter?
3. What differences did you notice when comparing persons of similar birth order in terms of the material discussed in this chapter?
4. What might you conclude about the effects of birth order based on your observations? Did you find that there really are consistent effects of birth order, or did you find that the effects have been "overdramatized and overemphasized"?

Personal Application 1: Reflecting on What You Learned

Consider what you read in Chapter 11, then answer the following questions:
1. What information in this chapter did you already know?
2. How can/do you use that information in your own life?
3. What information in this chapter was totally new to you?
4. How can you use that new information in your own life?
5. What information in this chapter was different from what you previously believed?
6. How was this information different?
7. How do you account for the differences between what you believed and what you learned in the chapter?
8. What is the most important thing you learned from reading this chapter?

Personal Application 2: Consider Your Own Development
(Your Parents' Parenting Style)

As discussed in the text, Diana Baumrind describes four primary styles of parenting: authoritative, authoritarian, neglectful, and indulgent. None of us is perfectly consistent, and two parents may often have different parenting styles. Further, as discussed in the text, parents may shift their style and, for example, become less controlling as their children grow up. Consider your own parents and the style(s) they used with you and your siblings (they may have used different styles of parenting for each child—this is not a really clear-cut system). Indicate which style was used primarily by each of your parents, together with the types of behaviors that would indicate to you that this was the style that parent used; then indicate what other styles might have been used and the situations that elicited that style. Also indicate the style(s) used for your siblings and any changes in parenting style as you got older. After filling in the chart, answer the questions that follow.

	Primary Style with You	Other Style(s) with You	Primary Style with Siblings
Mother (you were a toddler)			
Mother (you were in early childhood)			
Mother (you were in middle and late childhood)			
Mother (you were an adolescent)			
Father (you were a toddler)			
Father (you were in early childhood)			
Father (you were in middle and late childhood)			
Father (you were an adolescent)			

1. What was the primary parenting style each of your parents used with you? What other style(s) did they use? When?
2. How consistent were your parents in terms of their parenting style? If they were not consistent, what do you think accounted for the lack of consistency?
3. Did both of your parents use the same parenting style?
4. If your parents used different styles, how do you think that affected you?
5. Did they change parenting styles as you got older? In what way?
6. If you can, describe these styles to your parents and ask them which style they think best fits the one they used as you were growing up. Is this consistent with your assessment?
7. What effect do you think your parents' parenting styles have had on who you are today? How consistent is that with the research findings you have read in the text?

Internet Projects

Check out the McGraw-Hill Web site for this text (www.mhhe.com/santrockc9). You'll find numerous activities there, in particular, information that will help you research the answers and complete the exercises in the "Taking It to the Net" section at the end of the textbook chapter. Please note that all Web site addresses in this Study Guide have been checked and were correct at the time of publication; however, Web sites may be discontinued or addresses may change, so when you search a given site it may no longer be viable. If that occurs, I apologize for the inconvenience and would appreciate you notifying me so I can make appropriate revisions in future editions of this Study Guide.

Internet Project 1: The Effects of Television on Children

It should be clear from Chapter 11 that watching television is associated with both beneficial and detrimental outcomes. Check out two sites to find more information on this topic. First, go to the APA Web site (http://www.apa.org) and go to "Public Publications." On the top menu, type "children and television" in the search box at the top left of the page. Review some of the articles, then go to other search engines, such as Yahoo.com or Google.com to look more specifically at issues of gender inequity on television (do a search for "television + gender inequity"). After reviewing several articles about the effects on children of watching television, consider the following questions:

1. What are some important problems associated with watching television?
2. What are the benefits associated with watching television?
3. With respect to aggression and television violence, does watching violence make children more aggressive, or is it that the more aggressive children watch violent programs?
4. Did any of the articles or Web sites discuss the effects of providing strong female role models? What did they conclude?
5. How can parents use television to increase their children's sensitivity, empathy, and intellectual growth?
6. Consider the various guidelines presented in the text and the articles you've read online, then develop a set that you believe would be useful for people you know who have children (this may be you).

Internet Project 2: Child Physical and Sexual Abuse

Go to the Web site of the National Clearinghouse on Child Abuse and Neglect Information located at http://nccanch.acf.hhs.gov/index.cfm. Link to each of the topics, particularly the first two: "Preventing Child Abuse and Neglect" and "Overview of Child Abuse and Neglect." Consider what you've learned in the text together with what you learned from the information on this Web site. What are the issues here? What are the different types of child abuse discussed? How prevalent is child abuse in the United States? What would you conclude about the harm that occurs to a child (both as a child and later as an adult) resulting from physical and sexual abuse? What are the societal consequences of abuse? How can you use this information to reduce the occurrence of physical and sexual abuse in children? What can you, as an individual, do about this problem? If you would be willing to get involved in child abuse prevention, how would you go about doing that?

Another Web site to visit for ideas on what to do instead of losing control and harming a child is http://www.positivediscipline.com, which is aimed at raising young people to be responsible in a mutually respectful environment. A good non-Web source about the after effects of child sexual abuse is a book by Catherine Cameron, *Resolving Childhood Trauma: A Long-Term Study of Abuse Survivors* (2000, Sage Publications), which presents in a readable fashion the results of her longitudinal research with women who had been sexually molested as children.

Additional Internet Resources

American Academy of Pediatrics: http://www.aap.org

American Bar Association http://www.abanet.org/publiced/practical/books/family/chapter_7.pdf —The American Bar Association offers a chapter titled "Deciding Whether or Not to Divorce" (you can also go to http://www.abanet.org" and type "divorce" in the search box to find lots of others resources).

APS site: http://www.psychologicalscience.org.

Brown University: http://search.brown.edu/search/texis/webinator/search—An excellent site to search for articles and other information concerning gender equity (type "gender equity" in the search box and see what comes up).

Childabuse.org: http://childabuse.org—A Colorado organization that offers information about child abuse and neglect.

Children's Defense Fund (CDF): http://www.childrensdefense.org—The Web site for CDF, the organization headed by Marian Wright Edelman to promote child welfare (discussed in Chapter 1 of the text).

The Child Development Web site: http://childstudy.net—Provides information on children's topics and encourages social activism.

Drkoop.com: http://www.drkoop.com —A Web site full of information on medical topics and links to many others that provide information and links on a wide range of health issues, both psychological and physiological.

Early Childhood and Parenting Collaborative Information Technology Group: http://ecap.crc.uiuc.edu/info/—Offers a broad array of content and information to the early childhood community, including information on research and an online discussion group.

Early Childhood Care and Development: http://www.ecdgroup.com—Use the search option to find useful research and articles.

Emory University offers an excellent site for learning about Albert Bandura, the father of social learning theory, at http://www.emory.edu/EDUCATION/mfb/Bandura/Index.html. Here you will also learn about self-efficacy, an integral component of one's sense of self.

Healthfinder: http://healthfinder.gov

Mayo Clinic's Health Site: http://www.mayoclinic.com

Medscape: http://www.medscape.com—Free database of medical articles, plus access to medical dictionaries, drug databases, and breaking medical news.

National Institutes of Health: http://www.nih.gov—Starting point for getting into any subagency of NIH.

National Institute of Mental Health: http://www.nimh.nih.gov—Excellent resource for policy statements, NIMH research, and grants.

New England Journal of Medicine: http://www.nejm.org—Abstracts to articles, full text on letters and commentaries.

Positive Discipline: http://www.positivediscipline.com—A good site for parents and teachers to find useful solutions for discipline problems.

Psychology Matters: http://psychologymatters.org—An excellent resource for current research on many interesting and practical applications of psychology that are easy to read and understand. Type in a search topic or use the links on the left side of the page to find lots of useful information relating to topics in Chapter 11.

Scientific American: http://www.sciam.com—General scientific resource

Society for Research in Child Development (SRCD): http://www.srcd.org—The Web site for SRCD, an organization whose purposes are to promote multidisciplinary research in the field of human development, to foster the exchange of information among scientists and other professionals of various disciplines, and to encourage applications of research findings.

Web MD: www.webmd.com—Offers a wide variety of information for the medical profession and for consumers.

Zero to Three: www.zerotothree.com—A site for parents and professionals. Zero to Three is a nonprofit organization that focuses on promoting the healthy development of babies and toddlers.

CHAPTER 12: PHYSICAL DEVELOPMENT IN MIDDLE AND LATE CHILDHOOD

CHAPTER OUTLINE

WHAT CHANGES TAKE PLACE IN BODY GROWTH AND MOTOR DEVELOPMENT?

Skeletal and Muscular Systems
Tooth Development and Dental Care
Motor Development

WHAT ARE THE CENTRAL ISSUES IN CHILDREN'S HEALTH?

Nutrition
Exercise and Sports
Obesity in Children
Diseases
Accidents and Injuries

WHAT ARE THE PREVALENT DISABILITIES IN CHILDREN?

Who Are Children with Disabilities?
The Range of Disabilities
Educational Issues

REACH YOUR LEARNING GOALS

1. **WHAT CHANGES TAKE PLACE IN BODY GROWTH AND MOTOR DEVELOPMENT?**

   Skeletal and Muscular Systems

   Motor Development

   Tooth Development and Dental Care

2. **WHAT ARE THE CENTRAL ISSUES IN CHILDREN'S HEALTH?**

   Nutrition

   Accidents and Injuries

   Obesity

   Exercise and Sports

   Diseases

3. **WHAT ARE THE PREVALENT DISABILITIES IN CHILDREN?**

   Who Are Children with Disabilities

   Educational Issues

   The Range of Disabilities

Learning Goals

By the time you have completed this chapter, you should be able to reach the following goals:

1. Discuss changes in body growth and motor development in middle and late childhood.

2. Characterize children's health in middle and late childhood.

3. Summarize information about children with disabilities.

What are the most pronounced physical changes in middle and late childhood?	Explain the difference in the terms *children with disabilities* and *handicapped children*.
What basic, overall change takes place in motor development during middle and late childhood?	Describe the three criteria for diagnosing children with a learning disability.
Explain the relationship between television and exercise.	How is *dyslexia* different from typical reading problems? What is *dyscalculia*?
Describe both the positive and negative consequences of participation in sports for children.	Describe the characteristics of *attention deficit hyperactivity disorder (ADHD)*.
How is *obesity* determined? How predictive is childhood obesity of obesity in the adult years?	Compare the three speech disorders: *articulation disorders*, *voice disorders*, and *fluency disorders*.
What are the two leading causes of death in children between the ages of 5 and 14? What other diseases are particularly harmful to children's development?	Differentiate between *low vision* and *educationally blind*.

Children with disabilities: The current preferred term for the children (approximately 10%) who receive special education or related services for various disabilities; the term emphasizes the person rather than the handicap (as results from use of the term *handicapped children*).	**The most pronounced physical changes**: Skeletal and muscular systems (increased muscle mass and strength, decreased "baby fat," proportional changes; head and waist circumference and leg length decrease in relation to body height) and tooth development (primary teeth replaced by secondary teeth).
Three criteria for learning disabilities: A minimum IQ level; significant difficulty in a school-related area (especially reading or mathematics); and exclusion of severe emotional disorders, second-language background, sensory disabilities, and/or specific neurological deficits.	**Motor development**: becomes much smoother and more coordinated; gross motor skills involving large muscle activity improve, particularly for boys; increased myelination of the central nervous system is seen in improved fine motor skills.
Dyslexia: The most common form of learning disability; it is a category of reading problem reserved for individuals who have a severe impairment in their ability to read and spell. **Dyscalculia**: Learning disability involving difficulty in math computation (also called developmental arithmetic disorder); some children have both dyslexia and dyscalculia.	**Relationship between television and exercise**: Some experts suggest television is partially to blame for children's poor physical health. One study found children who watch little television to be significantly more physically fit than their heavy-television-watching peers; more television viewing is correlated with being overweight.
Attention deficit hyperactivity disorder (ADHD): A disability in which children consistently show one or more of the following over a period of time: inattention, hyperactivity, and impulsivity.	**Positive consequences:** exercise, opportunities to learn how to compete, self-esteem, and a setting to develop peer relations and friendships. **Negative consequences:** the pressure to achieve and win, physical injuries, distraction from academic work, and unrealistic expectations for success as an athlete.
Articulation disorders: Problems in pronouncing sounds correctly. **Voice disorders**: Speech that is hoarse, harsh, too loud, too high-pitched, too low-pitched; common in children with cleft palate. **Fluency disorder**: Involves stuttering, which occurs when speech has a spasmodic hesitation, prolongation, or repetition.	**Obesity**: An individual who is 20% over the expected weight for height is considered obese; in adults, body mass index (BMI) is used; for children this requires development of age- and gender-based reference graphs; obesity at age 6 results in approximately 25% chance of adult obesity, at age 12 it's about a 75% chance.
Low vision: Visual acuity of between 20/70 and 20/2000 with corrective lenses on the Snellen scale (20/20 is normal vision). **Educationally blind**: Cannot use their vision in learning and must use their hearing and touch to learn.	**Leading causes of death** for children between 5 and 14: the most common cause of severe injury and death is motor vehicle accidents; cancer (most commonly, leukemia) is the second leading cause of death in this age group. Diabetes, cardiovascular disease, and asthma are three other diseases that are harmful to children's development.

Compare *oral approaches* with *manual approaches* with regard to helping hearing-impaired children learn.	Explain the mandates of the *Individuals with Disabilities Education Act (IDEA)*.
Explain the restrictions involved in *orthopedic impairments*.	What is *instructional technology*?
What is *cerebral palsy*? What is its most common cause? Describe the "tools" that are often used to help children with cerebral palsy learn.	What is *assistive technology*?
What are *emotional and behavioral disorders*? What are the *autism spectrum disorders (ASD)*?	Describe an *individualized education plan (IEP)*.
Describe the characteristics of *autistic disorder*. When does it develop? How is it similar to and dissimilar from *Asperger syndrome*?	Describe the notion of the *least restrictive environment (LRE)*.
Explain the purpose of *Public Law 94–142*.	How is the term *inclusion* used in reference to the education of children with disabilities?

Individuals with Disabilities Education Act (IDEA): The new name for PL 94–142 as of 1990; spells out broad mandates for services to all children with disabilities, including evaluation and eligibility determination, appropriate education and the individualized education planr (IEP), and least restrictive environment (LRE).	Educational approaches to help children with hearing impairments: *Oral approaches* include lip reading, speech reading (relies on visual cues to teach reading), and whatever hearing the child has. *Manual approaches* involve sign language and finger spelling.
Instructional technology includes various types of hardware and software, combined with innovative teaching methods, to accommodate students' needs in the classroom; includes videotapes, computer-assisted instruction, and complex hypermedia programs.	*Orthopedic impairments* involve restrictions in movement because of muscle, bone, or joint problems; the amount of restriction depends on severity of the impairment; they can be caused by prenatal or perinatal problems, or from disease or accident during childhood years.
Assistive technology consists of various services and devices to help students with disabilities function within their environment; includes communication aids, alternative computer keyboards, and adaptive switches.	*Cerebral palsy*: Disorder involving lack of muscular coordination, shaking, or unclear speech; most common cause is lack of oxygen at birth; in the most common type (spastic) muscles are stiff and difficult to move; in ataxia (less common) muscles are rigid one moment, floppy the next. "Tools": computers, pen with light, speech and voice synthesizers, communication boards, talking notes, page turners.
Individualized education plan (IEP): A written statement that spells out a program specifically tailored for the student with a disability; in general, the IEP should be related to the child's learning capacity, specially constructed to meet the child's needs, and designed to provide educational benefits.	*Emotional and behavioral disorders*: Serious, persistent problems in relationships, aggression, depression, fears (personal and school matters), and other inappropriate socioemotional characteristics. *Autism spectrum disorder (ASD)*: Ranges from severe autistic disorder to milder Asperger syndrome; problems in social interaction, verbal and nonverbal communication, and repetitive behaviors.
Least restrictive environment (LRE): A setting for children with disabilities that is as similar as possible to the one in which children who do not have a disability are educated.	*Autistic disorder*: Severe autism spectrum disorder; onset in first 3 years of life; deficiencies in social relationships, abnormalities in communication, and restricted, repetitive, stereotyped patterns of behavior. *Asperger syndrome*: Mild autism spectrum disorder; relatively good verbal language, milder nonverbal language problems, restricted range of interests and relationships.
Inclusion: Educating a child with special education needs full-time in the general school program.	*Public Law 94-142*, passed in 1975 (called the Education for All Handicapped Children Act), requires all students with disabilities to be given a free, appropriate public education and allocates funding to help implement this education.

Self-Test A: Multiple Choice

1. During the period of middle and late childhood, children:
   a. grow an average of 2 to 3 inches a year.
   b. grow an average of an inch a year.
   c. have growth spurts that start and stop throughout this period.
   d. have moderate growth that is relatively gradual, with occasional spurts.

2. Norman, a typical child going through middle to late childhood, would experience all of the following EXCEPT:
   a. increased muscle mass.
   b. increased body fat.
   c. increased strength.
   d. decreased leg length in relation to body height.

3. What is the best way to reduce the risk of periodontal disease?
   a. conscientious brushing and flossing.
   b. orthodontic treatment.
   c. restricting use of fluoride in toothpaste.
   d. regular use of mouthwash.

4. Which activity is most likely to create fatigue for elementary school children?
   a. sitting
   b. running
   c. jumping
   d. bicycling

5. Increased myelination is seen in improvements in each skill EXCEPT:
   a. use of tools.
   b. tying shoe laces.
   c. bicycling.
   d. playing a musical instrument.

6. According to nutritionists:
   a. peers have a greater influence on children's eating patterns than parents do.
   b. when left to make their own decisions about food, children will develop healthy eating patterns.
   c. breakfast should make up about one-fourth of the day's calories.
   d. children should not be allowed to eat sweets or fats.

7. Which of the following is NOT a reason children today are not getting enough exercise?
   a. television
   b. schools
   c. diet
   d. families

8. A study in which elementary school children were randomly assigned either to a running program or to regular physical education classes found that children in the running program:
   a. got lower grades.
   b. had enhanced creativity.
   c. were more likely to be injured.
   d. had poorer cardiovascular health.

9. Critics of children's participation in sports express special concern about the appropriateness of:
   a. Special Olympics.
   b. highly competitive, win-oriented sports.
   c. gymnastics.
   d. highly physical interactive sports.

10. Although defining obesity is not a simple task, generally individuals who are _____ over the expected weight for height are considered obese.
    a. 5%
    b. 10%
    c. 15%
    d. 20%

11. Which child is at highest risk for obesity?
    a. Milly, an 8-year-old White girl whose mother is obese
    b. Maddy, an 8-year-old African-American girl with high levels of leptin
    c. Malcolm, an 8-year-old African-American boy who eats cereal for breakfast
    d. Martin, a White adolescent boy whose father is obese

12. An obese teenager is at risk for all of the following, EXCEPT:
    a. low self-esteem.
    b. low blood cholesterol levels.
    c. high blood pressure.
    d. pulmonary problems.

13. Dr. Lublin, an expert in childhood obesity, is most likely to recommend which treatment for an obese child?
    a. stomach surgery.
    b. psychotherapy to understand why the child is obese.
    c. a high-protein, low-carbohydrate diet.
    d. exercise, moderate reduction in calories, and behavior modification.

14. Comparisons of cancer in children and cancer in adults find that:
    a. cancer is usually found earlier in children.
    b. cancer in children is more likely to be caused by diet or exposure to cancer-causing agents.
    c. children with cancer are usually treated by their family physician or by pediatricians.
    d. children with cancer are likely to survive for a long period of time.

15. The Bogalusa, Louisiana, school system has implemented a program aimed at improving its students':
    a. cognitive skills.
    b. cardiovascular health.
    c. math scores.
    d. verbal and math skills.

16. The most common cause of severe injury and death in middle and late childhood is:
    a. cancer.
    b. skate-boarding.
    c. ingestion of poisons.
    d. motor vehicle accidents.

17. Children with a learning disability have all of the following characteristics, EXCEPT:
    a. normal or above-normal intelligence.
    b. difficulties in at least one academic area.
    c. their difficulty is not attributable to some other diagnosed problem or disorder.
    d. hypervigilance.

18. Which of the following children has the most common learning disability?
    a. Draco, who has dyslexia
    b. Harry, who has difficulty with handwriting
    c. Ron, who has dyscalculia
    d. Hermione, who has ADHD

19. Angel is inattentive, hyperactive, and impulsive. He would most likely be diagnosed with:
    a. mental retardation.
    b. ADHD.
    c. autism.
    d. Asperger syndrome.

20. Classification of a child with ADHD typically occurs:
    a. soon after birth.
    b. in preschool.
    c. in elementary school.
    d. in high school.

21. Adderall has been prescribed for several children with ADHD at Hogwarts School. Which child would be most likely to benefit from this drug?
    a. Neville, whose problems focusing are helped with behavior therapy
    b. Luna, who has high levels of anxiety
    c. Percy, who has recently graduated
    d. Ginny, who has relatively mild symptoms

22. Which of the following children has an articulation disorder?
    a. Jason, whose voice is hoarse and harsh
    b. Kelly, who has problems pronouncing sounds correctly
    c. Lamar, who speaks in a loud, high-pitched voice
    d. Marty, who stutters

23. Helen is educationally blind. We would expect that in school she will be helped by use of:
    a. a touch system such as Braille.
    b. a magnifying glass.
    c. large-print books.
    d. special lamps to help her see.

24. Eddie is hearing impaired and uses manual approaches to help him learn in school. This would involve use of:
    a. sign language.
    b. lip reading.
    c. speech reading.
    d. listening closely.

25. _____ consist(s) of serious, persistent problems involving relationships, aggression, depression, fears associated with personal or school matters, and other inappropriate socioemotional characteristics.
    a. Cerebral palsy
    b. Emotional and behavioral disorders
    c. Attention deficit hyperactivity disorder
    d. Learning disabilities

26. Six-year-old Ricky rarely seeks affection or interaction with others; he becomes distressed when his mother makes even the smallest change in the house (such as moving a vase from one side of the coffee table to the other side); he uses no language; and he becomes absorbed in rocking back and forth. Ricky most likely has:
    a. ADHD.
    b. Asperger syndrome.
    c. dyslexia.
    d. autistic disorder.

27. In 1990, Public Law 94–142 was renamed the Individuals with Disabilities Education Act (IDEA). This act requires that students with disabilities have:
    a. special classrooms to enhance their education.
    b. restrictive placement in regular classrooms.
    c. an individualized education plan.
    d. tutors or aides to assist them.

28. Under the provisions of the Individuals with Disabilities Education Act (IDEA):
    a. children are evaluated within a month after school begins each fall.
    b. children's needs must be reevaluated at the beginning of each school year.
    c. in addition to the school evaluation, parents must obtain independent evaluations.
    d. technology devices and services must be provided if necessary to ensure a free, appropriate education.

29. The IEP (individualized education plan) requires that each student with a disability have a program specifically tailored to that student. This would mean that the IEP should be all of the following, EXCEPT:
    a. related to the child's learning capacity.
    b. similar to options that are available to other children.
    c. specially constructed to meet the child's individual needs.
    d. designed to provide educational benefits.

30. The current trend concerning children with disabilities is to:
    a. include them in the regular classroom.
    b. provide them with separate programs because they are more effective for disabled children.
    c. provide separate programs because it is disruptive to other students to have classrooms and lessons adapted for the needs of disabled students.
    d. provide separate programs because it is disruptive for teachers to have classrooms and lessons adapted for the needs of disabled students.

Self-Test B: Matching

Match each of the following persons or terms with the statement that fits best:

1. Sharla Peltier
2. Sharon McLeod
3. James Kauffman
4. Linda Siegel
5. Heart Smart
6. Adderall
7. IDEA
8. Asthma
9. Motor vehicle accidents
10. Dyslexia

a. Study designed to improve children's cardiovascular health.
b. Trains Native American parents in improving communication skills with their children.
c. Helps children cope with their health-care experiences through therapeutic play and developmentally appropriate activities.
d. This is the most common chronic disease among children.
e. Most common cause of severe injury and death in middle/late childhood.
f. Severe impairment in reading/spelling; most common learning disability.
g. Believed that children with disabilities need an individualized approach that does not always involve full inclusion.
h. Stimulant medication commonly prescribed to treat ADHD.
i. Created three-prong criteria for diagnosing learning disabilities.
j. Act that spells out broad mandates for services to children with disabilities.

Self-Test C: True-False

T/F   1. The period of middle and late childhood involves slow, consistent growth.

T/F   2. During the period of middle and late childhood children need to reduce their activity levels.

T/F   3. As children progress through the period of middle and late childhood, girls usually have better gross motor skills and boys generally have better fine motor skills.

T/F   4. Children in the middle and late childhood years need to consume fewer calories than when they were younger.

T/F   5. Contrary to popular beliefs, indications are that children in the United States get sufficient exercise.

T/F   6. For most children, middle and late childhood is a time of excellent health.

T/F   7. The most common chronic disease in children is asthma.

T/F   8. The term "children with disabilities" is used today rather than "handicapped children" so the focus will be on the child, not on the disability.

T/F   9. Most children with learning disabilities are mentally retarded.

T/F   10. The trend in education today is to educate children with disabilities in special education classes as much as possible.

Self-Test D: OLC

1. The incidence of cancer in children is _____.

2. Inclusion
   a. has been replaced by the term "mainstreaming."
   b. means educating a child with special education needs part-time in the general school program and part-time in a special education program.
   c. can be very costly and time consuming.
   d. violates the least restrictive environment provision of IDEA.

3. T/F   Elementary school children become more fatigued by long periods of passivity than by engaging in physical activity.

4. T/F   The current consensus is that autism in children is the result of an emotionally cold home environment.

Essay Questions

1. Your next-door neighbor has told you that her 7-year-old daughter came home from school asking for permission to join the gymnastics team. She also told her mother that the gymnastics coach told her she would have to "go on a diet" if she wanted to join. Your neighbor is concerned about whether he should allow his daughter to join the team and how he should handle her concerns about dieting. You have watched this little girl grow up and she doesn't seem overweight to you. What will you tell your neighbor?

2. Knowing you are taking this class in child development, two of your friends approach you for your guidance. They've recently watched the Special Olympics and began thinking about opening a school for handicapped children. They've heard about mainstreaming, but think that perhaps these children would do better in a more protected environment. They also want to know what kinds of handicaps they might expect to see. Enlighten them.

Key to Self-Test A: Multiple Choice

1. a (LG1)	11. a (LG2)	21. a (LG3)
2. b (LG1)	12. b (LG2)	22. b (LG3)
3. a (LG1)	13. d (LG2)	23. a (LG3)
4. a (LG1)	14. d (LG2)	24. a (LG3)
5. c (LG1)	15. b (LG2)	25. b (LG3)
6. c (LG2)	16. d (LG2)	26. d (LG3)
7. c (LG2)	17. d (LG3)	27. c (LG3)
8. b (LG2)	18. a (LG3)	28. d (LG3)
9. b (LG2)	19. b (LG3)	29. b (LG3)
10. d (LG2)	20. c (LG3)	30. a (LG3)

Key to Self-Test B: Matching

1. b
2. c
3. g
4. i
5. a
6. h
7. j
8. d
9. e
10. f

Key to Self-Test C: True/False

1. True
2. False. During middle and later childhood children should be activity-oriented and very active.
3. False. Boys are usually better at gross motor skills, girls at fine motor skills.
4. False. During middle and late childhood children need to consume more (not fewer) calories than when they were younger (however, a balanced die is important—they should not be filling up on "empty calories").
5. False. Every indication suggests the children in the United States are not getting enough exercise.
6. True
7. True
8. True
9. False. To be diagnosed with a learning disability, IQ must be at least average.
10. False. The trend today is toward including children with disabilities full-time in the regular classroom.

Key to Self-Test D: OLC

1. increasing
2. c
3. True
4. False. The current consensus is that autism involves a brain dysfunction; there is no evidence that family socialization causes autism.

Key to Essay Questions

1. There are two primary issues here. First is the caution about involving children in sports, as discussed in the section on sports as well as in the "Caring for Children" section titled "Parents and Children's Sports." To answer this question you will need to discuss both the positive and negative consequences for children who participate in sports, with special concern for children in high-pressure sports settings; also consider the role of the parents in children's sports. Second, there would be a major concern about a teacher or coach who suggests that a young child be on a diet, particularly when that child is not overweight, so you should be discussing the concerns about dieting for young children.

2. The first two things you need to tell your friends are that the term used today is "children with disabilities," to keep the focus on the child not the disability, and that the trend today, based on legislation first passed in 1975 (Public Law 94–142, revised in 1990 as the Individuals with Disabilities Education Act [IDEA]), is for inclusion of children with disabilities into regular classrooms (tell your friends the term "mainstreaming" is no longer used). Next, explain why these children are being included (e.g., reducing the stigma of being disabled, although there is controversy about whether the regular classroom is the best place for many disabled children) and how they are able to be included (e.g., elaborate on some of the special equipment). You will also need to discuss the wide range of disabilities (e.g., learning disabilities such as dyslexia and dyscalculia, ADHD, autism spectrum, visual, speech, etc.) and ways that these different problems are treated. You would probably advise your friends that many years of training in education and special education are needed before jumping into this challenging field.

Research Project 1: Fine and Gross Motor Activity

This is a way to see developmental changes in fine and gross motor activity over time. After obtaining parental permission and the permission of the children with whom you will be working, have five children from five different age groups (ranging from 2 through 10) write (or print, as appropriate) their first name and their age and draw a picture of themselves (note that only one chart is provided—be sure to make four more copies before using this one). Compare the handwriting and the drawings in terms of what you have learned so far (feel free to incorporate what you have learned about children's drawings from Chapter 9). Then answer the questions the following questions:

1. What similarities and what differences did you notice in how the children held their writing/drawing utensil (pencil, crayon, etc.)?

2. What patterns of development did you notice when comparing the writing and drawing of the children in terms of the material discussed in this chapter?

3. Were your observations consistent with what you might expect from the research described? Explain your response.

4. What might you conclude about development of these skills based on your observations?

Name:	Age:

Self-Portrait:

Research Project 2: Dealing with Childhood Obesity

It should be clear from Chapter 12 (and other sections of the textbook as well) that obesity is a critical problem for children in the United States today. The text has mentioned some causes of obesity, some of the problems that children currently have and will have in the future as a result of being obese, and some ways to deal with the problem. It is now up to you to go beyond the textbook. Interview pediatricians, cardiologists, child psychologists, and other health care professionals who work with children and are familiar with this issue. Also, check with local hospitals and HMOs to see what information and programs they provide to the public. Then either use the chart below or create one of your own to organize what you have learned in terms of what the experts say.

	Expert #1	Expert #2	Expert #3	Health Care Institution (Hospital, HMO, etc.)
Expert's Profession/ Experience				
Causes of Childhood Obesity				
Consequences: Current				
Consequences: Future				
Ways to Alleviate the Problem				
Cautions About Various Types of Treatment				
Other Comments				

1. What have you learned about the causes and current and future consequences of childhood obesity?
2. What have you learned about different ways to treat childhood obesity? Are some more effective than others, and what potential dangers are there in some of the suggested treatments?
3. What other comments did these professionals (or organizations) offer that provide more insight into this problem and its effective treatment?
4. How can you incorporate what you learned into an effective program to ensure children's healthy development?
5. How can you use what you learned in terms of advancing your own knowledge about children and their optimal development?

Personal Application 1: Reflecting on What You Learned

Consider what you read in Chapter 12, then answer the following questions:

1. What information in this chapter did you already know?
2. How can/do you use that information in your own life?
3. What information in this chapter was totally new to you?
4. How can you use that new information in your own life?
5. What information in this chapter was different from what you previously believed?
6. How was this information different?
7. How do you account for the differences between what you believed and what you learned in the chapter?
8. What is the most important thing you learned from reading this chapter?

Personal Application 2: Reflecting on Learning Disabilities

Referring back to the "Review and Reflect" section toward the end of this chapter, you will see that Dr. Santrock asks you to think about your own schooling and issues concerning children with disabilities: were they diagnosed; were you aware that there were children in your class with disabilities; were these children helped either by teachers or by specialists? If you are still in touch with any of those students from your elementary school years who did have a learning disability, interview them now about their school experiences and their suggestions for improving the ways that schools (e.g., teachers, administrators, boards of education) work with children who have learning disabilities. If you had (or continue to have) a learning disability, consider your own experiences when answering these questions.

Also consider the recommendations of Linda Siegel listed in the chapter for helping children with learning disabilities. Do you (or your classmates) remember any of these strategies being used when you were in elementary school? Are there any strategies listed that you might find useful now, either in your personal life or when interacting with others (who may or may not have a learning disability)? How could you apply any of these in your own personal or professional life?

Internet Projects

Check out the McGraw-Hill Web site for this text (www.mhhe.com/santrockc9). You'll find numerous activities there, in particular, information that will help you research the answers and complete the exercises in the "Taking It to the Net" section at the end of the textbook chapter. Please note that all Web site addresses in this Study Guide have been checked and are correct at the time of publication; however, Web sites may be discontinued or addresses may change, so when you search a given site it may no longer be viable. If that occurs, I apologize for the inconvenience and would appreciate you notifying me so I can make appropriate revisions in future editions of this Study Guide.

Internet Project 1: Autism

The text presents a snapshot of autism, a disorder that typically leaves children isolated and, in previous times, had them sent off to institutions to live out their lives withdrawn from the world. Go to the Web site for the National Institute of Mental Health (http://www.nimh.nih.gov/publicat/autism.cfm) and check out the NIMH publication on autism, which you may print out if you wish. After reading this publication, go to http://www.templegrandin.com/ and read about Temple Grandin, an extraordinary woman who was diagnosed with autism when she was 3-1/2 years old. After reading about the autistic spectrum disorders at both Webs ites, answer the following questions:

1. What are the characteristics of autism and how early are they noticed?
2. What other disorders are included in the autistic spectrum disorders, and how are they similar to and different from autistic disorder (i.e., autism)?
3. How can understanding autism help you understand normal development?
4. How can understanding autism help you understand brain function? What factors affect brain development?
5. Read the story of Temple Grandin and think about what that story says about how to work with an autistic child (or adult) and the hope for autistic children to become valuable, contributing members of society. What do you think it was about Temple and her family that helped her develop her talents to become who she is today? (You might note that at the beginning of the brochure it is stated that the individuals referred to are not real, but their stories are; however, Temple Grandin is a real person and this is a true story about her.)
6. What are the different approaches to treating autism and other autistic spectrum disorders? How would you go about selecting the best treatment for someone you know who has one of these disorders?
7. Are there elements of treatment for autism that you think would be appropriate to incorporate into the standard classroom setting? Describe what they are and how they could be used.
8. What other thoughts came to mind as you read this material?

Internet Project 2: Sports and Exercise

As indicated in Chapter 12, getting sufficient exercise is a major concern for children today—it often seems they are either "couch potatoes" who stuff themselves in front of the television set and get too little exercise or they are overly concerned with diet and push themselves beyond health limits in competitive sports. Check out what the "experts" are saying by going to Dr. Koop's Web site (http://www.drkoop.com) and doing a search for "children and sports"; then go to the National Center for Sports Safety site at http://www.sportssafety.org/ to see what coaches, parents, and young athletes need to know to ensure their safety and enjoyment when engaging in sports (although there are some interesting articles available through links, for most benefit you'll need to register—it's free).

1. How does the information of each site compare with what you learned at the other?
2. How does the information compare with what you have read in the chapter?
3. What additional information did you learn?
4. Based on what you learned, what advice would you give to parents about their children's (and their own) participation in sports?
5. Based on the information in the text and from the Web sites, what type of intervention would you design to ensure that school children today are protecting their health in terms of diet, nutrition, and exercise?

Additional Internet Resources

APS site: http://www.psychologicalscience.org

American Sports Medicine Institute: http://www.asmi.org/—Provides information for professionals and non-professionals, including important safety information for children.

California Childcare Health Program: http://www.ucsfchildcarehealth.org/ —Offers a wealth of information on keeping children safe and healthy.

Children's Defense Fund (CDF): http://www.childrensdefense.org—The Web site for CDF, the organization headed by Marian Wright Edelman to promote child welfare (discussed in Chapter 1 of the text).

The Child Development Web site: http://childstudy.net—Provides information on a variety of children's topics.

The Consultative Group on Early Childhood Care and Development: http://www.ecdgroup.com

Early Childhood and Parenting Collaborative Information Technology Group: http://ecap.crc.uiuc.edu/info/—Offers a broad array of content and information technology services to the early childhood community.

Healthfinder: http://healthfinder.gov—A treasure trove of health information from the federal government.

Mayo Clinic's Health Site: http://www.mayoclinic.com

Medscape: http://www.medscape.com—Free database of medical articles, plus access to medical dictionaries, drug databases, and breaking medical news.

Middle Childhood Physical Development: http://www.fractaldomains.com/devpsych/midchildphys.htm —A site that adds additional perspectives about physical development (and obesity) in middle childhood to the information contained in the text.

The National Institute of Child Health: http://www.nichd.nih.gov—One of the many information sites of the National Institutes of Health. This one is devoted to all aspects of children's health.

National Institutes of Health: http://www.nih.gov—Starting point for getting into any subagency of NIH.

National Institute of Health *Consensus Statements: 110. Diagnosis and Treatment of Attention Deficit Hyperactivity Disorder,* http://odp.od.nih.gov/consensus/cons/110/110_statement.htm—An in-depth look at all aspects of ADHD.

National Institute of Mental Health: http://www.nimh.nih.gov—Excellent resource for policy statements, NIMH research, and grants.

New England Journal of Medicine: http://www.nejm.org—Abstracts to articles, full text on letters and commentaries.

O.A.S.I.S. (Online Asperger Syndrome Information and Support): Asperger's Guide for Teachers: http://www.udel.edu/bkirby/asperger/teachers_guide.html—Discusses the skills and limitations of children with Asperger syndrome.

Pediatric Neurological Associates: http://www.pediatricneurology.com/autism.htm—This site offers extensive information about the autistic spectrum disorders (eight different specific disorders and the relationship with ADHD), and offers an excellent guide for working with Asperger disorder.

Scientific American: http://www.sciam.com—General scientific resource.

Society for Research in Child Development (SRCD): http://www.srcd.org—The Web site for SRCD, an organization whose purposes are to promote multidisciplinary research in the field of human development, to foster the exchange of information among scientists and other professionals of various disciplines, and to encourage applications of research findings.

Web MD: http://www.webmd.com—Offers a wide variety of information for the medical profession and for consumers.

Zero to Three: http://www.zerotothree.com—Although this is primarily a site for information about infants and toddlers, there are many useful links for information about autism and eating disorders. One cautionary note is that many of the links are advertisements, so you may need to sift carefully to find the informational articles (it's worth the effort).

CHAPTER 13: COGNITIVE DEVELOPMENT IN MIDDLE AND LATE CHILDHOOD

CHAPTER OUTLINE

WHAT IS PIAGET'S THEORY OF COGNITIVE DEVELOPMENT IN MIDDLE AND LATE CHILDHOOD?

Concrete Operational Thought
Piaget and Education
Evaluating Piaget's Theory

WHAT IS THE NATURE OF CHILDREN'S INFORMATION PROCESSING?

Memory
Thinking
Metacognition

HOW CAN CHILDREN'S INTELLIGENCE BE DESCRIBED?

What Is Intelligence?
Multiple Intelligences
Controversies and Issues in Intelligence
The Extremes of Intelligence

WHAT CHARACTERIZES CHILDREN'S ACHIEVEMENT?

Extrinsic and Intrinsic Motivation
Mastery Orientation
Self-Efficacy
Goal Setting, Planning, and Self-Monitoring
Ethnicity and Culture

WHAT CHANGES IN LANGUAGE DEVELOPMENT OCCUR IN MIDDLE AND LATE CHILDHOOD?

Vocabulary and Grammar
Reading
Bilingualism

REACH YOUR LEARNING GOALS

1. **WHAT IS PIAGET'S THEORY OF COGNITIVE DEVELOPMENT IN MIDDLE AND LATE CHILDHOOD?**

   Concrete Operational Thought

   Evaluating Piaget's Theory

   Piaget and Education

2. **WHAT IS THE NATURE OF CHILDREN'S INFORMATION PROCESSING?**

   Memory

   Metacognition

   Thinking

3. **HOW CAN CHILDREN'S INTELLIGENCE BE DESCRIBED?**

   What Is Intelligence

   Controversies and Issues in Intelligence

   Multiple Intelligences

   The Extremes of Intelligence

4. **WHAT CHARACTERIZES CHILDREN'S ACHIEVEMENT?**

   Extrinsic and Intrinsic Motivation

   Self-Efficacy

   Ethnicity and Culture

   Mastery Orientation

   Goal Setting, Planning, and Self-Regulation

5. **WHAT CHANGES IN LANGUAGE DEVELOPMENT OCCUR IN MIDDLE AND LATE CHILDHOOD?**

   Vocabulary and Grammar

   Bilingualism

   Reading

Learning Goals

By the time you have completed this chapter, you should be able to reach the following goals:

1. Discuss Piaget's stage of concrete operational thought, apply Piaget's theory to education, and evaluate his theory.
2. Describe changes in information processing in middle and late childhood.
3. Characterize children's intelligence.
4. Explain the development of achievement in children.
5. Summarize language development in middle and late childhood.

Explain the task of *seriation*. What is the role of *transitivity* in reasoning?	What is *creativity*? How does creativity relate to *convergent thinking* and *divergent thinking*? What role does *brainstorming* play in the creative process?
What do the neo-Piagetians believe in terms of children's cognitive development?	What role does *metacognition* play in helping children become better critical thinkers?
Describe *long-term memory*. What does *schema theory* say about memory? Explain the role of *schemas* with regard to long-term memory. What is the premise of *fuzzy trace theory*?	What is *intelligence*? What is the relevance of individual differences to intelligence?
Explain the role of *expertise* and *strategies* with regard to long-term memory. How are *elaboration* and *imagery* important strategies for learning?	What is the relationship of *mental age* to the *intelligence quotient (IQ)*? What is the relevance of a *normal distribution* to IQ?
Explain the relationship between critical thinking and cognitive processes. How can teachers help students become critical thinkers?	Contrast Spearman's notions of general and specific intelligence described in his *two-factor theory*. What is *factor analysis*?
Describe the *FCL (Fostering a Community of Learners)* program created by Brown and Campione and the strategies used in the program to encourage critical thinking.	Contrast Thurstone's *multiple-factor theory* with Gardner's *theory of multiple intelligences*.

Creativity is the ability to think in novel, unusual ways, come up with unique solutions to problems; *convergent thinking*: produces one correct answer (like the kinds of thinking tested by standardized intelligence tests); *divergent thinking*: produces many answers to a question (characteristic of creativity); *brainstorming*: come up with ideas in a group, play off each other's ideas, say what comes to mind.	*Seriation* is the concrete operation that involves ordering stimuli along a quantitative dimension (such as length). *Transitivity*: In concrete operational thought, a mental concept that underlies the ability to logically combine relations to understand certain conclusions (focus: reasoning about the relations between classes).
Metacognition is cognition about cognition, or knowing about knowing. Pressley believes helping students develop a rich repertoire of problem-solving strategies is the key to education; critical thinkers use strategies and effective planning to solve problems, know when and where to use strategies; summarize and get the gist of what author says when reading; and plan, organize, reread, and write drafts when writing.	*Neo-Piagetians*: Developmentalists who have elaborated on Piaget's theory, arguing that he got some things right and it is important to describe some general developmental changes in children's cognition; however, they reinterpret his theory from an information-processing perspective, emphasizing how children use attention, memory, and strategies to process information.
Intelligence includes problem-solving skills and the ability to learn from and adapt to the experiences of everyday life. *Individual differences* are the stable, consistent ways in which people are different from each other; interest in intelligence has often focused on individual differences and assessment.	*Long-term memory*: Relatively permanent type of memory that holds huge amounts of information for a long period of time. *Schema theory*: People mold memories to fit information already in their minds. *Schemas*: Mental concepts that organize concepts and information. *Fuzzy trace theory* says that memory is best understood by considering verbatim memory and gist.
Mental age (MA): Binet's measure of one's level of mental development compared to that of others; dividing that number by a person's chronological age and multiplying the answer (quotient) by 100 gives the *Intelligence quotient (IQ). (IQ = MA/CA x 100)*; IQ scores fall within a *normal distribution*, a symmetrical distribution with 68% of scores falling in the middle of the possible range and fewer scores at the extremes.	*Expertise*: Organized factual knowledge about a particular content area; involves what a person already knows about a topic. *Elaboration*: A strategy of engaging in more extensive processing of information. *Imagery*: Use of visual images helps older (not younger) children remember verbal information better.
Two-factor theory: Spearman's theory that individuals have both general intelligence, which he called *g*, and a number of specific intelligences, referred to as *s*. *Factor analysis*: A statistical procedure that correlates test scores to identify underlying clusters, or factors.	*Critical thinking*: involves grasping the deeper meaning of ideas, keeping an open mind about different approaches and perspectives, and deciding for oneself what to believe or do. Teachers can help students develop open-mindedness, intellectual curiosity, planning and strategy, and intellectual carefulness.
Multiple-factor theory: Thurstone's theory that intelligence consists of seven primary mental abilities; verbal comprehension, number ability, word fluency, spatial visualization, associative memory, reasoning, and perceptual speed. *Gardner's multiple intelligences* include the following skills: verbal, mathematical, spatial, bodily-kinesthetic, musical, interpersonal, intrapersonal, and naturalist.	*FCL uses: Children teaching children*: Older students teach younger students (cross-age teaching) face-to-face and via e-mail; talk about learning, offer responsibility and purpose; fosters collaboration among peers. *Reciprocal teaching*: Students take turns leading small-group discussions to discuss complex passages, collaborate, and share individual expertise and perspectives. Also use modified jigsaw classroom.

What are the components of *Sternberg's triarchic theory*?	Explain the role of *achievement motivation* (need for achievement) in success.
Describe the concept of *emotional intelligence*.	Differentiate *intrinsic motivation* from *extrinsic motivation*.
Describe how *adoption studies* are used and what *heritability* is with regard to assessing the influence of heredity on intelligence.	Describe how *helpless orientation*, *mastery orientation*, and *performance orientation* differ.
Explain the purpose of *culture-fair tests*. What types of culture-fair tests have been devised?	What is *self-efficacy* and how does it relate to achievement? Explain the importance of goal setting, planning, and self-regulation for achievement.
Describe the three types of *mental retardation* discussed in the text.	Explain how the *whole-language approach* differs from the *basic-skills-and-phonetics approach* of reading instruction.
What does it mean to say that a child is "*gifted*"? What are the characteristics of gifted children?	What is *bilingualism*? Explain the goal of bilingual education.

Achievement motivation (need for achievement): The desire to accomplish something, to reach a standard of excellence, and to expend effort to excel.	***Sternberg's triarchic theory***: Intelligence comes in three forms: *analytical* (ability to analyze, judge, evaluate, compare, contrast); *creative* (ability to create, design, invent, originate, imagine); and *practical* (ability to use, apply, implement, put into practice).
Intrinsic motivation: The desire to be competent and to do something for its own sake; based on internal factors, such as self-determination, curiosity, challenge, and effort. ***Extrinsic motivation***: The motivation produced by external rewards and punishments.	***Emotional intelligence*** is the ability to perceive and express emotions accurately and adaptively, to understand emotion and emotional knowledge, to use feelings to facilitate thought, and to manage emotions in oneself and others.
Helpless orientation: One seems trapped by the experience of difficulty and attributes difficulty to a lack of ability. ***Mastery orientation***: One is task oriented and instead of focusing on ability, is concerned with learning strategies. ***Performance orientation***: Focus is on achievement outcomes, winning is what matters most, and happiness is thought to result from winning.	***Adoption studies*** are inconclusive about the relative importance of heredity in intelligence; some studies find some behaviors of adopted children is more like that of their biological than their adopted parents. ***Heritability*** is the fraction of variance in IQ in a population that is attributed to genetics.
Self-efficacy: Belief that one can master a situation and produce favorable outcomes. Bandura: this a critical factor in whether students achieve. ***Goal setting, planning, and self-regulation***: important dimensions of achievement; goal setting and planning often work in concert—when individuals set goals, they need to plan how to reach those goals; self-regulation involves self-generation and self-monitoring of thoughts, feelings, and behaviors to reach the goal.	***Culture-fair tests***: Tests designed to be free of cultural bias. One type includes items familiar to people from all socioeconomic and ethnic backgrounds (or at least familiar to the individuals taking the test); the other has no verbal items. Although designed to be culture-fair, students with more education score higher than students with less education.
Metalinguistic awareness is knowledge about language. ***Whole-language***: Instruction should parallel children's natural language learning; reading materials should be whole and meaningful. ***Basic-skills-and-phonetics***: Phonetics and basic rules are necessary to translate symbols into sounds; early reading instruction should involve simplified materials.	***Mental retardation***: Limited mental ability in which an individual has a low IQ, usually below 70 on a traditional IQ test, and has difficulty adapting to everyday life. ***Organic retardation***: Retardation caused by a genetic disorder or brain damage in which the IQ is between 0 and 50. ***Cultural-familial retardation***: characterized by no evidence of organic brain damage; individual's IQ is between 50 and 70.
Bilingualism: The ability to speak two languages (this has a positive effect on children's cognitive development). ***Bilingual education***: An educational approach whose aim is to teach academic subjects to immigrant children in their native languages (most often Spanish) while gradually adding English instruction.	***Gifted children***: Have above-average intelligence (an IQ of 130 or higher) and/or a superior talent for something. Characteristics include precocity (master an area earlier than their peers); marching to their own drummer; a passion to master.

Self-Test A: Multiple Choice

1. Mental actions that allow children to do mentally what they had done physically before are referred to in Piagetian terms as:
   a. operations.
   b. seriations.
   c. reversals.
   d. cognitions.

2. Piaget believed that _____ thought appears when the child is about 7 years of age.
   a. sensorimotor
   b. preoperational
   c. concrete operational
   d. formal operational

3. An important characteristic of concrete operations is that they are:
   a. reversible.
   b. transitive.
   c. sensory.
   d. egocentric.

4. Annie is asked to arrange 12 dolls of different sizes, going from the smallest to the largest. As a concrete operational thinker, she is able to do this, demonstrating which type of task?
   a. transitivity
   b. seriation
   c. conservation
   d. reversibility

5. Which of the following is an application of Piaget's ideas to education?
   a. We need to know how children understand the world to teach them effectively.
   b. Children's illogical or distorted ideas about the world make it hard for them to learn.
   c. The pattern of mental development is universal, so one curriculum could be developed and used for all children.
   d. By the third or fourth grade, children are ready for abstract learning.

6. Mr. Washington wants to apply Piaget's theory to teaching his fourth-grade class. He would probably incorporate all of the following, EXCEPT:
   a. take a constructivist approach.
   b. direct the children's learning.
   c. consider the child's knowledge and level of thinking.
   d. turn the classroom into a setting of exploration and discovery.

7. Which of the following is NOT one of Piaget's many contributions?
   a. He presented a vision of children as active, constructive thinkers.
   b. He created a theory that generated a huge volume of research on children's cognitive development.
   c. His careful observations offer inventive ways to learn about children and important things to look for in cognitive development.
   d. He demonstrated that children's concepts of the world emerge spontaneously.

8. A valid criticism of Piaget's theory is that:
   a. some cognitive abilities emerge earlier than Piaget thought, and others can emerge later.
   b. his theory neglects developmental synchrony.
   c. children at any given cognitive stage cannot be trained to reason at a higher cognitive stage.
   d. culture and education exert a much weaker influence on children's development than Piaget believed.

9. Lucienne, a 9-year-old, is most likely to remember events through the process of:
   a. reflection.
   b. reconstruction.
   c. exact recall.
   d. abstraction.

10. According to fuzzy trace theory, memory is best understood by considering:
    a. verbatim memory trace and gist.
    b. strategic methods.
    c. fuzzy traces of memory.
    d. information that already exists in one's mind.

11. Tina has been told that a good way to remember something is to think of examples of how the information is useful, or apply the new information to what she already knows. These suggestions are examples of:
    a. elaboration.
    b. imagery.
    c. rote strategies.
    d. critical thinking.

12. Although some teachers shy away from using this technique because they do not think it's "polite" or nice," Mr. Hughes is following a suggestion for incorporating critical thinking into his sixth-grade classroom. This suggestion is to encourage students to:
    a. define and describe what they have learned about sex in their science class.
    b. memorize important ideas news stories about American colonialism.
    c. discuss both sides of controversial issues.
    d. learn to analyze adult love poems.

13. Creativity is defined as the ability to:
    a. see all sides of an argument.
    b. think in novel and unusual ways.
    c. come up with many solutions to a problem.
    d. use previous knowledge to solve problems.

14. Guy was asked, "How many quarts make up a gallon?" This type of question tests:
    a. convergent thinking.
    b. divergent thinking.
    c. critical thinking.
    d. creative thinking.

15. Aaron is aware of his thinking and understands that he uses certain strategies to help him remember. These skills demonstrate:
    a. memory.
    b. cognition.
    c. metacognition.
    d. abstract reasoning.

16. _____ is defined as problem-solving skills and the ability to adapt to and learn from life's everyday experiences.
    a. Creativity
    b. Intelligence
    c. Metacognition
    d. Wisdom

17. The first intelligence test was developed in:
    a. France.
    b. Germany.
    c. the United States.
    d. Russia.

18. Ashley has a mental age of 13 and a chronological age of 10. Thus her intelligence quotient (IQ) is:
    a. 130.
    b. 100.
    c. 77.
    d. 10.

19. A goal of applying Gardner's theory to children's education is to:
    a. allow students to discover and explore domains they find interesting.
    b. encourage student interaction.
    c. promote critical thinking.
    d. help children become creative and critical thinkers.

20. Robert Sternberg's triarchic theory of intelligence includes all of the following abilities, EXCEPT:
    a. analytical.
    b. creative.
    c. motivational.
    d. practical.

21. Paolo sells souvenirs on the streets of Salvador, Brazil. He cares for his brother and sister, who live on the streets with him. Although he never went to school, he has become successful in his business and caring for his siblings. In Sternberg's terms, Paolo has which type of intelligence?
    a. analytical
    b. creative
    c. practical
    d. all three factors

22. Daniel Goleman's theory of emotional intelligences emphasizes which aspects of intelligence?
    a. interpersonal
    b. intrapersonal
    c. practical
    d. all of these

23. All of the following are potential problems with IQ tests, EXCEPT:
    a. scores on an IQ test can easily lead to stereotypes.
    b. IQ tests might be used as the sole indicator of a person's competence.
    c. there may be problems in interpreting the meaningfulness of the overall IQ score.
    d. IQ tests cannot be used to predict how well a student might be expected to perform in school.

24. Melody has Down syndrome. She has an IQ of 50. Her retardation would likely be considered:
    a. organic.
    b. social.
    c. profound.
    d. cultural-familial.

25. Ellen Winner has described three criteria that characterize gifted children. Which of the following is NOT a criterion?
    a. ingenuity
    b. precocity
    c. marching to their own drummer
    d. a passion to master

26. Which of the following is NOT likely to increase children's internal motivation?
    a. giving children choices
    b. providing children with opportunities for personal responsibility
    c. offering children opportunities to set goals and monitor their progress
    d. providing children with structured guidelines to help them achieve their goals

27. Bobby often instructs himself to pay attention, think carefully, and remember strategies that worked for him before. Bobby demonstrates a:
    a. helpless orientation.
    b. performance orientation.
    c. mastery orientation.
    d. achievement orientation.

28. Mrs. Blum read her first graders *The Little Engine That Could.* The part of the story where the engine asserts, "I know I can, I know I can," illustrates Bandura's notion of:
    a. self-efficacy.
    b. self-concept.
    c. self-esteem.
    d. self-assurance.

29. Mrs. Kumin believes that in early reading instruction, children should be presented with materials in their complete form, such as stories and poems. Which approach does Mrs. Kumin support?
    a. whole-language
    b. basic-skills-and-phonetics
    c. balanced
    d. classical

30. Researchers have found that bilingualism:
    a. has a negative effect on children's cognitive development.
    b. has a positive effect on children's cognitive development.
    c. confuses children in regard to language development.
    d. results in children scoring lower than monolingual children on intelligence tests.

Self-Test B: Matching

Match each of the following persons with the statement or theory that most closely reflects his or her perspective:

1.	Alfred Binet	a.	Discovered rapid worldwide increase in intelligence test scores.
2.	Howard Gardner	b.	Created first test to determine children who would do well in school.
3.	James Flynn	c.	Proposed a theory of eight kinds of intelligence.
4.	Ellen Winner	d.	Developed the triarchic theory of intelligence.
5.	Robert J. Sternberg	e.	Distinguished between convergent and divergent thinking.
6.	J.B. Guilford	f.	Found academically gifted children to be socially well adjusted.
7.	Lewis Terman	g.	Thought that few schools teach students to think critically.
8.	Jacqueline Brooks	h.	Found that social qualities (respect, responsibility, consideration) are important domains of intelligence among Luo culture of Kenya.
9.	Elena Grigorenko	i.	Memory is best understood by considering verbatim memory trace and gist.
10.	Charles Brainerd	j.	Described gifted children in terms of precocity, marching to one's own drummer, and passion.

Self-Test C: True-False

T/F   1. The landmark of concrete operations is abstract reasoning.

T/F   2. Piaget's constructivist approach has been applied to education to focus on the teacher as a guide rather than a director.

T/F   3. Children's memory is characterized by remembering exact copies of events.

T/F   4. Creativity is the ability to think about something in novel and unusual ways and to come up with unique solutions to problems.

T/F   5. Emotional intelligence is the ability to perceive and express emotion accurately and adaptively, to understand emotion and emotional knowledge, to use feelings to facilitate thought, and to manage emotions in oneself and others.

T/F   6. Heritability is the strongest component of intelligence.

T/F   7. Mental retardation involves an IQ below 100 and problems in adapting to everyday life.

T/F   8. Giving children choices and providing opportunities for personal responsibility increases intrinsic motivation.

T/F   9. The whole-language approach to instruction stresses phonetics and basic rules to translate symbols into sounds.

T/F   10. Bilingualism has a negative effect on children's cognitive development.

Self-Test D: OLC

1. Offering a child money in exchange for good grades in an example of _____ motivation.

2. Which of the following have researchers found to improve children's self-efficacy and achievement?
   a. setting distal rather than proximal goals.
   b. setting goals that are easy to reach to avoid getting discouraged.
   c. setting concrete, specific goals.
   d. being monitored by a teacher or parent rather than encouraged to monitor themselves.

3. T/F   Howard Gardner believed that traditional tests of IQ were too narrow, and proposed the triarchic theory of intelligence.

4. T/F   Bilingualism has a positive effect on children's cognitive development.

Essay Questions

1. You have been approached by your favorite elementary school teacher, who has asked you for your ideas on creating a healthy, holistic atmosphere for his students. He wants to address their physical, emotional, and cognitive needs, but he also wants a special emphasis on teaching children to read. Bearing in mind all of the developmental issues you have studied in this chapter, what would you suggest?

2. An acquaintance knows that you are taking this class in child development. He approaches you at a party and tells you about a couple of books he has read that definitively state that intelligence is inherited and that this has been proven through twin studies. He goes on to say that it is clear from cross-cultural studies that people in Western cultures are smarter than people in Eastern and third-world cultures. How do you respond?

Key to Self-Test A Multiple Choice

1. a (LG1)	11. a (LG2)	21. c (LG3)
2. c (LG1)	12. c (LG2)	22. d (LG3)
3. a (LG1)	13. b (LG2)	23. d (LG3)
4. b (LG1)	14. a (LG2)	24. a (LG3)
5. a (LG1)	15. c (LG2)	25. a (LG3)
6. b (LG1)	16. b (LG3)	26. d (LG4)
7. d (LG2)	17. a (LG3)	27. c (LG4)
8. a (LG2)	18. a (LG3)	28. a (LG4)
9. b (LG2)	19. a (LG3)	29. a (LG5)
10. a (LG2)	20. c (LG3)	30. b (LG5)

Key to Self-Test B: Matching

1. b
2. c
3. a
4. j
5. d
6. e
7. f
8. g
9. h
10. i

Key to Self-Test C: True/False

1. False. Abstract thought develops in the formal operational stage, not the concrete operational stage.
2. True
3. False. Children's memory is characterized by reconstructing the past rather than remembering an exact copy of it.
4. True

5. True
6. False. Although many studies show a strong heritability component is involved in intelligence, environmental influences are also critically important.
7. False. Mental retardation involves an IQ below 70 together with problems adapting to everyday life; average IQ is 100.
8. True
9. False. The whole-language approach is based on the idea that instruction should parallel children's natural language learning and reading materials should be whole and meaningful; the approach stressing phonetics and basic rules to translate symbols into sounds is the basic-skills-and-phonetics approach.
10. False. Bilingualism has a positive effect on cognitive development.

Key to Self-Test D: OLC

1. extrinsic
2. c
3. False. While Gardner argues that traditional types of intelligence tests are too narrow, it was Sternberg who developed the triarchic theory of intelligence.
4. True

Key to Essay Questions

1. Your answer here should encompass the entire chapter. For extra points, you may want to incorporate information from the previous chapter, too, including physical changes in the skeletal and muscular systems and increased motor skills (gross and fine) and how these changes relate to proper diet and the need to exercise, as well as the positive and negative consequences of participating in sports; sensitivity to various issues of children's disabilities (e.g., learning disabilities, ADHD) and socioeconomic issues. Then move on to the developmental changes in children's cognitive abilities (they are now in the concrete operational stage), addressing application of Piaget's theory to education and what information-processing theory says about development during this period (e.g., memory, metacognition, critical thinking). Then address the issues of intelligence, creativity, language development, and the debate on teaching reading using the whole-language approach or the basic-skills-and-phonetics approach. After addressing all of these developmental issues, suggest how you would use this information to assist your teacher in creating a model classroom with a developmentally appropriate curriculum to achieve optimal outcomes for all of the students. (To *really* be a star, you might also want to discuss the benefits of bilingualism and how it would be appropriate for children at this age to start to learn a second language if they do not come from a bilingual home.)

2. First, acknowledge that you are familiar with the research of Arthur Jensen and of Richard Herrnstein and Charles Murray, and are aware that adoption studies have shown a strong heritability component in intelligence. Then discuss the flaws in Jensen's research (e.g., more recent research shows a much smaller difference in IQ scores between identical and fraternal twins, noting that this lessens the power of Jensen's findings) and in that of Herrnstein and Murray (e.g., as the economic gap narrows between African Americans and White Americans, so does the gap in IQ scores, and that there are flaws in the validity of IQ tests). Next, discuss the impact of the environment on intelligence and the research suggesting that families, schools, and socioeconomic status have a huge impact on cognitive processes, and that interventions that enrich a child's environment can raise a child's IQ. Also, discuss the fact that heritability refers to groups, not individuals, and it cannot provide information about differences *between* groups. It is also important to consider how intelligence is being tested, noting that there are many reasons why someone would or would not do well on an "intelligence" test. This brings you to a

discussion of cross-cultural comparisons, noting that different cultures consider different traits when determining what does (or does not) constitute intelligence (e.g., Eastern cultures value community, many African communities consider social competence to be a more important component of intelligence than "rational thinking"). Also, all tests, no matter how "culture fair," are culturally biased. Finally, you might want to bring up all the various theories about exactly what constitutes intelligence (considering, for example, those of Spearman, Sternberg, and Thurstone) to suggest that your acquaintance might want to come up with a good idea of what intelligence is; then he needs to balance heritability with environmental influences and cultural considerations.

Research Project 1: Motivation for Learning—Where Does It Go?

It is often said that children enter school eager to learn and by the time they are in fourth grade they have lost their enthusiasm for education. Review what has been written by the psychologists, educators, and researchers discussed in this chapter on effective ways for children to learn. Then observe several different classrooms and several different grades. Are the teachers using the methods that are suggested? Do the children seem motivated to learn? Can you see a relationship between the teaching techniques used and the children's eagerness to learn? Based on your review of the literature and your observations, prepare a proposal for keeping children motivated to learn.

Research Project 2: Conservation Tasks

Work with two children, one between the ages of 4 and 5, the other between 6 and 7. Be sure to obtain written consent from the parents; it is also appropriate to have the children sign (or print, as the case may be) the consent form indicating their willingness to participate—even if they don't sign the consent form, you should be sure to ask them for permission to work with them. Usually if you tell them you are working on a project for school and ask if they would be willing to help you out, they are more than happy to do so. In the event that the parent and/or child wishes to have the parent present while you are doing these tasks, instruct the parent to say nothing, merely to observe. Also, be sure that you do not have both of these children present and observing each other because that might influence the outcome.

Referring back to Chapter 10 of the text, look at the figures that contain conservation tasks. You may administer any or all of these to the children to demonstrate differences in conservation ability. For example, to do the conservation of liquid (volume) task, you will need a pitcher of colored water (use a couple of drops of food coloring), two glasses (glasses A and B) that are the same size, and one glass (glass C) that is taller and thinner than the other two. In the presence of the child, pour water into glass A; then, as you pour water into glass B, ask the child to tell you when there is exactly the same amount of water in glass B as in glass A. When the child is sure they're the same, ask: "Do both of these glasses have the same amount of water?" If the child says yes, then pour water from glass B into glass C, saying: "I'm pouring the water from this glass into this glass. I'm not adding any; I'm not taking any away." After you have poured all the water into glass C, ask the child: "Do both glasses have the same amount of water, or does one have more?" Typically, the younger child will say one has more. If so, ask: "Which has more?" In either case, whether the child says one has more or they're the same, ask: "How do you know?" Then pour the water back into glass B and ask: "Are they both the same, or does one have more?" Unless you've spilled some in the process, the child will almost always say they're the same. Repeat the entire process again.

You can do a similar task for conservation of number using 12 objects of the same size, shape, and color (pennies, the plastic tops of water bottles, whatever). Lay them out in two rows of six, being sure that they are completely aligned with each other. Ask the child whether there are the same amount (don't say "number") of pennies (or whatever) in the top row as in the bottom row. Then spread out the bottom row and ask the child again if there are the same amount in the top row as in the bottom row. Whatever the answer, ask: "How do you know?" Then put the items back into aligned rows and repeat the process.

You can do similar tasks with all of the forms of conservation discussed in Figure 10.5. You may also wish to look at the children's degree of animism—whether they consider inanimate objects to be alive. A well-used question is: "Have you ever watched the moon at night when you're riding in a car? What does it do?" The typical animistic (preoperational) response is: "It follows me."

Using the charts below, record the two children's responses. Then answer the questions that follow.

Task	Child 1 (age:__/sex__) Response 1	Reason for Response	Child 1 (age:__/sex__) Response 2	Reason for Response
Conservation of Liquid				
Conservation of Number				

Task	Child 2 (age:__/sex__) Response 1	Reason for Response	Child 2 (age:__/sex__) Response 2	Reason for Response
Conservation of Liquid				
Conservation of Number				

1. What similarities and differences did you notice in how the children responded?

2. What patterns of development did you notice when comparing the responses of the children in terms of the material discussed in Chapters 10 and 13?

3. Were your observations consistent with what you might expect from the research described? Explain your response.

4. Recalling the criticisms of and support for Piaget's theory, how were the responses of the children you observed consistent or inconsistent with what Piaget and his critics would predict?

5. What might you conclude about development of these skills based on your observations?

Personal Application 1: Reflecting on What You Learned

Consider what you read in Chapter 13, then answer the following questions:
1. What information in this chapter did you already know?
2. How can/do you use that information in your own life?
3. What information in this chapter was totally new to you?
4. How can you use that new information in your own life?
5. What information in this chapter was different from what you previously believed?
6. How was this information different?
7. How do you account for the differences between what you believed and what you learned in the chapter?
8. What is the most important thing you learned from reading this chapter?

Personal Application 2: Sternberg's Triarchic Theory

Think about your own intellectual growth over the years, including where you are today. Consider the three components of Sternberg's triarchic theory of intelligence and use the following chart to indicate what evidence you have concerning your own strengths and challenges in each of these categories as you have developed.

	Analytical	Creative	Practical
Early Childhood			
Middle to Late Childhood			
Adolescence			
Present Time			
Comments:			

Internet Projects

Check out the McGraw-Hill Web site for this text (www.mhhe.com/santrockc9). You'll find numerous activities there, in particular, information that will help you research the answers and complete the exercises in the "Taking It to the Net" section at the end of the textbook chapter. Please note that all Web site addresses in this Study Guide have been checked and were correct at the time of publication; however, Web sites may be discontinued or addresses may change, so when you search a given site it may no longer be viable. If that occurs, I apologize for the inconvenience and would appreciate you notifying me so I can make appropriate revisions in future editions of this Study Guide.

Internet Project 1: How Intelligent Are the Intelligence Tests?

This is a really fun project. Go to http://www.queendom.com/tests/iq/classical_iq_r2_access.html and select the Classical Intelligence Test-R. Take the test (it takes about 30 to 45 minutes, depending on how quickly you read, how many interruptions you have, and how fast your connection is). Two notes: (1) You do not have to pay to take these tests, this site has many that are free; and (2) *Please do not take this too seriously—we spend a lot of time taking classes on how to administer and evaluate tests, so just do this as a fun project* (my first series of assessment classes were an entire academic year, and I've taken several others since then, but this can give you some idea about the verbal, spatial, and mathematical nature of a classic intelligence test). After completing the test, consider the following:

1. How accurate do you think this test is?
2. What parts were most challenging for you?
3. Several questions on the test ask you to determine which of five words does not fit. What are the different classifications that you can think of for those questions? Can you think of other ways that the words could be classified so that an answer other than the one considered "correct" might be correct (although they don't tell you what the "correct" answers are)?
4. Parents often ask whether they should test their children's IQ. Considering what you have learned from the chapter and what you gained from this browsing this Web site, how would you answer that question?
5. To what degree do you think this test is culturally biased?
6. What problems might someone from another culture have taking a test like this?
7. How might you put the results of a test like this to good use?

Feel free to take any of the other tests at that Web site—a relatively new area of interest is in emotional intelligence, so you might want to look at that as well. You might also want to try the Culture-Fair IQ Test to see if you think it really is culture-fair. And, while you're there, explore the whole site—there are lots of interesting articles, polls, tests, etc. Have fun with this!

Internet Project 2: Bilingualism

The controversy regarding bilingualism is not limited to the United States; however, it certainly has become a major issue over the past few decades. In many states, documents such as election ballots, driver's license applications, and other official forms are printed with both English and Spanish on the same form. The text discusses some of the issues involved in the controversy and, of course, the bottom line for education would seem to be whether bilingual education (however that is defined) is beneficial or detrimental to *all* students, not just those whose native language is not English. Check out this controversy by going to a couple of Web sites and looking at the divergent views. First, go to the

ProEnglish—English Language Advocates site at http://www.proenglish.org/ and read their statements, particularly the one titled "Why 'Official English'? Our positions and data resources"; look at the other topics as well. Then go to http://www.cal.org/resources/faqs/index.html, which is the Center for Applied Linguistics FAQS site. While exploring the wondrous wealth of information that's available, check out the various links as well as the FAQs and other resources. You can also do a search of your own.

After becoming familiar with these diverse positions, what conclusions can you reach about the value of bilingual education? What are the problems inherent in bilingual education? Why do you think the United States, unlike so many other nations around the world, does not begin teaching a second language early in the curriculum? Do you think that helps or hinders our children as they mature into adults? What effect does that have on our own ability to communicate throughout the world? What suggestions do you have with regard to this debate?

Additional Internet Resources

American Academy of Pediatrics: http://www.aap.org

American Medical Association: http://www.ama-assn.org

APS site: www.psychologicalscience.org

The Child Development Web site: http://childstudy.net—Provides information on a multitude of children's topics.

Creativity Links: http://www.goshen.edu/art/ed/creativitylinks.html#links —Here's a really fun site with a wide range of links (skip the ones to ozemail.com.au/~caveman because they are restricted), but do jump around to other links, especially to the box at the bottom, "Visit These Art Education Links" for excellent activities and fun things to do.

Drkoop.com: http://www.drkoop.com—A Web site full of information on medical topics and links to many others that provide information on a wide range of health issues, both psychological and physiological.

Early Childhood and Parenting Collaborative Information Technology Group: http://ecap.crc.uiuc.edu/info/—Offers a broad array of content and information to the early childhood community, including information on research and online discussion groups.

Early Childhood Care and Development: http://www.ecdgroup.com

Kidsource: http://www.kidsource.com/—This site is a forum for parents and educators to talk about children and a wide range of topics; of particular interest in relation to this chapter are learning disabilities and giftedness as well as bilingualism (especially check out "K-12" and "Education" in the links on the left). If you scroll all the way down to the bottom, you'll find the "search" link where you can search for any topic you'd like.

Memoryzine: http://www.memoryzine.com—A source for information about memory throughout the life span.

The National Association for the Education of Young Children (NAEYC): http://www.naeyc.org

National Institutes of Health: http://www.nih.gov—Starting point for getting into any subagency of NIH.

National Institute of Mental Health: http://www.nimh.nih.gov—Excellent resource for policy statements, NIMH research, grants, and more (you might want to check out information about gifted programs and resources for children with mental retardation).

New England Journal of Medicine: http://www.nejm.org—Abstracts to articles, full text on letters and commentaries).

Project Zero: http://pzweb.harvard.edu—Harvard's Project Zero conducts longitudinal research in adults' and children's learning processes—a wonderful site to explore.

Scientific American: http://www.sciam.com—General scientific resource.

Society for Research in Child Development (SRCD): http://www.srcd.org—The Web site for SRCD, an organization whose purposes are to promote multidisciplinary research in the field of human development, to foster the exchange of information among scientists and other professionals of various disciplines, and to encourage applications of research findings.

Web MD: http://www.webmd.com—Offers a wide variety of information for the medical profession and for consumers; you may particularly want to check out information about the various forms of retardation.

CHAPTER 14: SOCIOEMOTIONAL DEVELOPMENT IN MIDDLE AND LATE CHILDHOOD

CHAPTER OUTLINE

WHAT IS THE NATURE OF EMOTIONAL AND PERSONALITY DEVELOPMENT IN MIDDLE AND LATE CHILDHOOD?

The Self
Emotional Development
Moral Development
Gender

WHAT ARE SOME PARENT–CHILD ISSUES AND SOCIETAL CHANGES IN FAMILIES?

Parent–Child Issues
Societal Changes in Families

WHAT CHANGES CHARACTERIZE PEER RELATIONSHIPS IN MIDDLE AND LATE CHILDHOOD?

Friends
Peer Statuses
Social Cognition
Bullying

WHAT ARE SOME IMPORTANT ASPECTS OF SCHOOLS?

Contemporary Approaches to Student Learning and Assessment
The Transition to Elementary School
Socioeconomic Status and Ethnicity

REACH YOUR LEARNING GOALS

1. **WHAT IS THE NATURE OF EMOTIONAL AND PERSONALITY DEVELOPMENT IN MIDDLE AND LATE CHILDHOOD?**

   The Self   Moral
                               Development

   Emotional   Gender
   Development

2. **WHAT ARE SOME PARENT–CHILD ISSUES AND SOCIETAL CHANGES IN FAMILIES?**

   Parent–Child   Societal Changes
   Issues   in Families

3. **WHAT CHANGES CHARACTERIZE PEER RELATIONSHIPS IN MIDDLE AND LATE CHILDHOOD?**

   Friends   Social Cognition

   Peer Statuses   Bullying

4. **WHAT ARE SOME IMPORTANT ASPECTS OF SHCOOLS?**

   Contemporary   Socioeconomic
   Approaches   Status and
   to Student Learning and   Ethnicity
   Assessment

   The Transition
   to Elementary
   School

Learning Goals

By the time you have completed this chapter, you should be able to reach the following goals:

1. Discuss emotional and personality development in middle and late childhood.
2. Describe parent–child issues and societal changes in families.
3. Identify changes in peer relationships in middle and late childhood.
4. Characterize some important aspects of elementary school education.

Flashcards: Chapter 14-1

What are the three key characteristics of *self-understanding* in middle to late childhood?

What is Kohlberg's second level of moral development? What are the two stages in this level?

Differentiate between *self-esteem* and *self-concept*.

What is Kohlberg's highest level of moral development? What are the two stages in this level?

What are the four ways indicated in the chapter that children's self-esteem can be improved?

Differentiate between the *justice perspective* and the *care perspective*.

What are the two extremes of Erikson's fourth stage of human development?

What factors relate to increased prosocial behavior during middle and late childhood? What is the specific prosocial behavior referred to as *altruism*? What is the *moral exemplar approach*?

What is seen as a key concept in understanding moral development?

Describe *gender stereotypes*. How universal are they?

What is Kohlberg's lowest level of moral development? What are the two stages in this level?

Differentiate between *rapport talk* and *report talk*.

Conventional reasoning: Internalization is intermediate; the person abides by certain standards (internal) but they are the standards of others (external), e.g., parents, laws. *Mutual interpersonal expectations, relationships, interpersonal conformity*: Person values trust, caring, loyalty as basis of moral judgments. *Social systems morality*: Moral judgments based on understanding social order, law, justice, duty.	Three key characteristics of self-understanding in middle to late childhood: shift toward defining self in terms of *internal* characteristics; include *social aspects* in self-descriptions; and self-understanding includes increasing reference to *social comparison*.
Postconventional reasoning: Morality completely internalized, not based on others' standards. *Social contract or utility and individual rights:* Values, rights, and principles undergird/transcend the law; laws and social systems examined with respect to extent they preserve/protect fundamental human rights and values. *Universal ethical principles*: Person has developed a moral standard based on universal human rights.	*Self-esteem* is the global evaluative dimension of the self (how one feels about oneself); also, self-worth or self-image. *Self-concept* is the domain-specific evaluations of the self, such as in academics, athletics, appearance. Self-esteem refers to global self-evaluations; self-concept refers to domain-specific evaluations.
Justice (Kohlberg): Focuses on individual rights; individuals stand alone and independently make moral decisions. *Care (Gilligan)*: Views people in terms of connectedness with others; emphasizes interpersonal communication, relationships with and concern for others. Both are moral perspectives.	*Four ways to improve self-esteem:* (1) identify causes of low self-esteem and areas of competence important to the self; (2) provide emotional support and social approval; (3) help children achieve; and (4) encourage coping skills.
Factors that contribute to age-related increase in *prosocial behavior* include advances in perspective-taking skills, moral judgment, and self-regulation. *Altruism*: Unselfish interest in helping another person. *Moral exemplar approach*: Emphasizes development of personality, character, and virtue in terms of moral excellence.	*Erikson's fourth stage:* Industry versus inferiority—children attempt to master many skills and either develop a sense of competence or incompetence (industry: children are interested in how things are made and how they work); inferiority is encouraged when efforts at making things are seen as "mischief" or "making a mess."
Gender stereotypes: Broad categories that reflect impressions and beliefs about females and males. 30-country study: males seen as dominant, independent, aggressive, achievement-oriented, enduring; females seen as nurturant, affiliative, less esteemed, more helpful; similarity between sexes is greater in more highly developed nations.	*Internalization*: The developmental change from behavior that is externally controlled to behavior controlled by internal standards and principles; this is a key concept for understanding moral development.
Rapport talk: The language of conversation and a way of establishing connections and negotiating relationships. *Report talk*: Talk that gives information (e.g., public speaking). Males hold center stage through report talk; females prefer rapport talk (Tannen, 1990).	*Preconventional reasoning*: Lowest level in Kohlberg's theory of moral development; no internalization of moral values; moral reasoning is controlled by external rewards/punishments. *Heteronomous morality*: Moral thinking is tied to punishment. *Individualism, instrumental purpose, and exchange*: Individuals pursue their own interests and let others do the same; what is right involves equal exchange.

Contrast expressions of **aggression** observed in males and females.	Contrast the descriptions of **neglected children** with those of **rejected children**.
Explain the term **androgyny**. What is **gender-role transcendence**? How does it occur?	Explain what **controversial children** are.
Describe the process of **coregulation** that generally occurs during middle to late childhood.	Discuss the importance of **social cognitions** during middle and late childhood.
Describe the term **latchkey children**. What special problems do they face?	Describe the **direct instruction approach** to education.
What are the major functions of **friendship**?	Contrast the **cognitive constructivist approaches** to teaching with the **social constructivist approaches**.
Contrast the descriptions of **popular children** with those of **average children**.	Describe the strategies listed for improving relations between ethnically diverse students.

Neglected children: Infrequently nominated as a best friend but not disliked by peers; low rates of interaction with peers, often described as shy. ***Rejected children***: Infrequently nominated as a best friend and actively disliked by peers; have more serious adjustment problems than children who are neglected.	***Physical aggression***: In all cultures boys are more physically aggressive than girls early in development. ***Verbal aggression*** (e.g., yelling): Females are often as aggressive or even more so than males. ***Relational aggression*** (e.g., spreading malicious rumors): Females are more likely than males to engage in relational aggression.
Controversial children: Frequently nominated both as someone's best friend and as being disliked.	***Androgyny*** is the: presence of a high degree of masculine and feminine characteristics in the same person ("andro" = male; "gyno" = female). ***Gender-role transcendence***: When personal competence is at issue, it should be conceptualized on a personal basis rather than on the basis of masculinity, femininity, or androgyny; occurs through rearing competent children.
Social cognitions involve thoughts about social matters; children's social cognitions about peers become increasingly important for understanding peer relationships in middle and late childhood.	***Coregulation*** refers to the gradual transfer during middle and late childhood in which some control is transferred from parent to child; the major shift occurs around age 12 or later.
Direct instruction approach: Teacher-centered approach characterized by teacher direction and control, mastery of academic skills, high expectations for students, and maximum time spent on learning tasks.	***Latchkey children***: Children who are given the key to their home, take the key to school, then use it to let themselves into the home while their parents are still at work; they are largely unsupervised 2 to 4 hours a day during the school week; for the entire day—5 days/week during the summer; they have greater responsibility and greater likelihood to get in trouble.
Cognitive constructivist approaches: Emphasize child's active, cognitive construction of knowledge and understanding (e.g., Piaget's theory). ***Social constructivist approaches***: Focus on importance of collaboration with others to produce knowledge and understanding (e.g., Vygotsky's theory).	***Major functions of friendship*** include companionship, stimulation, physical support, ego support, social comparison, and intimacy/affection.
Strategies to improve relations among ethnically diverse students: Use jigsaw classroom strategy; use technology to foster cooperation with students from around the world; encourage positive personal contact with diverse other students; encourage perspective taking; help students think critically and be emotionally intelligent about cultural issues; reduce bias; view school and community as a team to help support teaching efforts; be a competent cultural mediator.	***Popular children*** are frequently nominated as a best friend, are rarely disliked by peers; many social skills contribute to their being well liked (e.g., give out reinforcements, listen carefully, open lines of communication with peers, happy, control negative emotions, act like themselves, have concern for others, self-confident. ***Average children*** receive an average number of both positive and negative nominations from peers.

Self-Test A: Multiple Choice

1. Nora, a typical 9-year-old, is more likely than her 5-year-old sister to define herself in terms of:
   a. her age.
   b. her eye color.
   c. how tall she is.
   d. how she compares with other children her age.

2. _____ refers to domain-specific evaluations of the self.
   a. Self-efficacy
   b. Self-esteem
   c. Self-concept
   d. Self-perception

3. Which of the following is NOT a text suggestion for increasing self-esteem?
   a. setting high goals with a need to succeed
   b. identifying the causes of low self-esteem and the domains of competence important to the self
   c. providing emotional support and social approval
   d. helping children achieve and effective coping

4. Amalia, a third grader, is interested in how things are made and how they work. According to Erikson, Amalia would be in which stage of development?
   a. trust versus mistrust
   b. autonomy versus shame and doubt
   c. initiative versus guilt
   d. industry versus inferiority

5. Hermione is experiencing emotional changes characteristic of children in elementary school. Thus we would expect her to exhibit all of the following, EXCEPT:
   a. use of self-initiated strategies to redirect her feelings.
   b. increased understanding that more than one emotion can be experienced in a particular situation.
   c. improved ability to conceal negative emotions.
   d. emotions becoming more externalized.

6. Ms. Evans has been trained to work with children who experience extreme trauma. She is most likely to do all of the following EXCEPT:
   a. help them make sense of what happened.
   b. encourage them to talk about their feelings, worries, and daydreams.
   c. reassure them that nothing like this will ever happen to them again.
   d. be patient in listening to them retell events..

7. Kohlberg's theory of moral development was an outgrowth of _____'s developmental theory.
   a. Piaget
   b. Freud
   c. Erikson
   d. Watson

8. According to Kohlberg, moral development is based primarily on:
   a. moral behavior.
   b. moral reasoning.
   c. reinforcements and punishments.
   d. development of conscience.

9. "Heinz should steal the drugs. It isn't like they really cost $2,000, and he owes it to his wife because they love each other." This is characteristic of which stage of morality?
   a. heteronomous morality
   b. individualism, instrumental purpose, and exchange
   c. mutual interpersonal expectations, relationships, and interpersonal conformity
   d. social contract and individual rights

10. A pacifist who is thrown in jail for refusing to obey the draft laws because he believes that killing is morally wrong is at what stage of moral development?
    a. individualism, purpose, and exchange
    b. mutual interpersonal expectations
    c. social contract and individual rights
    d. universal ethical principles

11. Criticisms of Kohlberg's theory of moral development include all of the following, EXCEPT:
    a. it places too much emphasis on moral thought, not enough on moral behavior.
    b. it is culturally biased.
    c. it considers family processes essentially unimportant in children's moral development.
    d. it places females at a higher level of morality than males.

12. According to Bandura, before engaging in harmful or immoral conduct, people generally:
    a. justify the morality of their actions to themselves.
    b. understand the consequences of their actions and decide their personal gain is worth it.
    c. don't bother to think about the consequences of their actions.
    d. are not concerned with the effect their actions will have on others.

13. Research on Kohlberg's theory of moral development in 27 diverse cultures around the world has found:
    a. no universal support for this theory.
    b. support for the universality of the first four stages only.
    c. support for the universality of all six stages.
    d. that his scoring system does not recognize higher-level moral reasoning in certain cultural groups.

14. Gilligan believes Kohlberg underplayed the importance of a care perspective for all of the following reasons EXCEPT:
    a. he was a male.
    b. his research was conducted over a short period of time.
    c. he used male responses as a model for his theory.
    d. most of his research was with males.

15. Damon found that by the time children enter elementary school, they share with others:
    a. for the fun of the social play ritual.
    b. out of imitation of older people.
    c. out of obligation, but don't think they need to be as generous to others as they are to themselves.
    d. from a sense of fairness.

16. Research on gender stereotypes has found:
    a. although men and women are seen as having different traits, the traits for each are viewed favorably.
    b. traits attributed to men are viewed more favorably than those attributed to women.
    c. traits attributed to women are viewed more favorably than those attributed to men.
    d. men and women are seen as having similar traits.

17. When comparing differences between males and females, it is important to remember:
    a. even when differences are found, most of the individuals in the groups are virtually identical.
    b. it is unfair to compare the groups because almost all gender differences are the result of uncontrollable biological factors.
    c. it is only when statistically significant scores are found that you can conclude there is little overlap between male and female scores.
    d. even when differences are reported, there is considerable overlap between the sexes.

18. With respect to male and female brains:
    a. portions of the corpus callosum tend to be larger in males than in females.
    b. a part of the hypothalamus involved in sexual behavior is larger in females.
    c. an area of the parietal lobe relating to visuospatial skills is larger in females.
    d. female brains are smaller than male brains, but female brains have more folds and thus more surface brain tissue.

19. A study by the U.S. Department of Education found that:
    a. girls significantly surpassed boys in math skills.
    b. boys significantly surpassed girls in verbal skills.
    c. boys did slightly better than girls at math and science, but girls were better students than boys.
    d. girls did slightly better than boys at math and science, and were also better students than boys.

20. Sara met Susan and engaged her in a personal conversation on mutual feelings about boys, parents, and other friends through which they strengthened their friendship. In terms of socioemotional development, Sara and Susan were engaging in:
    a. rapport talk.
    b. report talk.
    c. girl talk.
    d. gossip.

21. A consistent gender difference that appears early in all cultures is:
    a. males are consistently more aggressive than females.
    b. males are consistently more physically aggressive than females.
    c. females are consistently more aggressive in subtle ways than males.
    d. males are more verbally aggressive, females are more socially aggressive.

22. Mischa rates high in androgyny on the Bem Sex-Role Inventory, suggesting he:
    a. scored high in masculine traits, low in feminine traits.
    b. scored high in feminine traits, low in masculine traits.
    c. scored high in both masculine and feminine traits.
    d. scored low in both masculine and feminine traits.

23. An alternative view to androgyny is gender-role transcendence, which suggests that parents should:
    a. rear their children to develop masculine traits because they are more highly respected in our society.
    b. rear their children to develop feminine traits because they are more nurturing.
    c. rear their children to be competent individuals rather than masculine, feminine, or androgynous.
    d. teach their boys to develop masculine traits, and their girls to develop feminine traits.

24. During the elementary school years, co-regulation results in:
    a. more control taken by parents.
    b. moment-to-moment self-regulation by children, but general parental supervision.
    c. transfer of control to children.
    d. no change from early childhood in the amount of control exercised by parents.

25. Marlene, a single parent, works full time, so her 11-year-old daughter, Beth, is an after-school latchkey child. To minimize the negative impact of this situation, Marlene should:
    a. encourage Beth to make friends that she can hang out with after school.
    b. use authoritative parenting and monitor Beth's activities.
    c. explain the importance of independence and provide at-home responsibilities so Beth learns independent living.
    d. hire a baby-sitter.

26. Teri is infrequently nominated as a best friend, but she is not disliked by her peers. Teri would be classified as:
    a. a popular child.
    b. an average child.
    c. a neglected child.
    d. a rejected child.

27. Mr. James wants to start a program to help rejected children gain popularity with their peers. He should encourage them to:
    a. join a group of peers, but avoid asking them questions.
    b. talk about items of personal interest to themselves, even if the items are of no interest to others.
    c. get peers to pay attention to them through some positive activity.
    d. ask questions, listen in positive ways, and say things about themselves that relate to their peers' interests.

28. To reduce bullying, the text suggests all of the following, EXCEPT:
    a. have older peers serve as monitors for bullying and intervene when it takes place.
    b. suspend bullies from school for victimizing other children.
    c. form friendship groups for children who are regularly bullied by peers.
    d. incorporate the anti-bullying message into community activities where the children are involved.

29. Mr. Herman, an elementary school principal, wants an academic curriculum in which his teachers create opportunities for students to learn with the teachers and with peers in co-constructing understanding. Mr. Herman is proposing which approach?
    a. direct instruction
    b. cognitive constructivist
    c. cognitive behavioral
    d. social constructivist

30. John Santrock suggests teachers use all of the following strategies to improve relations between ethnically diverse students, EXCEPT:
    a. turn the class into a jigsaw classroom.
    b. teach students the harmful effects of segregation.
    c. encourage students to engage in perspective taking.
    d. be a competent cultural mediator.

Self-Test B: Matching

Match the following persons with the statement or theory that most closely reflects his or her perspective:

1. Carol Gilligan
2. Sandra Bem
3. Deborah Tannen
4. William Damon
5. Lawrence Kohlberg
6. Albert Bandura
7. Elliot Aronson
8. John Ogbu
9. Jonathan Kozol
10. Alice Eagly

a. Described some of the problems children of poverty face in school.
b. Found gender differences to be stronger than feminists acknowledge.
c. Devised an inventory to measure gender orientation.
d. Believed that minority students are in a position of subordination and exploitation.
e. Sociologist who says boys and girls grow up in different worlds of talk.
f. Described a developmental model of children's altruism.
g. Stressed that moral development is based on moral reasoning.
h. A critic of Kohlberg; distinguished between justice and care perspectives.
i. Says that people usually justify the morality of their actions before engaging in harmful conduct.
j. Created the jigsaw classroom.

Self-Test C: True-False

T/F   1. The internal, social, and socially comparative selves become more prominent in middle and late childhood.

T/F   2. Moral development involves increased externalization when moving from lower to higher levels.

T/F   3. Children's altruism is guided by the motivation to obey adult authority figures.

T/F   4. Gender stereotypes are widespread around the world.

T/F   5. Parental control during middle and late childhood becomes stricter than it was earlier.

T/F   6. The majority of children in stepfamilies do not have adjustment problems.

T/F   7. Popular children are frequently nominated as a best friend but are often resented by peers.

T/F   8. Aggressive boys are likely to have a clear understanding of other children's actions and intentions.

T/F   9. Bullying can have long-term negative effects for both bullies and their victims.

T/F   10. Many critics believe that schools have not done a good job of educating low-income, ethnic minority students.

Self-Test D: OLC

1. The view that there is too much talk about gender and that people should be evaluated as persons is called _____.

2. The androgynous person would exhibit which traits?
   a. high masculine, low feminine
   b. high feminine, low masculine
   c. both high masculine and high feminine
   d. both low masculine and high feminine

3. T/F   Rapport talk is associated more with men than with women.

4. T/F   Constructivist approaches to education place the learner, not the teacher, at the center of the education process.

Essay Questions

1. As a newly elected member of your local school board, you are faced with a crisis in the educational system: student scores on national tests are low from the schools in your district. You are now being barraged with questions about how the board is going to address this situation. People are concerned about how students are being taught and they bring up concerns about the great diversity in ethnic

and socioeconomic populations within your schools. What issues will be at the forefront of your plan to improve this situation?

2. You have decided to open a day care center for elementary schoolchildren to provide an optimum environment for them between the hours that school lets out and the time their parents finish working. You've already talked to some of the parents and, while they may not tell you *their* child has problems, each has been open about some of the other children's problems, including low self-esteem, difficulties establishing friendships, and even bullying. The parents have also asked if you would be willing to help their children (not to mention the others!) develop in a morally appropriate manner, but they come from different religious perspectives, so they want to keep religion out of the picture in your center. Further, it appears that all five "peer statuses" (i.e., popular, average, neglected, rejected, and controversial) are represented among the population of children you anticipate enrolling. How would you help all of these children have the best possible growth experience in your day care facility? How would you assist them in developing a healthy sense of self-esteem, altruism, and a solid foundation for moral development?

Key to Self-Test A: Multiple Choice

1. d (LG1)	11. d (LG1)	21. b (LG2)
2. c (LG1)	12. a (LG1)	22. c (LG2)
3. a (LG1)	13. d (LG1)	23. c (LG2)
4. d (LG1)	14. b (LG1)	24. b (LG3)
5. d (LG1)	15. d (LG1)	25. b (LG3)
6. c (LG1)	16. b (LG2)	26. c (LG4)
7. a (LG1)	17. d (LG2)	27. d (LG4)
8. b (LG1)	18. d (LG2)	28. b (LG5)
9. c (LG1)	19. c (LG2)	29. d (LG5)
10. d (LG1)	20. a (LG2)	30. b (LG5)

Key to Self-Test B: Matching

1. h
2. c
3. e
4. f
5. g
6. i
7. j
8. d
9. a
10. b

Key to Self-Test C: True/False

1. True
2. False. Moral development is characterized by increased internalization (not externalization).
3. False. Adult authority has only a small influence on children's sharing and altruism; the give-and-take of peer requests and arguments is the most immediate stimulation for children's altruistic behavior.
4. True
5. False. During middle to late childhood discipline changes and control becomes more coregulatory.
6. True
7. False. Popular children are frequently nominated as a best friend and are rarely (not frequently) disliked by their peers.
8. False. Aggressive boys are more likely to perceive another child's actions as hostile when the child's intention is ambiguous.
9. True
10. True

Key to Self-Test D: OLC

1. gender-role transcendence
2. c
3. False. Rapport talk (relationships) is associated more with women than with men; men are more likely to engage in report (informational) talk with each other.
4. True

Key to Essay Questions

1. First, you will need to explore the ways in which children might be taught, looking at the direct instruction approach, the cognitive constructivist approach, and the social cognitive approach, addressing the benefits and problems in each of these. Next, discuss accountability and consider such issues as reasons for state-mandated testing and the negative consequences of these tests. Then look at the obstacles faced by children from low-socioeconomic backgrounds, including some observations of Jonathan Kozol about aspects of these children's environment that place them at an academic disadvantage, including ongoing segregation in schools and other forms of institutional racism. Next, provide some suggestions for improving ethnic relations in schools and state how these strategies can also generally improve education. Finally, based on the foregoing discussion, give a clear outline of the type of system that you suggest for educating children in the elementary grades.

2. You will need to describe the five peer statuses, explain the stages of moral development and development of altruism, and describe how these can be facilitated in children. You will also need to address self-esteem building and the various domains where a child can learn to acquire skills; and you will need to address how to incorporate the less socially competent students (e.g., rejected) into supportive peer groups. Finally, you will need to address the issues concerning bullying both in terms of reducing (hopefully, eliminating) the behavior and helping the victimized children learn not to be bullied.

Research Project 1: The Jigsaw Classroom

Elliot Aronson and his colleagues (1986) developed the jigsaw classroom in response to a major crisis in the education system in Austin, Texas. As described in your text, students from different cultural backgrounds are placed in a cooperative group in which they have to construct different parts of a project to reach a common goal. Each student is responsible for one part of the project (e.g., learning about ways to improve relations among ethnically diverse students); each student learns his or her part, then all of the students come back and teach their respective parts to the entire group. A great deal of research indicates that the best way to smooth out relations among persons of diverse views is to have them cooperate with each other on a project where they have a common goal. Try this technique either with your classmates or with a group of children from different cultural orientations (making sure to get permission from the children and their parents).

Take note of (a) how the individuals interact with each other *before* the intervention; (b) their scores on tests/quizzes *before* the intervention; (c) how they interact with each other *after* the intervention; and (d) their scores on tests/quizzes *after* the intervention. What differences do you notice? Did the results of your intervention coincide with those found in the literature? If they are different, what do you think would explain the difference?

Research Project 2: Helping the "Challenged" Child

Consider the problems of the rejected, neglected, and controversial children discussed in this chapter, as well as the problem of bullying. View some films or videos about youngsters who have become violent, killing schoolmates, teachers, and parents, and take note of specific traits they exhibit that would be useful in categorizing them into one of the peer groups discussed in the chapter and/or as bullies, victims of bullies, or alternating between the two. Understand that these children may become the bane of society in years to come, so it would benefit us all to have some early intervention. Design a program that looks at the underlying factors that lead to these children adopting their respective behaviors, then present appropriate interventions to teach them to interact effectively with other children and with adults. This will need to include development of friendships, perspective taking, altruism, and morality. Present your ideas to your professor for critique and streamlining, then present it to your local school districts or community center to see if they would be willing to put your ideas into action.

1. When designing this program, what do you believe are the underlying factors that will lead a child to attain a status of rejected, neglected, or controversial, or to become a bully or the victim of a bully?
2. Would the same types of interventions help all of these children? What will work for each?
3. Considering their current level of development (ignoring their peer status), based on the research, what could reasonably be expected from them in terms of perspective taking, altruism, and moral development?
4. How can you teach these children to develop friendships, perspective taking, altruism, or morality, or to become more assertive or less aggressive?

Personal Application 1: Reflecting on What You Learned

Consider what you read in Chapter 14, then answer the following questions:

1. What information in this chapter did you already know?
2. How can/do you use that information in your own life?
3. What information in this chapter was totally new to you?
4. How can you use that new information in your own life?
5. What information in this chapter was different from what you previously believed?
6. How was this information different?
7. How do you account for the differences between what you believed and what you learned in the chapter?
8. What is the most important thing you learned from reading this chapter?

Personal Application 2: Consider Your Own Development

Chapter 14 addresses such school-based issues as children's interactions with each other, as well as those issues more directly affecting academics. How would you describe your elementary school peer status? Were you affected by bullying (as a bully, a victim, or in some other way)? Were you affected by gender roles or expectations? What approach toward education did your elementary school take? How diverse was your elementary school? What strategies did your teachers or other school officials use that fit within the guidelines suggested in this chapter? Use the chart below to describe your category or classification (e.g., popular child, victim of bullying, etc.), the effects of each of these issues on your development, and any other comments you feel are relevant.

	Category/ Classification	Positive Effects	Negative Effects	Comments
Peer status				
Bullying				
Gender roles				
Educational approach				
School diversity				
Strategies used by teachers/other school personnel				
Other issues				

1. How consistent was your school experience with what is described in Chapter 14? How did it differ?

2. In what ways were you positively affected by your experience?

3. In what ways were you negatively affected by your experience?

4. Have these experiences had a long-term effect? If so, explain in what ways. If not, what do you think intervened to change what might otherwise have been a long-term outcome?

5. What have you learned from these experiences that can help you in your personal life and in terms of your future career? What have you learned from these experiences that might help you be a better parent?

6. If you feel that the consequences of these experiences have been primarily negative, how can you turn them around to offer a more positive effect?

7. In what ways has looking at these experiences provided you with more insight into the person you are today?

Internet Projects

Check out the McGraw-Hill Web site for this text (www.mhhe.com/santrockc9). You'll find numerous activities there, in particular, information that will help you research the answers and complete the exercises in the "Taking It to the Net" section at the end of the textbook chapter. Please note that all Web site addresses in this Study Guide have been checked and were correct at the time of publication;

however, Web sites may be discontinued or addresses may change, so when you search a given site it may no longer be viable. If that occurs, I apologize for the inconvenience and would appreciate you notifying me so I can make appropriate revisions in future editions of this Study Guide.

Internet Project 1: Talking to Kids About Tough Issues

The Kaiser Family Foundation has an excellent Web site titled "Talk with Your Kids," located at http://www.talkingwithkids.org. The suggestion is to start children talking about tough issues when they are between ages 8 and 12; if children haven't received guidance by the time they are teenagers, it becomes much harder to establish good communication with them. When you go to the site, consider the following questions:

1. What topics on the site are related to Chapter 14?
2. Are there other topics at this site that you might consider including in a chapter on socioemotional development for elementary schoolchildren that weren't already included? (Remember, of course, that no textbook can include everything—students would have to be in the class for a year or two!)
3. What have you learned from this site about ways to talk to children about difficult issues?
4. Is there someone you know who could benefit from this information? How would you go about approaching such a discussion (or would you just send them to the Web site and say, "After you've looked at it, come back and let's talk")?

If you'd like, you can order the booklet free from the Foundation at the Web site.

Internet Project 2: What to Do About Bullying

Research presented in Chapter 14 states clearly that bullying has negative consequences, both short-term and long-term, not only for victims but also for perpetrators and for society at large. A search at Google.com will provide innumerable resources to help understand and deal effectively with this problem. Although I'll make a few suggestions here, it's a good idea to do a search yourself to see how many sites come up, what information the sites offer, and where the sites are based—I was surprised to see so many sites from around the world, suggesting that this is a universal problem.

For this project, first go to http://www.cde.ca.gov/ls/ss/se/bullyres.asp and read the prevention manual prepared by the California Department of Education ("Bullying at School"). What are the different types of bullying described (see Chapter 2 of the publication)? How prevalent is this problem? In what ways are we all hurt by bullying? What interventions, strategies, and activities are suggested for dealing with this problem?

A few other sites are www.education.unisa.edu.au/bullying/, www.bullying.org, www.bullying.co.uk/, and http://www.bullyonline.org/schoolbully/index.htm. Go to http://www.nobully.org.nz/added.pdf to view an excellent guide for schools that wish to create an anti-bullying program (note that this site is from New Zealand, but certainly is applicable to the United States). After reading this guide, what have you learned in regard to problems inherent in passively permitting bullying to continue, bullies' characteristics, characteristics of victims, and what can be done to stop bullying? Although the focus in these sites is bullying in schools, think about the other areas of our lives in which people are or can be bullied, such as at work, in interpersonal relationships, and in families. What effect does bullying have on each of us, individually and as a society?

Based on what you've learned from the text and from the various sites you've visited, design a program to identify bullies and their victims, and then design an intervention to help bullies, their victims, and all the other people (including you and me) who are affected by what is actually a serious societal problem.

Additional Internet Resources

APS site: http://www.psychologicalscience.org

The Child Development Web site: http://childstudy.net—Provides information on children's topics.

Children's Defense Fund (CDF): http://www.childrensdefense.org—The Web site for CDF, the organization headed by Marian Wright Edelman to promote child welfare (discussed in Chapter 1 of the text).

Kids' Health: http://kidshealth.org/teen/your_mind/families/divorce.html—This page of Kids' Health (Dealing with Divorce) offers useful advice and information to help kids understand and deal with their parents' divorce.

Latchkey Children: http://www.ci.phoenix.az.us/FIRE/keykids.html—An excellent site for information about these children and how to keep them safe.

NLDLine: http://www.nldline.com/dr.htm—A great site by Dr. Stephen Rothenberg about self-esteem and social skills; Dr. Rothenberg presents some case studies of children who have problems with social skills and different therapeutic strategies that could be useful.

The Psi Café (sponsored by Massachusetts School of Professional Psychology): http://www.psy.pdx.edu/PsiCafe/KeyTheorists/Kohlberg.htm—Provides discussion about Kohlberg's theory of moral development, including evaluation and application, as well as some information about Kohlberg himself.

Psychology Matters: http://search3.apa.org/pm/results.cfm—Some of the articles presented here deal specifically with bullying, others with violence or other relevant concerns.

Society for Research in Child Development (SRCD): http://www.srcd.org—The Web site for SRCD, an organization whose purposes are to promote multidisciplinary research in the field of human development, to foster the exchange of information among scientists and other professionals of various disciplines, and to encourage applications of research findings.

CHAPTER 15: PHYSICAL DEVELOPMENT IN ADOLESCENCE

CHAPTER OUTLINE

WHAT IS THE NATURE OF ADOLESCENCE?

WHAT ARE THE PHYSICAL AND PSYCHOLOGICAL ASPECTS OF PUBERTY?

Determinants of Puberty
Growth Spurt
Sexual Maturation
Secular Trends in Puberty
Psychological Dimensions
The Brain

WHAT ARE THE DIMENSIONS OF ADOLESCENT SEXUALITY?

Developing a Sexual Identity and Sexual Activity
Contraceptive Use
Sexually Transmitted Infections
Adolescent Pregnancy

HOW CAN ADOLESCENT PROBLEMS AND HEALTH BE CHARACTERIZED?

Risk Factors and Assets
Risk-Taking Behavior
Substance Use and Abuse
Eating Disorders
Adolescent Health

REACH YOUR LEARNING GOALS

1. **WHAT IS THE NATURE OF ADOLESCENCE?**

2. **WHAT ARE THE PHYSICAL AND PSYCHOLOGICAL ASPECTS OF PUBERTY?**

Determinants of Puberty	Sexual Maturation	Psychological Dimensions
Growth Spurt	Secular Trends in Puberty	The Brain

3. **WHAT ARE THE DIMENSIONS OF ADOLESCENT SEXUALITY?**

Developing a Sexual Identity and Sexual Activity	Sexually Transmitted Infections
Contraceptive Use	Adolescent Pregnancy

4. **HOW CAN ADOLESCENT PROBLEMS AND HEALTH BE CHARACTERIZED?**

Risk Factors and Assets	Substance Use and Abuse	Adolescent Health
Risk-Taking Behavior		Eating Disorders

Learning Goals

By the time you have completed this chapter, you should be able to reach the following goals:

1. Discuss the foundations of adolescence and today's youth.

2. Describe puberty's determinants, developmental changes, and psychological dimensions.

3. Characterize adolescent sexuality.

4. Summarize adolescent problems and health.

How valid is G. Stanley Hall's notion of *storm and stress*?	What are the primary male and female hormones?
Define *puberty*.	Contrast the functions of *testosterone* and *estradiol*.
Explain the role of *hormones* within the human body.	Explain the two phases of puberty that are linked with hormonal changes.
Describe the role of the *hypothalamus*.	Describe how *menarche* and *spermarche* relate to *gonadarche*. What is the *secular trend* and how does that relate to timing of menarche?
What is the *pituitary gland*?	What is the current thinking about the role played by the hormone *leptin* in puberty?
What are *gonads*?	What are the three most noticeable pubertal changes in boys and the two most noticeable pubertal changes in girls described in the text?

Androgens: The main class of male sex hormones. **Estrogens**: The main class of female hormones.	**The storm-and-stress view:** G. Stanley Hall's concept that adolescence is a turbulent time charged with conflict and mood swings. Cross-cultural research by Offer et al. instead found that most adolescents have positive images of themselves and thus contradicted the stereotype that most adolescents have problems or are disturbed in some way.
Testosterone: An androgen with an important role in male pubertal development; associated with the development of external genitals, an increase in height, and a change in voice. **Estradiol**: An estrogen with an important role in female pubertal development; associated in girls with breast, uterine, and skeletal development.	**Puberty**: A period of rapid physical maturation involving hormonal and bodily changes that occurs primarily during early adolescence.
Adrenarche: Involves hormonal changes in the adrenal glands, which are located above the kidneys; they begin from about 6 to 9 years of age. **Gonadarche**: Involves sexual maturation and development of reproductive maturity; begins at approximately 9 to 10 years in Caucasian girls, around 8 to 9 in African American girls in the U.S., and about 10 to 11 in boys.	**Hormones**: Powerful chemical substances secreted by the endocrine glands and carried through the body by the bloodstream; the endocrine system's role in puberty involves the interaction of the hypothalamus, the pituitary gland, and the gonads (sex glands).
Gonadarche culminates in **menarche,** female's first menstrual period; age for onset of menstruation has been declining at an average of about 4 months per decade for the last 150 years (referred to as the "**secular trend**"); **spermarche**—male's first ejaculation of semen.	**Hypothalamus**: A structure in the higher portion of the brain that monitors eating, drinking, and sex.
Leptin has been proposed as a possible signal of the beginning and progression of puberty; it may be one of the messengers that signals the adequacy of fat stores for reproduction and maintenance of pregnancy at puberty.	**Pituitary gland**: An important endocrine gland that controls growth and regulates other glands.
Three of the most noticeable areas of sexual maturation in boys: penis elongation, testes development, and growth of facial hair. **Two of the most noticeable areas of sexual maturation in girls**: growth of pubic hair and breast development.	**Gonads**: The sex glands—the testes in males, the ovaries in females.

Describe the psychological dimensions of physical change in adolescence.	What causes *syphilis*? How is it transmitted?
Explain some of the developmental changes that occur in the brain during adolescence.	Describe *genital herpes* and its possible consequences.
What factors are involved in developing a *sexual identity*?	Explain the consequences of teen pregnancy.
What are the primary risk factors for not taking appropriate safeguards when engaging in sexual activity? How are *sexually transmitted infections (STIs)* contracted?	What does the term *risk factor* mean? How are risk factors used? What factors predict adolescent problems?
What is *AIDS*? How is it transmitted? Describe risk factors for contracting AIDS.	What effects are of particular concern with regard to adolescent drug use?
What is *chlamydia*? What might the consequences be of contracting chlamydia?	Contrast the eating disorders that may appear in adolescence: *anorexia nervosa* and *bulimia nervosa*.

Syphilis: A sexually transmitted infection that can ultimately cause death; caused by a tiny bacterium, it is transmittable via intercourse, kissing, intimate body contact; treated by use of penicillin.	*Psychological accompaniments of physical change include:* preoccupation with bodies, develop individual images of what the body is like; early-maturing boys perceive selves more positively and have better peer relations than late maturers; early-maturing girls have more problems in school and other problems (e.g., more likely to smoke, drink, be depressed, have eating disorders, etc.), but more independence and popularity with boys.
Genital herpes: A sexually transmitted infection; symptoms include irregular cycles of sores and blisters in the genital area; the virus is potentially dangerous—babies exposed to the active virus during birth are vulnerable to brain damage or death, and women with herpes are 8 times more likely to get cancer than those without the virus; there is no known cure.	*Emotional information*: Brain activity for adolescents is more pronounced in the amygdala than in the frontal lobe (reverse of adult activity), suggesting growth continues in the frontal lobe from adolescence to adulthood. The prefrontal cortex is not adequately developed to control strong emotions. Changes in the reward/pleasure aspects of the limbic system lead adolescents to seek novelty and stimulation.
Teen pregnancy: Infants born to adolescent mothers are more likely to have low birth weights, which is related to infant mortality; neurological problems; childhood illnesses; adolescent mothers often drop out of school, have problems finding work or have low-paying/low-status jobs; their children have lower achievement test scores and more behavioral problems than other children.	*Developing a sexual identity*: An individual's sexual identity (homosexual or heterosexual) involves a combination of sexual behavior together with physical, social, and cultural factors.
Risk factor: There is an elevated probability of a problem outcome in groups of people who have that factor, although not all members of the group will experience the problem (e.g., teen pregnancy, substance abuse). Risk factors such as poverty, ineffective parenting, and mental disorders in parents are used to predict adolescent problems.	*Major risk factors for sexual activity without appropriate safeguards:* Ineffective use of contraception leads to early unintended pregnancy and *sexually transmitted infections (STIs). STIs* are diseases contracted primarily through sexual contact, which is not limited to vaginal intercourse but includes oral-genital and/or anal-genital contact as well.
Prescription painkillers and OTC drugs: Easy access and the false belief that they are safer than street drugs and not addictive has led to increased use. *Alcohol*: rates are down since 1980, but one-third of high school seniors engage in binge drinking. *Cigarettes*: serious problem; causes permanent genetic changes in lungs that increase risk of lung cancer.	*AIDS (Acquired Immune Deficiency Syndrome)*: Sexually transmitted disease caused by the human immunodeficiency virus (HIV), which destroys the body's immune system; high-risk populations: drug users, people with other sexually transmitted diseases, young homosexual males, individuals living in low-income circumstances, Latinos and African Americans; recently, heterosexual transmission has increased.
Anorexia nervosa: Relentless pursuit of thinness through starvation; among the many debilitating health consequences, the most critical is that anorexia nervosa can eventually lead to death. *Bulimia nervosa*: The individual consistently follows a binge-and-purge eating pattern (purging typically involves induced vomiting and/or use of laxatives).	*Chlamydia*: A sexually transmitted infection named for the bacteria that cause it. Males with chlamydia experience a burning sensation during urination and a mucoid discharge; females experience painful urination or a vaginal discharge; untreated, it can affect the entire reproductive tract and can prevent pregnancy.

Self-Test A: Multiple Choice

1. What is the effect of genes in adolescent development?
   a. They are subordinated to the influences of the environment.
   b. They interact with social conditions to influence thought and behavior.
   c. They no longer play an important role.
   d. Their influence is stronger than it was in childhood.

2. G. Stanley Hall's belief that "storm and stress" is a prevailing feature of adolescence:
   a. has been supported by the research.
   b. was true in the early part of this century, but is no longer true.
   c. is exaggerated and provides a view of adolescence that is too negative.
   d. has been disproved.

3. Daniel Offer's 1988 study found that:
   a. most adolescents around the world have a healthy self-image.
   b. most adolescents around the world have a low self-image.
   c. adolescents in developed nations have a healthier self-image than their counterparts in poorer countries.
   d. adolescents in developed nations have a lower self-image than their counterparts in poorer countries.

4. Adults' perceptions of adolescents are:
   a. more positive than reality.
   b. objective and accurate.
   c. based on personal experience and media portrayals, which are not objective.
   d. based on personal experience and media portrayals, which are highly objective.

5. What can be said about adolescents today?
   a. their lives are easier than the lives of teens in previous generations.
   b. their lives are more difficult than the lives of teens in previous generations.
   c. they do not make up a homogeneous group.
   d. they seem more radical to adults than did teens in previous generations.

6. The situation for adolescents today suggests:
   a. the transition from childhood to adulthood is less positive than that which is portrayed in the media.
   b. many adolescents lack adequate opportunities and support to become competent adults.
   c. they have a more solid environment than adolescents of 10 to 20 years ago.
   d. a steady increase in drug use as a result of their exposure to complex lifestyle options.

7. _____ is a period of rapid physical maturation involving hormonal and bodily changes that occur primarily during early adolescence.
   a. Puberty
   b. Menarche
   c. Spermarche
   d. Gonadarche

8. Hormones are chemical substances secreted by the _____ and carried through the body by the bloodstream.
   a. endocrine glands
   b. adrenal glands
   c. lymph nodes
   d. sex glands

9. _____ is responsible for development of genitals, increase in height, and changes in boys' voices, and _____ is associated with breast, uterine, and skeletal development in girls.
   a. Testosterone; estradiol
   b. Estradiol; testosterone
   c. Estrogen; progesterone
   d. Serotonin; dopamine

10. Judy has had her first period. In technical terms, this is referred to as:
    a. menopause.
    b. menarche.
    c. spermarche.
    d. adrenarche.

11. During puberty, the most noticeable changes in body growth for females include all of the following, EXCEPT:
    a. height spurt.
    b. tendency toward obesity.
    c. breast growth.
    d. growth of pubic hair.

12. The "secular trend" suggests that:
    a. adolescents today are less religious than in previous generations.
    b. adolescents today are more involved in politics than in previous generations.
    c. over the past many generations, the average age for onset of puberty has declined.
    d. eventually puberty will commence during childhood.

13. Which statement is MOST accurate with respect to body image during puberty?
    a. In general, girls are more happy with their bodies than boys.
    b. In general, girls are less happy with their bodies than boys.
    c. As pubertal change proceeds, girls tend to become more satisfied with their bodies.
    d. As pubertal change proceeds, boys tend to become more dissatisfied with their bodies.

14. Recent research about puberty suggests all of the following, EXCEPT:
    a. it is advantageous to be an early-maturing rather than a late-maturing boy.
    b. early-maturing girls experience more problems in school than late-maturing girls.
    c. in late adolescence, early-maturing girls show less satisfaction with their figures than do late-maturing girls.
    d. pubertal variations are less dramatic than is commonly thought.

15. Joshua is 15 and his cousin Caleb is 22. With regard to processing emotional information, we could expect that:
    a. both will process the information primarily in the frontal lobe.
    b. both will process the information primarily in the amygdala.
    c. Joshua will process the information in his amygdala, and Caleb in his frontal lobe.
    d. Joshua will process the information in his frontal lobe, and Caleb in his amygdala.

16. Sexual activity and interest during adolescence is:
    a. normal.
    b. aberrant.
    c. unhealthy.
    d. the result of media attention.

17. Cross-cultural research on adolescent sexual activity finds:
    a. teenage females in the United States wait longer to engage in sexual intercourse than in most other Western cultures.
    b. By age 17, among the cultures studied, 75% of the males had engaged in sexual intercourse.
    c. Among 15- to 19-year-old males around the world, a majority who were sexually experienced were married.
    d. Among 15- to 19-year-old females around the world, a majority who were sexually experienced were married.

18. Adolescents who engage in homosexual behavior in adolescence:
    a. will increase their homosexual practices in adulthood.
    b. do not necessarily continue the practice into adulthood.
    c. may benefit from counseling aimed at helping them become heterosexual.
    d. are usually only exploring their newly budding sexuality.

19. Which statement is TRUE about homosexuality?
    a. The American Psychological Association considers homosexuality to be a mental illness.
    b. Homosexual males who are administered male sexual hormones often change their sexual orientation.
    c. Psychotherapists can modify sexual orientation with behavior therapy.
    d. Sexual minority youth have diverse patterns of initial attraction and may not be in love with individuals to whom they are physically or emotionally attracted.

20. Compared with younger adolescents, those over age 16 are more likely to use:
    a. the birth control pill.
    b. condoms.
    c. withdrawal.
    d. no form of contraception.

21. Tammy, age 15, has heard a lecture on sex in her health class. She found the lecture "disgusting." As a teen, she is likely to believe all of the following, EXCEPT:
    a. sexually transmitted infections always happen to "someone else."
    b. sexually transmitted infections can be easily cured without any harm done.
    c. sexually transmitted infections are too disgusting for a nice young person to get.
    d. to be on the safe side, she should use condoms whenever she has sex.

22. Which U.S. adolescent has the lowest risk for contracting the HIV virus?
    a. Jenny, who is a lesbian.
    b. Jeremy, who is gay.
    c. Jonathan, who is a drug user.
    d. Juana, a low-income Latina.

23. Researchers suggest that U.S. adolescent pregnancy rates are higher than other Western nations because those other nations hold all of the following attitudes EXCEPT:
    a. childbearing is seen as an adult activity.
    b. lower tolerance of adolescents having sex.
    c. access to family planning services.
    d. clear messages about sexual behavior.

24. All of the following are health risks for infants of adolescent mothers, EXCEPT:
    a. low birthweight.
    b. neurological problems.
    c. childhood illness.
    d. chlamydia.

25. An alarming trend that has recently emerged in adolescent drug use involves the increasing use by adolescents of:
    a. prescription painkillers
    b. marijuana and heroine.
    c. ecstasy.
    d. alcohol.

26. Who is at highest risk of permanent genetic changes in the lungs that will increase the risk of lung cancer?
    a. Lucy, who smoked two packs a day from age 21 until she quit at age 30.
    b. Lance, who smoked a pack a day from age 12 until he quit at age 25.
    c. Luisa, who smoked two packs a day from age 19 until she quit at age 45.
    d. Leon, who began smoking a few cigarettes a day at age 18, increased to a pack a day by 19, and by age 35 continues to smoke a pack a day.

27. Elvira has an eating disorder that involves the relentless pursuit of thinness through starvation, which ultimately may lead to her death. Elvira suffers from:
    a. bulimia nervosa.
    b. anorexia nervosa.
    c. body dysphoric disorder.
    d. failure to thrive syndrome.

28. Research by Carskadon and her colleagues suggested that older adolescents are often more sleepy during the day than younger adolescents because of:
   a. academic work pressures.
   b. social pressures.
   c. changes in their biological clocks.
   d. family stress.

29. Which of the following is NOT one of the primary barriers to better health services for adolescents?
   a. awareness of the problem
   b. cost
   c. lack of special training to work with adolescents
   d. availability of health services

30. The three leading causes of death in adolescence are:
   a. accidents, homicides, and suicides.
   b. homicide, cancer, and eating disorders.
   c. homicide, suicide, and cancer.
   d. accidents, suicide, and drug overdose.

Self-Test B: Matching

Match each of the following persons with the statement or theory that most closely reflects his or her perspective:

1. G. Stanley Hall
2. Charles Nelson
3. David Hamburg
4. Lloyd Johnston
5. Lynn Blankenship
6. Daniel Offer
7. Roberta Simmons
8. Laurence Steinberg
9. Peter Benson
10. Mary Carskadon

a. Showed that though adolescents are capable of strong emotions, their prefrontal cortex isn't developed enough to allow them to control their passions.
b. Said that adolescence is filled with "storm and stress."
c. One of three researchers who surveyed adolescents about their drug use.
d. Contradicted the stereotype that most adolescents are disturbed.
e. Believes adolescents should be taught accurate information about their bodies.
f. Found that early-maturing girls have more school problems than late-maturing girls.
g. Has students learn about babies' needs by having them care for automated babies.
h. Suggests classes start later to reduce grogginess, inattention, and poor performance.
i. Says that the reward and pleasure aspects of the limbic system may be involved in adolescents' difficulty controlling their behavior.
j. Assets such as family support and good schools help adolescents competently transition from adolescence to adulthood.

Self-Test C: True-False

T/F   1. According to G. Stanley Hall, adolescence is a time of storm and stress.

T/F   2. The majority of adolescents today successfully negotiate the path from childhood to adulthood.

T/F   3.   The major hormonal and bodily changes of puberty take place primarily in later adolescence.

T/F   4.   Androgens are male sex hormones and estrogens are female sex hormones.

T/F   5.   Secular trends in puberty suggest that physical development is occurring much later now than in previous decades.

T/F   6.   Adolescent sexual identity includes sexual orientation, activities, interests, and styles of behavior.

T/F   7.   The primary causes of homosexuality are now thought to be environmental.

T/F   8.   The major risk of not using contraception during sexual intercourse is the potential for becoming pregnant.

T/F   9.   The United States has the highest adolescent drug-use rate of any industrialized nation.

T/F   10. The leading cause of death in adolescence is accidents.

Self-Test D: OLC

1.   The sex glands are called the _____.

2.   Public attitudes about adolescence that emerge from personal experience and media portrayals are:
    a.   relatively accurate.
    b.   generally inaccurate.
    c.   consistent with researchers' findings about adolescents' behaviors.
    d.   accurate from personal experiences, inaccurate from media portrayals.

3.   T/F   Adrenarche involves sexual maturation and the development of reproductive maturity.

4.   T/F   Motor vehicle accidents are the leading cause of death in adolescents and emerging adults from 15 to 24 years of age.

Essay Questions

1.   Your former high school counselor has invited you to speak to the students at your old high school. She has asked you to talk to them about high-risk behaviors—what they are, how kids get involved with them, the consequences, and how to avoid getting involved. Which issues would be important for you to address, what would you tell them about each of these, and what suggestions would you have for avoiding them?

2.   When you come home from campus one day you walk by your 12-year-old sister's bedroom and hear her and her best friend giggling. Unable to resist, you knock on the door to find out what's so funny. After giggling some more, then hesitating, and looking at each other, they finally confide in you that at a slumber party they attended over the weekend, two girls they know were under a blanket together and when someone lifted up the blanket, the two girls were kissing. Another girl started to call them lesbians, then the others joined in. The two girls called their parents to come pick them up, now EVERYONE in school is talking about how these girls are lesbians. Your sister looks at you and

says, "What's a lesbian?" You think it's time to talk to her about developing sexuality. What do you tell her?

<table>
<tr><td colspan="2">

Key to Self-Test A: Multiple Choice

</td><td>

Key to Self-Test B: Matching

</td></tr>
</table>

1. b (LG1)	11. b (LG2)	21. d (LG3)	1.	b
2. c (LG1)	12. c (LG2)	22. a (LG3)	2.	a
3. a (LG1)	13. b (LG2)	23. b (LG3)	3.	e
4. c (LG1)	14. d (LG2)	24. d (LG3)	4.	c
5. c (LG1)	15. c (LG2)	25. a (LG4)	5.	g
6. b (LG1)	16. a (LG2)	26. b (LG4)	6.	d
7. a (LG2)	17. d (LG2)	27. b (LG4)	7.	f
8. a (LG2)	18. b (LG2)	28. c (LG4)	8.	i
9. a (LG2)	19. d (LG2)	29. a (LG4)	9.	j
10. b (LG2)	20. a (LG3)	30. a (LG4)	10.	h

Key to Self-Test C: True/False

1. True
2. True
3. False. The hormonal and bodily changes of puberty take place primarily in early adolescence.
4. True
5. False. The onset of puberty is occurring increasingly earlier as the decades progress.
6. True
7. The causes of homosexuality have not been clearly determined, but as with heterosexuality, it is believed to involve a combination of physiological, psychological, and environmental factors.
8. False. Although pregnancy is certainly *one* of the risks of not using contraception during sexual intercourse, there are other problems, particularly the risk of contracting sexually transmitted infections.
9. True
10. True

Key to Self-Test D: OLC

1. gonads
2. b
3. False. Adrenarche is a prepubertal event that involves hormonal changes in the adrenal glands.
4. True

Key to Essay Questions

1. You would need to address the issues of dropping out of school, drug use, adolescent pregnancy, suicide and homicide, accidents, sexually transmitted infections (STIs), and eating disorders. First, describe what each of these problems is, how they interfere with healthy development, problems they may create for society at large, and the risk factors involved in their development. Then present ways to avoid these problems, such as developing effective ways to cope rather than turning to drugs, learning about contraception, working on ways to increase self-esteem, and so on.
2. Begin by discussing issues of developing a sexual identity, first addressing sexual feelings (e.g., arousal and attraction) and the importance of learning to manage those feelings and learning the skills to regulate sexual behavior to avoid undesirable consequences (something the two girls at the slumber party seem not to have done well). Also, talk about developing intimacy with another person, differentiating between friendships and sexual attractions. Explain how developing a sexual

identity means understanding your own sexual orientation (whether you are attracted to males or females—or both) but also that experimentation with someone of your own sex does not "make" you homosexual—many people explore different forms of sexuality as they go through adolescence (so labeling the two girls as lesbians was not only immature, but also premature). Explain, too, the wide range of sexual behaviors in terms of comfort level, arousal, and sexual activity (or the choice to refrain from sexual activity). Next tell the girls about the progression of sexual behaviors, from necking to intercourse and oral sex, and be sure they know that when they eventually choose to engage in sex, it is critically important to use contraception to protect themselves not only from pregnancy, but also from sexually transmitted infections. You may also want to talk about the various STIs and the difficulties associated with adolescent pregnancy. Finally, to address the issue of homosexuality a bit more, touch on some of the research on the biological bases of homosexuality, plus the issues that homosexual adolescents may have to face socially, noting that they are similar to heterosexuals in their wide range of attitudes, behaviors, and adjustments.

Research Project 1: Helping Youth Avoid Problem Behaviors

Consider all of the problem behaviors presented in this chapter. What do you believe are the antecedents of such behaviors? What are the consequences? What can be done to avoid each of these problem behaviors? What type of interventions would be useful?

Behavior	Antecedents	Consequences	Prevention/Intervention
Dropping Out of School			
Alcohol & Other Drug Use/Abuse			
Smoking Cigarettes			
STDs			
Adolescent Pregnancy			
Accidents & Suicides			
Eating Disorders			

On the basis of what you have learned about these problems, design a program that could be implemented in middle schools, junior high schools, and/or high schools to help confront and eliminate these problems. Meet with a local high school counselor and/or principal to discuss your ideas, then report your findings and your revised (or not revised) program to your class.

Prepare a resource guide that can be distributed to teens and preteens offering them help with problems they face. There are many toll-free numbers for organizations, such as Covenant House (crisis intervention, referral, and information services for troubled teens and their families: 1-800-999-9999); Youth Crisis Hotline (counseling and referrals for teens in crisis: 1-800-448-4663 [1-800-HIT-HOME]); the Centers for Disease Control and Prevention's National STD Hotline (1-800-232-4636); United States Department of Health and Human Services Substance Abuse & Mental Health Services Administration (SAMHSA: 1-800-729-6686); and National Runaway Switchboard (24-hour hotline for runaway and homeless youth and their families: 1-800-786-2929—1-800-RUNAWAY). Alcoholics Anonymous (AA), AlAnon, AlaTeen, and Narcotics Anonymous (NA) are all listed in local phone books. Check out the Internet section for this chapter for some online resources that can be included as well.

Research Project 2: Dealing with Your Teen's Pubertal Development

Parents may not be ready for their adolescents' pubertal development. Research the literature on parental reactions to adolescent development, then interview parents and teens to determine if the research is consistent with what you learn in real life. On the basis of what you learn, design a presentation for parents to help them understand and deal with the changes in their teens.

Personal Application 1: Reflecting on What You Learned

Consider what you read in Chapter 15, then answer the following questions:

1. What information in this chapter did you already know?
2. How can/do you use that information in your own life?
3. What information in this chapter was totally new to you?
4. How can you use that new information in your own life?
5. What information in this chapter was different from what you previously believed?
6. How was this information different?
7. How do you account for the differences between what you believed and what you learned in the chapter?
8. What is the most important thing you learned from reading this chapter?

Personal Application 2: Consider Your Own Physical Development

Consider your own physical development during adolescence.

Aspects of Physical Development	Early/Late/ On-Time	Effect on Life Satisfaction	Effect on Self-Image
Menarche (Females) Penile Growth (Males)			
Height Spurt			
Weight Gain			
Breast Growth (Females)/ Testicular Development (Males)			
Growth of Pubic Hair			

1. Was your development consistent with that described in the text?
2. Were you early, late, or on-time?
3. What effect did that have on your adjustment and satisfaction with yourself and your life?
4. Did you find adolescence to be a time of "storm and stress," or, as Daniel Offer suggests, did you have a positive self-image?
5. What other observations can you make when you compare your own development with the information in Chapter 15?

Internet Projects

Check out the McGraw-Hill Web site for this text (www.mhhe.com/santrockc9). You'll find numerous activities there, in particular, information that will help you research the answers and complete the exercises in the "Taking It to the Net" section at the end of the textbook chapter. Please note that all Web site addresses in this Study Guide have been checked and were correct at the time of publication; however, Web sites may be discontinued or addresses may change, so when you search a given site it may no longer be viable. If that occurs, I apologize for the inconvenience and would appreciate you notifying me so I can make appropriate revisions in future editions of this Study Guide.

Internet Project 1: Teen Pregnancy

Although rates of adolescent pregnancy have decreased somewhat in the past few years, this still remains a major problem, particularly for adolescent girls and their babies. It can also create problems for adolescent fathers, even if they choose not to accept responsibility. Go to the site for Planned Parenthood, http://www.plannedparenthood.org/pp2/portal/, and explore the many options available. Particularly check out the many links at "Health Info" (if you go to "pregnancy," you can find information about adolescent pregnancy; there is also a link to issues of teen health) and "Education." From investigating the Planned Parenthood site and the links suggested above, what did you learn about the problems inherent in a teenager having a child (include physical, social, economic, educational, and emotional)? Consider not only the problems encountered by the mother, but also those faced by the child, the child's father, the grandparents, and society. What are the risk factors that might predict teen pregnancy?

Based on what you learned from this site and from the text, design an intervention that could (1) help reduce teen pregnancy and (2) offer assistance to adolescent parents, their children, and their families to prevent the negative consequences (e.g., dropping out of school) of starting a family early.

Internet Project 2: Sexually Transmitted Infections

AIDS, HIV, and other STIs are considered a pandemic problem today (i.e., they are spreading quickly among populations around the world). Go to the Dr. Koop Web site (http://www.drkoop.com) and check out "Sexually Transmitted" at the links on the left, then type "adolescence" in the search box at the top of the page.

1. What types of articles did you find?
2. As you read these articles, did you notice that there are many more types of sexually transmitted infections than were described in Chapter 15?

3. What suggestions were offered for reducing the risks of acquiring a sexually transmitted infection?
4. Based on what you read, what types of interventions do you believe would be helpful in getting adolescents to use "safe sex" practices?
5. What would you suggest to an adolescent about sexual behavior? State your reasons.
6. If you were to design a global intervention to stop the spread of HIV, AIDS, and other STDs around the world, what would that intervention look like?

Additional Internet Resources

Alcoholics Anonymous: http://www.alcoholics-anonymous.org/—The official website of AA.

American Medical Association: http://www.ama-assn.org/ama/pub/category/1947.html—AMA's site where you can read articles about adolescent health.

APA site: http://www.apa.org—Offers a multitude of options for learning about pregnancy, childbirth options, and other topics covered in this chapter.

Centers for Disease Control and Prevention (CDC): http://www.cdc.gov/—Sponsored by the U.S. Department of Health and Human Services, the CDC conducts research and investigation (and applies research findings) to improve people's daily lives; also responds to health emergencies throughout the United States.

The Child Development Web site: http://childstudy/net—Provides information on children's topics.

Children's Defense Fund (CDF): http://www.childrensdefense.org—The Web site for CDF, the organization headed by Marian Wright Edelman to promote child welfare (discussed in Chapter 1 of the text).

Children Now: http://www.childrennow.org/—Uses research and mass communications to provide information about children's issues; provides many links.

Covenant House: http://www.covenanthouse.org/—Dedicated to assisting runaway and homeless youth.

Drkoop.com: http://www.drkoop.com —A Web site full of information on medical topics and links to many others that provide information on a wide range of health issues, both psychological and physiological.

Early Childhood and Parenting Collaborative Information Technology Group: http://ecap.crc.uiuc.edu/info/—Offers a broad array of content and information to the early childhood community, including information on research and online discussion groups.

Fitness Jumpsite: http://www.primusweb.com/fitnesspartner—A variety of resources such as general fitness, health, sports medicine, private and government institutions, associations and organizations, FAQs.

Gay and Lesbian Alliance Against Discrimination (GLAAD): http://www.glaad.org/—The primary source of information about and resources for issues concerning homosexuality. In the words of GLAAD, the site is "dedicated to promoting and ensuring fair, accurate and inclusive representation of people and events in the media as a means of eliminating homophobia and discrimination based on gender identity and sexual orientation."

The Henry J. Kaiser Foundation: http://www.kff.org/ —Resources can be found for many of the issues covered in this chapter, including HIV/AIDS, youth and HIV/STIs, and women's health.

Intelihealth: http://www.intelihealth.com/IH/ihtIH—Offers health information from a variety of sources, including Harvard Medical School. Feel free to search the site for any of the topics covered in this chapter (and others), but I recommend that you do a search for "Dieting and Preteens" or "Dieting and Teens" to see how early eating problems arise. At this site, you can check out any of the topics discussed in Chapter 15.

Mayo Clinic Health Site: http://www.mayoclinic.com

Medscape: http://www.medscape.com—Free database of medical articles, plus access to medical dictionaries, drug databases, and breaking medical news.

Mothers Against Drunk Driving (MADD): http://www.madd.org/home/—The Web site for this political action group that was formed to stop drunk driving, prevent underage drinking, and to support those who have been victims of drunk drivers. The site offers information on how to join, news articles, statistics, chat rooms, etc.

National Clearinghouse for Alcohol and Drug Information: http://www.health.org—Provides information and links regarding any aspect of alcohol and other drug use.

National Institutes of Health: http://www.nih.gov—Starting point for getting into any subagency of NIH.

National Institute of Mental Health: http://www.nimh.nih.gov—Excellent resource for policy statements, NIMH research, and grants (you might want to check out postpartum depression at this site).

National Runaway Switchboard: http://www.nrscrisisline.org/ —Offers help, resources, and education to teens, parents, teachers, concerned adults, and law enforcement about issues involving runaways.

The Oregon Health and Science University: http://www.oregonbrains.org/outreach/baw/about/index.shtml—Offers a vast amount of information about the brain; be sure to check out the section on brain health.

Parents, Families and Friends of Lesbians and Gays: http://www.pflag.org—Look at the drop-down menus for information about support, education, advocacy, and about PFLAG.

Planned Parenthood: http://www.plannedparenthood.org/pp2/portal/—This site offers information and resources for individuals of all ages involving reproductive choices and optimal care during and after pregnancy, including health information, health services, and education.

Talking with Kids About Tough Issues: http://www.talkwithkids.org/ —Co-sponsored by Children Now and the Kaiser Foundation, this is an extraordinarily useful site for the issues facing young people today and how to talk to them about these issues. You can order free booklets or download them.

United States Department of Health and Human Services-Substance Abuse and Mental Health Services Administration: http://www.samhsa.gov/index/aspx—Offers information and resources on a wide range of physical and mental health topics for people of all ages (e.g., substance abuse resources, homelessness, HIV/AIDS, children and families, older adults).

Web MD: http://www.webmd.com—Offers a wide variety of information on physical and mental health for the medical profession and for consumers.

Youth Crisis Hotline: http://hometown.aol.com/garnierlaw/hithome.html—A 24-hour hotline for youth in crisis and for runaways.

CHAPTER 16: COGNITIVE DEVELOPMENT IN ADOLESCENCE

CHAPTER OUTLINE

HOW DO ADOLESCENTS THINK AND PROCESS INFORMATION?

Piaget's Theory
Adolescent Egocentrism
Information Processing

WHAT CHARACTERIZES ADOLESCENTS' VALUES, MORAL EDUCATION, AND RELIGION?

Values
Moral Education
Religion

WHAT ARE SCHOOLS FOR ADOLESCENTS LIKE?

The American Middle School
The American High School
High School Dropouts

HOW DO ADOLESCENTS EXPERIENCE CAREER DEVELOPMENT AND WORK?

Career Development
Work

REACH YOUR LEARNING GOALS

1. **HOW DO ADOLESCENTS THINK AND PROCESS INFORMATION?**

   Piaget's Theory   Information Processing

   Adolescent Egocentrism

2. **WHAT CHARACTERIZES ADOLESCENTS' VALUES, MORAL EDUCATION, AND RELIGION?**

   Values   Religion

   Moral Education

3. **WHAT ARE SCHOOLS FOR ADOLESCENTS LIKE?**

   The American Middle School   High School Dropouts
   High School

   The American High School

4. **HOW DO ADOLESCENTS EXPERIENCE CAREER DEVELOPMENT AND WORK?**

   Career Development   Work

Learning Goals

By the time you have completed this chapter, you should be able to reach the following goals:

1. Discuss different approaches to adolescent cognition.

2. Describe changes in values and religion in adolescence.

3. Characterize schools for adolescents.

4. Summarize career development and work in adolescence.

Describe how *formal operational thought* differs from *concrete operational thought*.	Describe the cognitive changes that allow improved critical thinking in adolescence.
Explain the concept of *hypothetical-deductive reasoning*.	Explain the relevance of values and how adolescent values have changed over the past 50 years.
Describe Elkind's notion of *adolescent egocentrism*.	What role does *service learning* play in education?
Define and give examples of the *imaginary audience*.	Describe the *hidden curriculum* in education.
Define and give examples of the *personal fable*.	What is *character education*?
What changes in memory take place during adolescence?	Explain the concept of *values clarification*.

Cognitive changes that allow improved critical thinking in adolescence: increased speed, automaticity, and capacity of information processing; more breadth of content knowledge; increased ability to construct new combinations of knowledge; greater range and more spontaneous use of strategies.	***Formal operational thought***: More abstract than concrete operational thought; adolescents are no longer limited to actual, concrete experiences as anchors for thought, they can conjure up make-believe situations, events that are hypothetical possibilities or abstract propositions, and try to reason logically about them; adolescents also begin to think about thought itself.
Values: Beliefs and attitudes about the way things should be; they influence our thoughts, feelings, and actions. Over past 20 years, adolescents have shown an increased concern for personal well-being/decreased concern for well-being of others; since 1968 emphasis on financial well-being increased as developing meaningful philosophy of life decreased; however, self-fulfillment and self-expression continue in importance since the 1960s.	***Hypothetical-deductive reasoning***: Piaget's formal operational concept that adolescents have the cognitive ability to develop hypotheses, or best guesses, about ways to solve problems, such as an algebraic equation; then they systematically deduce, or conclude, which is the best path to follow in solving the operation.
Service-learning is a form of education that promotes social responsibility and service to the community; students engage in various activities such as tutoring, helping the elderly, assisting at a day care center; important goal: for students to become less self-centered and more motivated to help others.	***Adolescent egocentrism***: Heightened self-consciousness of adolescents reflected in their belief that others are as interested in them as they are in themselves, and in their sense of personal uniqueness and invulnerability; consists of imaginary audience and personal fable.
Hidden curriculum: Dewey's concept that every school has a pervasive moral atmosphere even if it doesn't have a program of moral education; created by school and classroom rules, the moral orientation of teachers and school administrators, and text materials.	***Imaginary audience***: The adolescent's heightened self-consciousness that others are as interested in the adolescent as the adolescent is; attention-getting behavior motivated by a desire to be noticed, visible, and "on stage." ***Example***: An eighth-grade girl who thinks everyone is looking at the tiny blemish on her face.
Character education: A direct approach that involves teaching students a basic moral literacy to prevent them from engaging in immoral behavior and doing harm to themselves or others. (Teach students not to lie, steal, or cheat because such acts are wrong.)	***Personal fable***: The part of adolescent egocentrism that involves an adolescent's sense of uniqueness—so unique that no one can understand him or her—and invulnerability. ***Example***: Adolescent girl thinks her mother is totally incapable of sensing how hurt she is because her boyfriend broke up with her.
Values clarification: Approach to moral education that emphasizes helping people clarify what their lives are for/what is worth working for; encourages students to define their own values and understand others' values; differs from character education in not telling students what their values should be.	***Short-term:*** More storage space results in fewer errors on complex tasks (e.g., analogies). ***Working memory***: Increases/improves during adolescence and adulthood. ***Long-term***: Likely improves, but depends on the specific learning activities engaged in.

Describe *cognitive moral education*.	Explore the problems addressed by educators when defining a new mission for U.S. schools in the twenty-first century.
Explain the role of religion in adolescents' lives.	Which students are most likely to drop out of high school? What are the primary reasons for dropping out of school? What ways are suggested in the text for reducing the dropout rate?
Describe how Piaget's theory relates to religious development in children and adolescents.	Compare *developmental career choice theory* with *career self-concept theory*.
Discuss the major concerns of educators and psychologists concerning junior high and middle schools.	What is Holland's *personality-type theory*?
Explain the *top-dog phenomenon*.	Which sociocultural factors are important in influencing career development?
What does the Carnegie report (1989) recommend for improving our middle schools?	What effects does working have on adolescents in terms of school and other areas of their lives?

Flashcard Responses: Chapter 16-2

New mission for twenty-first century in American schools: More support to enable all students to graduate with knowledge and skills to succeed in postsecondary education and careers; higher expectations for student achievement; shorter, higher quality work experiences for high school students; strong, positive connections between students and adults.	**Cognitive moral education** is moral education based on the belief that students should develop such values as democracy and justice as moral reasoning develops; Kohlberg's theory has been the basis for several cognitive moral education programs.
High school dropouts: Rates are highest for Latinos and Native Americans; reasons for dropping out include school-related issues, economics, or personal reasons. **Reducing dropout rate**: Monitored work experiences; community/neighborhood services; redirected vocational education; guarantees of continuing education, employment, or training; career information and counseling; and school volunteer programs.	**Religion** is linked with positive outcomes for adolescents, e.g., better grades for low-income students; encourages socially acceptable behavior; internalization of message of care and concern for others; may initiate work efforts for inner-city youth, as well as provide answers to questions about meaning, purpose, and direction in life. **Religiousness** is linked with lower levels of sexual activity in adolescence.
Developmental career choice theory (Ginzberg): Children and adolescents go through three career-choice stages: fantasy, tentative, and realistic. **Career self-concept theory (Super)**: Individuals' self-concepts play central roles in their career choices; during adolescence, individuals first construct a career self-concept.	**Preoperational intuitive religious thought:** Children's religious thoughts are unsystematic and fragmented. **Concrete operational religious thought:** Children focus on particular details of pictures and stories. **Formal operational religious thought:** Adolescents reveal a more abstract, hypothetical religious understanding.
Holland's personality-type theory: An effort should be made to match an individual's career choice with his or her personality; six basic personality types: realistic ("masculine" traits; construction); intellectual (theoretical; math and science); social ("feminine" traits; teaching); conventional (structured; bank tellers); enterprising (dominating; sales, politics); artistic (artistic and unconventional; art and writing).	**One major concern of educators and psychologists about middle schools** is that they have become watered-down versions of high schools; curricular and extracurricular activities should reflect the wide range of differences in biological and psychological development and should be incorporated into the schools; schools should create a variety of pathways for students to achieve identity.
Sociocultural factors that influence career development: socioeconomic status, parents and peers, schools, gender, and ethnic minority status.	**Top-dog phenomenon**: The circumstance of moving from the top position (in elementary school, being the oldest, biggest, most powerful students in the school) to the lowest position (in middle/junior high school, being the youngest, smallest, least powerful); the transition to middle or junior high can be difficult.
Adolescent work experiences: They get little on-the-job training, rarely feel close to adult co-workers, but *do* learn to understand how the business world works, how to get and keep a job, how to manage money and budget their time, take pride in accomplishments, and evaluate goals. Working students tend to have lower GPAs (but this depends on how many hours of work per week); increase in problem behavior depends on SES.	**To improve middle schools, the Carnegie Report recommended**: develop small "communities" or "houses" to lessen the impersonal nature of large middle schools; reduce student–counselor ratios from several hundred:1 to 10:1; involve parents and community leaders in schools; curricula that produce literate students who understand the sciences and have a sense of health, ethics, and citizenship; team teaching in flexible time blocks; boost students' health and fitness.

Self-Test A: Multiple Choice

1. The primary characteristic of formal operational thought is:
   a. concrete reasoning.
   b. intuitive thought.
   c. abstract reasoning.
   d. principled morality.

2. All of the following qualities of thinking are unique to adolescence EXCEPT:
   a. thinking about thinking.
   b. logic based on concrete elements.
   c. idealism.
   d. the ability to think hypothetically.

3. When playing the modified "20 Questions" game in which she is supposed to determine which picture of 42 the experimenter has in mind, Elnora asks questions in a systematic way, such as "Is it in the top half of the display?" Elnora is exhibiting:
   a. hypothetical-deductive reasoning.
   b. hypothetical-inductive reasoning.
   c. concrete operational thought.
   d. preoperational thought.

4. Jean Piaget's ideas on formal operational thought are being challenged in all of the following ways, EXCEPT:
   a. not all adolescents are formal operational thinkers.
   b. not all adults in every culture are formal operational thinkers.
   c. there is more individual variation in the development of formal operations than Piaget thought.
   d. only those with scientific training use hypothetical-deductive reasoning.

5. One aspect of Elkind's adolescent egocentrism states that adolescents have a heightened self-consciousness, believing others are as interested in them as they are. Elkind refers to this phenomenon as the:
   a. imaginary audience.
   b. false-belief syndrome.
   c. personal fable.
   d. personal absorption syndrome.

6. Jennifer, who is having unprotected sex with her boyfriend, comments to her best friend, "Did you hear about Barbara? You know how she fools around so much. I heard she's pregnant. That would never happen to me!" This is an example of the:
   a. imaginary audience.
   b. false-belief syndrome.
   c. personal fable.
   d. adolescent denial syndrome.

7. Elkind argues that adolescent egocentrism occurs as the result of:
   a. reversion back to childhood caused by fear of increased responsibilities.
   b. development of formal operational thought.
   c. increased ability to think hypothetically.
   d. the emerging ability to step outside oneself.

8. Zachary's memory has increased considerably from the time he was 5 years old until the time he turned 16. This is likely for all of the following reasons, EXCEPT:
   a. he has more storage space in his short-term memory.
   b. he is more likely to use concrete strategies.
   c. he processes information more quickly.
   d. he processes information more efficiently.

9. It is likely that working memory:
   a. reaches peak capacity by the end of adolescence.
   b. continues to improve from childhood into adulthood.
   c. improves from childhood to adolescence, then declines with the transition to adulthood.
   d. declines somewhat in adolescence then improves with the transition to adulthood.

10. Max's parents want to improve his decision making about real-world choices, such as sex, drugs, and risky driving. They would be wise to do all of the following, EXCEPT:
    a. lecture him on the dangers of sex, drugs, and risky driving.
    b. be sure his high school provides opportunities to engage in role-playing related to sex, drugs, and risky driving.
    c. be sure his high school provides opportunities to engage in group problem solving related to sex, drugs, and risky driving.
    d. involve him in family decision making so that he perceives himself to be in control of what happens to him.

11. For the development of critical thinking skills during adolescence there must be:
    a. a solid basis of fundamental skills developed during childhood.
    b. a supportive school environment.
    c. a supportive home environment.
    d. the adolescent must have an IQ of at least 100.

12. _____ are beliefs and attitudes about the way things should be.
    a. Ideals
    b. Prejudices
    c. Values
    d. Metacognitions

13. Hannah grew up in the 1960s. Two values that her grandchildren are likely to share with her are:
    a. self-regulation and self-esteem.
    b. self-fulfillment and self-expression.
    c. personal well-being and the well-being of others.
    d. developing a meaningful philosophy of life and self-expression.

14. Cross-cultural research shows which family values to be consistently linked with adolescent concern for social welfare?
    a. cohesiveness and loyalty
    b. compassion and social responsibility
    c. love and conservatism
    d. respect and obedience

15. Ahmed is involved in a service-learning program at his school. We would expect that this will result in Ahmed having:
    a. improved grades.
    b. an easy time finding a job.
    c. a difficult time keeping up with his studies.
    d. a sense of being exploited.

16. John Dewey said that schools provide moral education through:
    a. a hidden curriculum.
    b. character education.
    c. service learning.
    d. religious education.

17. A direct approach that involves teaching students a basic moral literacy to prevent them from engaging in immoral behavior and harming themselves or others is:
    a. the hidden curriculum.
    b. character education.
    c. cognitive moral education.
    d. social moral education.

18. _____ is based on the belief that students should learn to value such aspects of life as democracy and justice as their moral reasoning develops.
    a. The hidden curriculum
    b. Character education
    c. Cognitive moral education
    d. Social moral education

19. Which response to the question "Why was Moses afraid to look at God?" would reflect concrete operational religious thought?
    a. "Because God had a funny face."
    b. "Because it was a ball of fire and Moses thought he might get burned."
    c. "God is holy and the world is sinful."
    d. "The awesomeness of God would make Moses feel like a worm in comparison."

20. Students experiencing the top-dog phenomenon are most likely to exhibit:
    a. high achievement motivation.
    b. decreased satisfaction with school.
    c. good relations with peers.
    d. power over other students.

21. The Carnegie Corporation's recommendations for improving middle schools in the United States included all of the following, EXCEPT:
    a. lower the student-to-counselor ratios to 10:1.
    b. get parents involved.
    c. integrate physical health into the curriculum.
    d. promote continuity by keeping all class sessions the same length.

22. American companies, concerned that high school graduates are ill-prepared for the demands of the modern workplace, indicate that they want prospective employees to have a set of basic skills, including:
    a. the ability to do advanced algebra.
    b. self-direction.
    c. self-discipline.
    d. the ability to read at relatively high levels.

23. Based on the research, which student is at highest risk for dropping out of school?
    a. Geraldo, a Latino
    b. Juana, a Latina
    c. Gerald, an African-American male
    d. Joey, a White, non-Latino male

24. All of the following are recommended to reduce school dropout rates EXCEPT:
    a. offer community service opportunities.
    b. make the curriculum more interesting.
    c. provide early reading programs and tutoring.
    d. offer mentoring and caring environments.

25. Carl, a senior in high school with a teaching internship, is preparing letters for fourth-grade teaching positions. Carl is in Super's vocational phase called:
    a. crystallization.
    b. specification.
    c. implementation.
    d. stabilization.

26. According to Holland's personality-type theory, the person with an enterprising personality is most likely to be:
    a. a bank teller.
    b. a politician.
    c. a carpenter.
    d. a social worker.

27. The channels of upward mobility open to lower-SES youth are largely:
    a. political.
    b. in business.
    c. educational.
    d. nonexistent.

28. Mr. Ramirez, a counselor helping ethnic minority youth plan their career goals, should know about all of the following EXCEPT:
    a. communication skills.
    b. all of the jobs that are available at local companies.
    c. the impact of language fluency.
    d. values regarding the importance of the family.

29. Which of the following is a benefit that adolescents have been found to derive from working part-time?
    a. They are able to get extensive on-the-job training.
    b. They learn how to budget their time.
    c. They learn to get along better with adults.
    d. Their grades typically improve.

30. Research on the link between part-time work during adolescence and problem behavior suggests that:
    a. low-income adolescents who work are more likely than their more affluent peers to exhibit problem behaviors.
    b. having a part-time job teaches students responsibility and lowers the risk of problem behaviors.
    c. working for more than 20 hours per week is associated with increased problem behavior.
    d. working more than 10 hours per week is associated with juvenile delinquency.

Self-Test B: Matching

Match each of the following persons with the statement or theory that most closely reflects his or her perspective:

1. Eli Ginzberg
2. Jean Piaget
3. David Elkind
4. Alan Baddeley
5. Lawrence Kohlberg
6. John Holland
7. John Dewey
8. Ellen Greenberger
9. Robert Sternberg
10. Armando Ronquillo

a. Stated that imaginary audience and personal fable are part of adolescent egocentrism.
b. Proposed the concept of working memory as a "mental workshop."
c. Believes an effort should be made to match career choice with a person's personality.
d. Says children go through fantasy, tentative, and realistic career choice stages.
e. Said schools provide moral education through a "hidden curriculum."
f. Recognized the importance of the moral atmosphere in schools.
g. Said adolescents can think about abstract ideas and hypothetical possibilities.
h. Noted that more storage space in short-term memory results in fewer problem-solving errors.
i. Guides students in obtaining the academic preparation they need to go to college.".
j. Found that working adolescents' grades are lower than adolescents who don't work.

Self-Test C: True-False

T/F   1. According to Piaget, adolescent development is characterized by formal operational thought.

T/F   2. Elkind says that adolescents believe they are unique and invulnerable.

T/F   3. Adolescents who are impulsive and seek sensation are often very effective decision makers.

T/F   4. Over the last two decades, first-year college students have shown a decreased concern for personal well-being and an increased interest in the welfare of others.

T/F   5. Dewey believed that every school has a moral atmosphere, even if morals are not directly taught.

T/F   6. Generally speaking, adolescents are likely to adopt the religious affiliation of their parents.

T/F   7. The Carnegie Council on Adolescent Development gave U.S. middle schools an extremely negative evaluation.

T/F   8. While high school dropout rates have decreased for Native Americans and Latinos, they have increased for African Americans.

T/F   9. Adolescents are more likely today than a hundred years ago to hold full-time jobs.

T/F   10. U.S. adolescents engage in more work than their counterparts in many other developed countries.

Self-Test D: OLC

1. When children say they want to grow up to be a sports star, they are in Ginzberg's _____ stage of career choice.

2. Research on religious beliefs in adolescence typically demonstrates that:
    a. most adolescents say they believe in God or a universal spirit.
    b. most adolescents are agnostics (they're not sure about the existence of a supreme being).
    c. most adolescents today are atheists and do not believe in a supreme being.
    d. while most adolescents believe in God or a higher power, the vast majority no longer attend religious services with their families on a regular basis.

3. T/F   Adolescents' thought is more abstract than younger children's thought.

4. T/F   The top-dog phenomenon reduces the stress of adolescents who are making the transition from elementary to middle school, making that transition easier.

Essay Questions

1. As you walk into the cafeteria, you notice two of your friends arguing about teaching morality in high school. They are having a heated debate about the pros and cons of teaching moral behavior. They also start to argue about whether adolescents should be "dragged" to religious services by their parents or should, instead, be left to develop their own identity, as Erikson predicts they are likely to do. What can you tell them about these issues?

2. One evening you decide to attend a school board meeting that is being held to discuss the current state of your community's schools. One person after another stands up and criticizes teachers, administrators, curriculum, and students. They complain that our students are not being educated, graduates can't compete in the global market, kids are dropping out, and graduates are not prepared to transition either to college or into the working world. Knowing you have some background in these matters, the superintendent calls upon you to offer some advice. What can you tell them about how to improve matters?

Key to Self-Test A: Multiple Choice

1. c (LG1)	11. a (LG1)	21. d (LG3)
2. b (LG1)	12. c (LG1)	22. d (LG3)
3. a (LG1)	13. b (LG1)	23. a (LG3)
4. d (LG1)	14. b (LG2)	24. b (LG3)
5. a (LG1)	15. a (LG2)	25. b (LG4)
6. c (LG1)	16. a (LG2)	26. b (LG4)
7. b (LG1)	17. b (LG2)	27. c (LG4)
8. b (LG1)	18. c (LG2)	28. b (LG4)
9. b (LG1	19. b (LG3)	29. b (LG4)
10. a (LG2)	20. b (LG3)	30. c (LG4)

Key to Self-Test B: Matching

1. d
2. g
3. a
4. b
5. f
6. c
7. e
8. j
9. h
10. i

Key to Self-Test C: True/False

1. True
2. True
3. False. Impulsive, sensation-seeking adolescents are often *not* very effective decision makers.
4. False. The opposite is true: First-year college students today exhibit an increased concern for personal well-being and a decreased interest in the welfare of others
5. True
6. False. While this is generally so when adolescents have a positive relationship with their parents and are securely attached to them, when conflict or insecure attachment characterizes parent–adolescent relationships the adolescent may seek a religious affiliation that differs from that of the parents.
7. True
8. False. Dropout rates have been decreasing for African Americans and remain high for Native Americans and Latinos.
9. False. Adolescents are not as likely to hold full-time jobs today as they were in the nineteenth century.
10. True

Key to Self-Test D: OLC

1. fantasy
2. a
3. True
4. False. The top-dog phenomenon is the experience of moving from the top position (in elementary school) to the lowest position (in middle school), which would increase rather than decrease stress.

Key to Essay Questions

1. Here you will need to explore the various aspects of moral education (e.g., explain the ideas of hidden curriculum and character education), noting the benefits that have been found for such things as service learning and character education before debating the worthiness of moral education. Be sure to look at values clarification and what both Kohlberg and Gilligan stated concerning moral education. After exploring those issues, discuss what you consider to be the pros and cons of moral education. Then move on to the developmental changes that occur in religiosity during adolescence, considering both Piaget's and Erikson's theories, as well as what the various researchers have found concerning such issues as religiousness and sexuality and the part played by families in nurturing their adolescents' religious attitudes.

2. First tell them their complaints have been validated by the research, as noted in the studies by the Carnegie Corporation. Then move on to the Carenegie Council's recommendations (e.g., smaller "communities" to lessen the impersonal nature of schools, parental involvement). Note that many American companies, finding high school graduates poorly prepared for college and the workplace, have now delineated the skills they want graduates to have, such as high levels of reading, word processing skills, problem-solving skills, and the ability to work effectively in highly diverse groups. Discuss some steps to take toward this end, such as having higher expectations for students, providing quality work experiences, and the coordination of curriculum for K–12. Finally, discuss ways to reduce the dropout rate (e.g., providing early reading programs, tutoring, mentoring, community service opportunities). One other thing you might want to bring up in terms of our students being able to function in the global community is the importance of learning more than one language, beginning in the primary grades.

Research Project 1: Critical Thinking

The text discusses developmental changes in decision making and critical thinking, provides some suggestions for improving adolescents' thinking skills, and offers insights into limitations on adolescents' abilities to make good decisions (e.g., an immature brain that processes emotional information in the amygdala rather than the frontal lobe—see Chapter 15; adolescent egocentrism; and Erikson's notion of identity formation, explored more deeply in Chapter 17). Consider some issues of importance to your community (e.g., your school, your city/town, etc.) or, if you are politically active (such a good thing to be!), consider some of the current "hot topics," such as education, the environment, separation of church and state, women's rights, etc., and select three or four to use in this project.

Once you have settled on your topics of interest, write unbiased questions about those topics (e.g., "What is your stand on abortion?" or "What is your position on stem cell research?"; biased phraseology that you need to avoid would be something like "Are you pro-choice or anti-choice?" or "Are you pro-life or in favor of abortions?" or "Do you think the war in Iraq is evil?"). Although these are open-ended questions that may result in long answers, they are less likely to contain subtle bias than asking closed-ended questions, like "Do you support the war in Iraq?" or "Do you oppose tax breaks for the wealthy?"

Next, check out several sources to develop a list of criteria to help you assess critical thinking. Your introductory psychology text is likely to have several, or you can go to the library and look at books specifically about critical thinking, or check the Internet. Our text offers some insights in this chapter—here are some suggestions for criteria: ask questions, identify and clarify the problem, gather information, evaluate the evidence, be flexible in your thinking and tolerate ambiguity, avoid emotional thinking and identify inherent biases and assumptions, be open yet skeptical, separate fact from opinion, don't oversimplify, consider other interpretations. Select five or six (or seven or eight) criteria for assessing critical thinking.

Create a chart that contains your questions (perhaps listed down the left-hand column) and your critical thinking criteria (across the top). When you begin your interviews, assure your respondents that their answers are confidential. Obtain basic demographic information from them, such as age, ethnicity, gender, religious affiliation, political affiliation, etc. (Note that if anyone chooses not to supply that information, you say "fine" or "okay" and move on—you don't want to make them uncomfortable or defensive!). After getting the demographics, move on to your questions. As you ask the questions, jot down the answers and check off on your chart whether they have met your criteria for critical thinking (instead of putting Y or N, yes or no, etc., use a different code like "-" or "/" because if they are watching your note-taking it may affect their responses—in fact, it may be easier to tape the interviews if they don't object and indicate whether the criteria have/have not been met afterwards). During the interview make mental notes that you can insert later, such as "highly emotional," or "based opinions on what she's heard," or "has done a lot of research on the topic," etc. (if they see you jotting down these comments, they are likely to get upset, which will confound your research). Be sure to ask how they got the information on which they base their comments.

After you complete the interviews and evaluate your responses, attempt some simple descriptive statistics so you can order the information by gender, age, political party, etc. You may make several graphs (histograms work well) for the different variables. Once you have evaluated your data, answer the questions that follow:

Age _____ Gender_____ Political Affiliation _____
Religious Affiliation _____ Highest Level of Education _____
Ethnicity_____

	Criterion 1	Criterion 2	Criterion 3	Criterion 4	Criterion 5
Question 1					
Question 2					
Question 3					

1. How many of your respondents met your critical thinking criteria? Did they meet all the criteria, or only a few? What criterion was met most frequently, and which one was met least frequently?
2. Did you find any differences based on the demographic information you gathered? If so, what differences did you find?
3. Based on the data you have gathered, do you think that people do/don't typically use critical thinking skills?
4. What seemed most obvious to you as you interviewed your respondents? What other observations have you made that you consider important to understanding how (whether) people think critically?
5. Based on what you observed, what suggestions would you have for educators about teaching critical thinking skills?
6. Based on what you observed, how will this affect (or not affect) your use of critical thinking skills?

Research Project 2: The Ideal School

Using the information contained in this chapter, material you gather from library research, and knowledge you gain from interviewing school officials, chart the types of schools in your area (for example, in my area we have public schools, charter schools, private schools for such specializations as the arts, and many parents who home-school their children) and the elements of the "ideal school" laid out in the chapter and/or from your research. Rank the schools in terms of how well they meet each of the criteria specified and design a program that you could present to the various schools in your area to help them maximize their students' educational experience.

For those schools that are nowhere near "ideal," you will likely encounter a great deal of resistance. What do you think is the basis for this resistance (e.g., finances, lack of expertise, power/ control issues, etc.)? How could you work with the school administration, parents, and other community officials to overcome these problems? What have you learned that can help you become a good parent, good educator, and good "educational consumer"?

Personal Application 1: Reflecting on What You Learned

Consider what you read in Chapter 16, then answer the following questions:

1. What information in this chapter did you already know?
2. How can/do you use that information in your own life?
3. What information in this chapter was totally new to you?

4. How can you use that new information in your own life?
5. What information in this chapter was different from what you previously believed?
6. How was this information different?
7. How do you account for the differences between what you believed and what you learned in the chapter?
8. What is the most important thing you learned from reading this chapter?

Personal Application 2: Consider Your Own Cognitive Development

Consider your own cognitive development during adolescence. Reflect on a variety of aspects, such as hypothetical-deductive reasoning, adolescent egocentrism, short-term memory, long-term memory, self-regulatory behavior, values development, moral reasoning, decision making, and religious orientation. Add any others that you think are particularly relevant to your life and your development.

Aspects of Cognitive Development	Early/Late/ On-Time	Effect on Life Satisfaction	Effect on Self-Image

1. Was your development consistent with that described in the text?
2. Were you early, late, or on-time?
3. What effect did that have on your adjustment and satisfaction with yourself and your life?
4. Did you find adolescence to be a time of "storm and stress," or, as Daniel Offer suggests, did you have a positive self-image?
5. Did you exhibit (or, if you are now a teen, are you exhibiting) any aspects of David Elkind's notion of adolescent egocentrism (consisting of the imaginary audience and the personal fable)? If so, explain.
6. What other observations can you make when you compare your own development with the information in Chapter 16?

Internet Projects

Check out the McGraw-Hill Web site for this text (www.mhhe.com/santrockc9). You'll find numerous activities there, in particular, information that will help you research the answers and complete the exercises in the "Taking It to the Net" section at the end of the textbook chapter. Please note that all Web site addresses in this Study Guide have been checked and are correct at the time of publication; however,

Web sites may be discontinued or addresses may change, so when you search a given site it may no longer be viable. If that occurs, I apologize for the inconvenience and would appreciate you notifying me so I can make appropriate revisions in future editions of this Study Guide.

Internet Project 1: Critical Thinking on the Web

Some people may find this weird, but every so often I get really excited when I find a Web site that makes me feel like that veritable "kid in a candy store." The History/Social Studies Website for K–12 Teachers (http://home.comcast.net/~dboals1/boals.html) is awesome. It offers a wide range of topics in the social sciences specifically aimed at kindergarten through 12th grade, but is also highly useful for college students and others interested in ongoing learning. The link that is particularly relevant to Chapter 16 is "Research/Critical Thinking," which offers a wealth of information on concept mapping, Web site evaluation, research skills, search tools and how to use them, and critical thinking and the Web (having now found this, this last one is going to be incorporated into my critical thinking classes). I suggest that you check out all of these sections, but particularly those on "research skills" and "critical thinking and the Web."

As you go through and look at the different articles and Web sites, consider how this information relates to Chapter 16 in terms of cognitive processes and critical thinking.

- How does what you learn about conducting research connect with the material in the chapter?
- In what ways have you expanded your own knowledge base by checking out the content of this Web site and some of the links provided?
- Thinking about metacognition (as discussed in Chapter 16), how can you use this information to enhance your own education?
- How else can you use the information in the chapter and from this Web site?

Internet Project 2: Character Education

There has been a great deal of controversy over the past few decades about prayer in school. Reading this chapter of your textbook should differentiate that debate from the issue of moral education—consider how the two are different. Having clarified that issue for yourself, move on to consider the issue of developing a sense of morality in our youth. Go to http://www.character.org (the Web site for the Character Education Partnership). The CEP site presents "Eleven Principles of Effective Character Education."

After exploring this site, consider what you've learned about character (or moral) education and answer the following questions:

1. What were your attitudes and opinions concerning moral education prior to reading about it in the text and at this site?
2. Has your attitude and/or opinion changed since you've learned more about it? If so, in what way and what was it that you learned that changed your attitude/opinion?
3. How would you describe moral education to someone else? What are the benefits? What problems does teaching moral education present?
4. If you were to develop a program to teach character/moral development, what areas would you target and what would that program look like?
5. How important do you think character or moral development is to our society today? Explain.

Additional Internet Resources

APA site: www.apa.org—At the "Public Publications" link you can access several other links; particularly go to the "Print and Media" links (you can do a comprehensive search for most topics by linking to *The Monitor*).

APS site: http://www.psychologicalscience.org

Career Counseling—Theorists and Theories: http://el.hct.ac.ae/Career/Theorists.htm —A wonderful resource with links to articles and other information about the theories discussed in this chapter.

The Child Development Web site: http://childstudy.net—Provides information on children's topics.

Children's Defense Fund (CDF): http://www.childrensdefense.org—The Web site for CDF, the organization headed by Marian Wright Edelman to promote child welfare (discussed in Chapter 1 of the text).

Children Now: http://www.childrennow.org—Uses research and mass communications to provide information about children's issues; provides many links.

Critical Thinking Links: http://psych.csufresno.edu/koswald/critical_thinking.htm —Useful guidelines, links, and information to encourage and help develop critical thinking skills.

Education Week on the Web: http://www.edweek.org—Independent K–12 education insight (you have to register to access information at the site, but registration is FREE, so do it and enjoy).

National Association for Single Sex Public Education at http://www.singlesexschools.org/—Addresses an ongoing debate about whether students succeed better in all girls' or all boys' education institutions or in coeducational settings.

National Institutes of Health: http://www.nih.gov—Starting point for getting into any subagency of NIH.

National Institute of Mental Health: http://www.nimh.nih.gov—Excellent resource for policy statements, NIMH research, and grants–you might want to check out postpartum depression at this site.

National Middle School Association: http://www.nmsa.org/ —Explains the concept of middle schools and has a good link to research articles concerning middle schools.

Northwest Regional Educational Laboratory: http://www.nwrel.org/scpd/sirs/6/cu11.html —An in-depth look at critical thinking, including terms, research, application, and references.

A Parent's Guide: Your Teen in the Working World: http://inside.bard.edu/academic/specialproj/darling/transition/group27/career.htm —Useful for helping to guide teens into the working world.

The Psi Café: http://www.psy.pdx.edu/PsiCafe/KeyTheorists/Erikson.htm—A wonderful resource for going more in-depth on Erik Erikson's theory and research; gives a critique of his theory.

Society for Research in Child Development: http://www.srcd.org

Texas GoCenter: http://www.gocenter.info—Offers information and services to help non-college-bound students create a future that includes college.

U.S. Department of Educational Publications in ERIC: http://www.ed.gov/about/pubs/intro/pubdb.html—Sponsored by the U.S. Department of Education, leads to numerous documents related to education.

CHAPTER 17: SOCIOEMOTIONAL DEVELOPMENT IN ADOLESCENCE

CHAPTER OUTLINE

WHAT CHARACTERIZES EMOTIONAL DEVELOPMENT AND SELF-DEVELOPMENT IN ADOLESCENCE?

Emotional Development
Self-Esteem
Identity

WHAT IS THE NATURE OF PARENT–ADOLESCENT RELATIONSHIPS?

Autonomy and Attachment
Parent–Adolescent Conflict

WHAT ASPECTS OF PEER RELATIONSHIPS ARE IMPORTANT IN ADOLESCENCE?

Friendships
Peer Groups
Peers and Culture
Dating and Romantic Relationships

WHY IS CULTURE AN IMPORTANT CONTEXT FOR ADOLESCENT DEVELOPMENT?

Cross-Cultural Comparisons
Ethnicity

WHAT ARE SOME SOCIOEMOTIONAL PROBLEMS IN ADOLESCENCE?

Juvenile Delinquency
Depression and Suicide
Successful Prevention/ Intervention Programs

REACH YOUR LEARNING GOALS

1. **WHAT CHARACTERIZES EMOTIONAL DEVELOPMENT AND SELF-DEVELOPMENT IN ADOLESCENCE?**

   Emotional Development   Identity

   Self-Esteem

2. **WHAT IS THE NATURE OF PARENT–ADOLESCENT RELATIONSHIPS?**

   Autonomy and Attachment   Parent–Adolescent Conflict

3. **WHAT ASPECTS OF PEER RELATIONSHIPS ARE IMPORTANT IN ADOLESCENCE?**

   Friendships   Peers and Culture

   Peer Groups   Dating and Romantic Relationships

4. **WHY IS CULTURE AN IMPORTANT CONTEXT FOR ADOLESCENT DEVELOPMENT?**

   Cross-Cultural Comparisons   Ethnicity

5. **WHAT ARE SOME SOCIOEMOTIONAL PROBLEMS IN ADOLESCENCE?**

   Juvenile Delinquency   Successful Prevention/ Intervention Programs

   Depression and Suicide

Learning Goals

By the time you have completed this chapter, you should be able to reach the following goals:

1. Discuss changes in emotional development and self-development during adolescence.

2. Describe changes that take place in adolescents' relationships with their parents.

3. Characterize the changes that occur in peer relations during adolescence.

4. Explain how culture influences adolescent development.

5. Identify adolescent problems in socioemotional development and strategies for helping adolescents with problems.

Which of Erikson's eight stages of psychosocial development takes place during adolescence?	What are "MAMA" cycles with regard to identity?
Contrast the concepts of **crisis** and **commitment** as used by James Marcia (1980, 1994).	Explain the two dimensions of **individuality**.
Explain Marcia's status of **identity diffusion**.	Explain the two dimensions of **connectedness**.
Explain Marcia's status of **identity foreclosure**.	How does Phinney define **ethnic identity**? What relationship did Phinney and Alipuria find between ethnic identity and self-esteem?
Explain Marcia's status of **identity moratorium**.	How do gender and culture affect autonomy-granting in adolescence?
Explain Marcia's status of **identity achievement**.	Characterize the nature and pattern of parent–teen conflict during the adolescent years in the United States.

"MAMA" cycles are cycles of moratorium-achievement-moratorium-achievement, which may be repeated throughout life. They suggest that throughout our lifespan, humans are continually exploring new alternatives and developing new commitments that are likely to facilitate our ability to cope with life changes.	***Erikson's fifth stage***: Identity achievement versus identity confusion; youth who successfully cope with conflicting identities (gap between security of childhood and autonomy of adulthood) develop a new, acceptable sense of self; those who don't either withdraw and isolate themselves or lose their identity in the crowd.
Individuality consists of two dimensions: self-assertion, the ability to have and communicate a point of view; and separateness, the use of communication patterns to express how one is different from others.	***James Marcia*** suggests that identity status is based on how we handle: ***Crisis***, the period of identity development during which the adolescent is choosing among meaningful alternatives. ***Commitment***, the part of identity development in which adolescents show a personal investment in what they are going to do.
Connectedness consists of two dimensions: mutuality, sensitivity to, and respect for others' views; and permeability, or openness, to others' views.	***Identity diffusion*** is Marcia's term for the status of adolescents who have not yet experienced a crisis (i.e., they have not yet explored meaningful alternatives) or made any commitments; they are undecided about occupational and ideological choices, and are likely to show little interest in such matters.
Ethnic identity: An enduring, basic aspect of the self that includes a sense of membership in an ethnic group and the attitudes and feelings related to that membership. ***Phinney and Alipuria***: Ethnic identity exploration was higher among ethnic minorities than among White American college students; the ethnic minority students who had thought about and resolved issues involving their ethnicity had higher self-esteem than their ethnic minority counterparts who had not.	***Identity foreclosure***: Marcia's term for the status of adolescents who have made a commitment but have not experienced a crisis; usually occurs when parents hand down commitments to adolescents, often in an authoritarian manner, so adolescents have not had adequate opportunities to explore different approaches, ideologies, and vocations on their own.
Boys are given more independence than girls, especially in families with a more traditional gender-role orientation. In a comparison of adolescents in the U.S. and Japan, those in the U.S. sought autonomy earlier and Japanese youth were less likely to live outside the family home than American youth transitioning to adulthood.	***Identity moratorium***: Marcia's term for the status of adolescents who are in the midst of a crisis, but their commitments are either absent or only vaguely defined; these adolescents are still attempting to define their specific ideologies, vocations, etc.
Parent–teen conflict typically stays stable during high school years, lessens as the adolescent reaches 17–20, and becomes more positive if adolescents go away to college. It is rarely as tumultuous as envisioned by Hall, and usually involves everyday events of family life (e.g., cleanliness, curfews). It facilitates the adolescent's transition to autonomy.	***Identity achievement***: Marcia's term for the status of adolescents who have undergone a crisis and have made a commitment; they are clear about their ideologies, vocations, etc.

What parental characteristics are most likely to promote competent adolescent development?	What is the purpose of *cross-cultural studies*?
Explain how peer pressure in adolescence can have both positive and negative outcomes.	What is the primary purpose of *rites of passage*? What is involved in rites of passage?
How do *crowds* and *cliques* differ from each other? How is clique membership related to self-esteem?	Differentiate between *assimilation* and *pluralism* with regard to value conflicts involving ethnic issues.
What purposes do early romantic relationships serve?	What is a *juvenile delinquent*? What are some risk factors for juvenile delinquency?
What are the common pathways followed by sexual minority youth?	Explain the reasons for differences between adolescent girls and boys with respect to depression.
What effect do values and religious beliefs have on adolescent dating practices?	What strategies have been found to be successful in preventing or reducing adolescent problems?

Cross-cultural studies involve the comparison of a culture with one or more other cultures; they provide information about the degree to which development is similar, or universal, across cultures, or the degree to which it is culture-specific.	***Parental characteristics likely to produce competent adolescents***: display warmth and mutual respect; sustained interest in adolescents' lives; recognize/adapt to cognitive/socioemotional development; communicate expectations for high standards of conduct/achievement; display authoritative, constructive ways to deal with problems and conflict.
Rites of passage are ceremonies or rituals that mark an individual's transition from one status to another; most rites of passage focus on the transition to adult status (some societies have elaborate ceremonies that signal the adolescent's move to maturity and achievement of adult status).	***Conformity to peer pressure*** can be negative by encouraging inappropriate behaviors (e.g., stealing, vandalizing, making fun of parents and teachers); can be positive by encouraging teens to engage in prosocial activities (e.g., clubs that raise money for worthy causes, cleaning up the beaches, mentoring younger children, etc.).
Assimilation: Absorption of ethnic minority groups into the dominant group; often involves loss of at least some of the behavior/values of the minority group. ***Pluralism***: The coexistence of distinct ethnic and cultural groups in the same society; individuals with a pluralistic stance usually advocate that cultural differences be maintained and appreciated.	***Cliques***: Small groups (average 5–6 individuals) with common interests, usually the same age and sex. ***Crowd***: larger than cliques, based on reputation. ***Jocks***: athletically oriented; ***populars***: well-known students, social leaders, and those not in cliques (independents), have highest self-esteem; ***nobodies***: low social skills and intellectual abilities, have lowest self-esteem.
Juvenile delinquent: Adolescent who breaks the law or engages in illegal behavior; ***risk factors***: conflict with authority, minor covert acts, then property damage and more serious acts, aggression, negative identity, cognitive distortions, low self-control, age (early start), male, low educational expectations, low achievement in early grades, heavy peer influence, low SES, little parental monitoring/ low support/discipline, delinquent older sibling, high-crime/urban neighborhood.	***Functions of romantic relationships***: Dating is a form of recreation, a source of status and achievement, and a setting for learning about close relationships, as well as maintaining its original function of mate selection Adolescents who are not involved in a romantic relationship may have more social anxiety than their counterparts who are dating or romantically involved.
Reasons for sex differences in depression: Females tend to ruminate, their self-images are more negative than males, and they face more discrimination than males; puberty occurs earlier for girls than boys.	***Romantic pathways for sexual minority youth***: Average age of initial same-sex activity for females is from 14 to18, and 13 to 15 for males; most common initial same-sex partner is a close friend; lesbians are more likely than gay adolescents to have sexual encounters with the opposite sex before same-sex activity.
Common components of successful programs to reduce adolescent problems: intensive individualized attention; community-wide multiagency collaborative approaches; early identification and intervention.	Values and religious beliefs of people in various cultures often dictate the age at which dating begins, how much freedom in dating is allowed, whether dates must be chaperoned, and the roles of males and females in dating.

Self-Test A: Multiple Choice

1. Emotional fluctuations in adolescence:
   a. are due primarily to hormonal changes.
   b. are more extreme in later adolescence than in early adolescence.
   c. may be due more to environmental than to biological causes.
   d. are serious and are likely to need therapeutic intervention.

2. Who is likely to have the lowest self-esteem?
   a. Maria, an 18-year-old female
   b. Martin, an 18-year-old male
   c. Maura, a 60-year-old female
   d. Maury, a 60-year-old male

3. Which of the following is NOT characteristic of identity formation?
   a. It involves commitment to a theoretical orientation.
   b. It involves commitment to a vocational direction.
   c. It involves commitment to an ideological stance.
   d. It involves commitment to a sexual orientation.

4. _____ is a period of identity development during which the adolescent is choosing among meaningful alternatives.
   a. Crisis
   b. Options
   c. Commitment
   d. Involvement

5. Because she has such varied interests, Valerie enrolls in 12 classes each semester, attends them all the first week, then drops half of them the second week. A junior in college, she has switched majors four times. According to Marcia, Valerie's identity status is:
   a. diffused.
   b. foreclosed.
   c. moratorium.
   d. achieved.

6. Identity status researchers refer to "MAMA" cycles, which suggest that:
   a. adolescents tend to get along better with their mothers than their fathers.
   b. some adolescents are seen by their peers to be too attached to their mothers.
   c. many individuals cycle through periods of moratorium and achievement throughout their lives.
   d. many individuals cycle through periods of mania and depression throughout their lives.

7. Two elements of family atmosphere that are important in promoting adolescent identity development are:
   a. separation and conflict.
   b. individuality and connectedness.
   c. obedience and self-regulation.
   d. family and peer relations.

8. Jean Phinney defined _____ as an enduring, basic aspect of the self that includes a sense of membership in an ethnic group and the attitudes and feelings related to that membership.
   a. ethnicity
   b. nationality
   c. culture
   d. ethnic identity

9. Phinney and Alipuria found that ethnic minority college students who had thought about and resolved issues involving their ethnicity had _____ than their counterparts who had not.
   a. lower self-esteem
   b. higher self-esteem
   c. no different self-esteem
   d. lower levels of anxiety

10. Olga's parents immigrated to the United States from Serbia. Olga's connection with her Serbian heritage is most likely to be linked to:
    a. political factors.
    b. religious factors.
    c. retention of the Serbian language.
    d. her experience with discrimination.

11. As the adolescent pushes for autonomy, the wise adult:
   a. insists on maintaining control for the sake of the child's well-being.
   b. gives up as much control as the adolescent feels is appropriate.
   c. relinquishes control in areas in which the adolescent can make reasonable decisions.
   d. keeps testing the adolescent to be sure that autonomy can be handled.

12. Talia, age 16, has a secure attachment with her parents. One might expect she will:
   a. have trouble breaking away from her parents to form peer relationships.
   b. tend to be more dependent in her relationship with her best friend.
   c. have a lower sense of self-worth.
   d. have higher social competence and well-being and lower probabilities of engaging in problem behaviors.

13. Which statement best characterizes the new model of parent–adolescent relationships?
   a. As adolescents mature, they detach from parents and move into a world of autonomy apart from parents.
   b. Parent–adolescent conflict is intense and stressful throughout adolescence.
   c. Everyday negotiations and minor disputes between parents and adolescents are harmful to developmental functions.
   d. Parents serve as important attachment figures and support systems for adolescents.

14. All of the following are likely to promote competent adolescent development EXCEPT:
   a. parental warmth and mutual respect.
   b. parental direction in adolescents' personal choices.
   c. parents communicating high standards of conduct and achievement.
   d. parental interest in their adolescents' lives.

15. With regard to adolescent friendships, Harry Stack Sullivan believed that:
   a. there is a dramatic increase in the psychological importance and intimacy of close friends during early adolescence.
   b. the psychological importance of close friendships decreases slightly during early adolescence, then increases in late adolescence.
   c. during early adolescence, the parent–child relationship remains more critical than the adolescent's relationship with friends.
   d. close friendships become increasingly more important than family attachments during adolescence.

16. Which of the following children is most likely to conform to peer pressure to engage in antisocial acts such as shoplifting or drawing graffiti?
   a. Andrew, who is in sixth grade
   b. Brandon, who is in ninth grade
   c. Charles, who is a high school sophomore
   d. Dale, who is a high school senior

17. Cliques are characterized by each of the following EXCEPT:
   a. they average about 5 to 6 individuals.
   b. they are based on reputation.
   c. their members engage in similar activities.
   d. their members share ideas.

18. A study of clique membership by Brown and Lohr revealed that the individuals with the lowest self-esteem were the:
   a. jocks.
   b. populars.
   c. druggies.
   d. nobodies.

19. Peer groups play the least prominent role in adolescents' lives in which culture?
   a. Japan
   b. the United States
   c. sub-Saharan Africa
   d. Spain

20. A recent study of 14- to 19-year-olds found that in comparison with their dating peers, adolescents who were not involved in a romantic relationship:
    a. had lower self esteem.
    b. had more social anxiety.
    c. were happier.
    b. felt more socially isolated.

21. Research addressing sexual minority youth has found that:
    a. their most stressful problem is disclosing their sexual orientation to their parents.
    b. they quietly struggle with same-sex attractions in childhood.
    c. they only have same-sex attractions.
    d. adolescents who sexually desire the same sex always fall in love with the same sex.

22. Research on adolescent romantic relationships suggests that when compared with their peers who are not in love, young adolescent girls who are in love:
    a. are happier.
    b. have a higher risk for depression.
    c. have lower grades.
    d. are more likely to engage in problem behaviors.

23. Compared with adolescents in other industrialized nations, adolescents in the United States:
    a. spend more time studying.
    b. have more discretionary time.
    c. spend more time watching television.
    d. are more helpful with household tasks.

24. A ceremony that marks an individual's transition from one status to another (such as adolescence to adulthood) is called a:
    a. rite of passage.
    b. transitory stage.
    c. period of transition.
    d. ritualistic transition.

25. Which of the following is TRUE regarding the rite of passage from adolescence to adulthood in American culture?
    a. There are many points of transition to adulthood in American culture.
    b. There is an abrupt entry into adulthood in American culture.
    c. The end of adolescence in American culture is more clearly marked by biological change than by social milestones.
    d. No specific event marks the end of adolescence in American culture.

26. One of the major limitations of studies on the effects of ethnicity is that_____ may play a larger causal role than ethnic heritage, but it is difficult to tease the two variables apart.
    a. race
    b. innate physical variation
    c. socioeconomic status
    d. language

27. Stanley Sue suggests that an appropriate way to address the issue of value conflicts in the context of discussing ethnic issues is to:
    a. emphasize values promoted by the dominant culture.
    b. emphasize values promoted by large minority groups.
    c. discuss the values of the dominant culture as well as those of ethnic minority groups.
    d. conceptualize the conflicting values in innovative ways.

28. Based on his interviews with adolescent killers, Garbarino concludes that:
    a. many young people are potential killers.
    b. there is a spiritual or emotional emptiness in which the youth sought meaning in the dark side of life.
    c. the clues to predict that these young people will become killers are being overlooked by parents and teachers.
    d. the spiral of violence will continue to increase until society begins to acknowledge the emotional needs of adolescents.

29. Which adolescent has the characteristic that is most commonly associated with suicide?
    a. Jeremy, who has just been told that he has failed his final exam in English
    b. Justin, who has just told his parents that he is gay
    c. Jillian, who has been depressed for the past 2 months and feels hopeless
    d. Julie, whose father just died

30. Joy Dryfoos has described the common components of programs that have been successful in preventing or reducing adolescent problems. These include all of the following, EXCEPT:
    a. intensive individualized attention.
    b. community-wide, multiagency, collaborative approaches.
    c. a more clear structure of appropriate behavior.
    d. early identification and intervention.

Self-Test B: Matching

Match each of the following persons with the statement or theory that most closely reflects his or her perspective:

1. James Marcia
2. Jean Phinney
3. Stanley Sue
4. Erik Erikson
5. Reed Larson
6. Harry Stack Sullivan
7. Vonnie McLoyd
8. James Garbarino
9. Joy Dryfoos
10. Richard Savin-Williams

a. Described components of successful programs for reducing teen problems.
b. Thought that intimacy needs intensify for teens and motivate them to have close friends.
c. Explored the hazards of contemporary life in families with adolescents.
d. Believed that ethnic minority youth have a disproportionate share of the adverse effects of poverty.
e. Developed the most comprehensive view of identity in adolescence.
f. Found a spiritual or emotional emptiness in youth killers.
g. Described four identity statuses involving crisis and commitment.
h. Found a relationship between ethnic identity and self-esteem.
i. Believes early studies of gay youth exaggerated suicide rates for gay adolescents because they only surveyed the most disturbed.
j. Says one way to resolve value conflicts about sociocultural issues is to redefine them in innovative ways.

Self-Test C: True-False

T/F 1. Moodiness is a normal aspect of early adolescence.

T/F 2. Although commitment is integral to identity achievement, crisis is not.

T/F 3. A hallmark of adolescence is the adolescent's push for autonomy.

T/F 4. Adolescents' attachment to parents decreases the probability that the adolescent will be socially competent.

T/F 5. The pressure to conform to peers is especially strong during the eighth and ninth grades.

T/F 6. Children's groups are more formal, more heterogeneous, and more single-sex than adolescent groups.

T/F 7. In the United States, rites of passage into adulthood are clearly defined.

T/F 8. Ethnic minority groups are not homogeneous.

T/F 9. An increasing concern with regard to the socioemotional development of adolescents is the high rate of violence currently seen among youth.

T/F 10. Common components of programs designed to prevent or reduce adolescent problems provide individual attention to high-risk adolescents, develop community-wide interventions, and include early identification and intervention.

Self-Test D: OLC

1. Many identity status researchers believe that a common pattern of individuals who develop positive identities is to follow what are called _____ cycles.

2. Which of the following is TRUE about self-esteem?
    a. At most ages, females report higher self-esteem than males.
    b. Self-esteem often decreases during and just after many life transitions.
    c. On average, self-esteem decreases as people age.
    d. There is a pronounced drop in self-esteem during adolescence.

3. T/F An 18-year-old girl who has agreed, at her parents' request, to work for the family business without exploring any other career options is identity foreclosed.

4. T/F U.S. adolescents have less discretionary time than their peers in other industrialized countries.

Essay Questions

1. The director of the local chapter of Big Brothers/Big Sisters has approached you because she is concerned with what she perceives to be major socioemotional problems facing some of the youngsters in the group. She knows there are not enough mentors to help all the children in the community who need a Big Brother or Big Sister and she's concerned about issues of juvenile delinquency, depression, and suicide. She asks you to address a community meeting to outline risk factors and what can be done to help these youngsters. What will you tell those attending the meeting?

2. The principal and school counselor of your former high school have asked for your advice on dealing with issues of diversity they are facing at school. The diversity is being noticed in terms of the cliques that are forming, as well as racial and ethnic conflict that seems to be a growing problem. What advice could you give them?

Key to Self-Test A: Multiple Choice

1. c (LG1)	11. c (LG1)	21. a (LG3)
2. a (LG1)	12. d (LG2)	22. b (LG3)
3. a (LG1)	13. d (LG2)	23. b (LG3)
4. a (LG1)	14. b (LG2)	24. a (LG4)
5. c (LG1)	15. a (LG3)	25. d (LG4)

Key to Self-Test B: Matching

1. g
2. h
3. j
4. e
5. c

6. c (LG1)	16. b (LG3)	26. c (LG4)	6. b
7. b (LG1)	17. b (LG3)	27. d (LG4)	7. d
8. d (LG1)	18. d (LG3)	28. b (LG4)	8. f
9. b (LG1)	19. a (LG3)	29. c (LG5)	9. a
10. c (LG1)	20. b (LG3)	30. c (LG5)	10. i

Key to Self-Test C: True/False

1. True
2. False. Both crisis (a period during which the adolescent is choosing among meaningful alternatives) and commitment (a point at which adolescents who a personal investment in what they are going to do) are the two critical aspects of identity achievement.
3. True
4. False. Attachment to parents during adolescence increases the probability that an adolescent will be socially competent.
5. True
6. False. Children's groups are less (not more) formal, heterogeneous, and single-sex than adolescents' groups.
7. False. Although rites of passage are often well defined in nonindustrial cultures, in contemporary America (and other industrialized cultures) they are often ill-defined.
8. True
9. True
10. True

Key to Self-Test D: CD

1. "MAMA"
2. b
3. True
4. False. Adolescents in the United States have more discretionary time than their peers in other countries.

Key to Essay Questions

1. First address juvenile delinquency, beginning by defining what it is and discussing some of the statistics (e.g., 8 of 10 juvenile delinquents are males, although rates for females are increasing), the types of offenses committed, and issues concerning juvenile delinquents and the judicial system (e.g., economically disadvantaged minorities are also disadvantaged legally, adult court vs. juvenile court, recidivism, etc.), and go in-depth on some of the antecedents of delinquency (e.g., conflict with authority, negative identity, low self-control, etc.). Move into issues concerning the increase in youth violence and some of the theories about why these youngsters are so violent (e.g., Garbarino's notion of spiritual emptiness). Then discuss depression and suicide in adolescence, looking at why females have higher rates of depression and addressing some of the factors leading to depression (e.g., family factors, peer relationships, life experiences), and talk about the prevalence of suicide (it is the third leading cause of death among adolescents). Provide statistics and descriptions of who is at highest risk and describe risk factors. Finally, present information about successful prevention and intervention programs, describing common components of successful programs and specifically detailing what some of the programs are, what they've done, and what they've accomplished.

2. Explore the notions of ethnicity and socioeconomic status to understand whether they are dealing with one or both of these issues, so they know how to proceed. It is important to discuss the stigmas associated with minority status, as well as the cultural differences (e.g., different customs and different values) that may or may not exist, including parenting practices and how they affect the adolescents' behavior. Note Stanley Sue's contention that value conflicts are often involved when individuals respond to ethnic issues, thus it would be important to teach the students to conceptualize or redefine these conflicts in innovative ways. Also important here is the research (e.g., by Phinney & Alipuria) concerning the outcome of students' explorations of their ethnic identity and the finding that students who do explore their ethnic identity tend to have higher self-esteem. Based on this research, suggest ways to reduce the conflict that is becoming a problem.

Research Project 1: Observing Developmental Periods

In several places throughout this chapter of your textbook, the author discusses various prosocial activities such as peer tutoring and peer mentoring. Organize your classmates into a peer-tutoring group. Decide which topics each of you will tutor, then approach the appropriate person at your college (e.g., dean of students, learning resources center) or at local high schools (e.g., principal, counselor) and offer your services. Before beginning the tutoring, it is helpful to get assistance on effective ways to teach both peers and younger students; also, at the beginning of this project, chart each group member's grades to use for comparison after you have begun tutoring. Keep track of grades (e.g., midterms and papers throughout the term, or, if you continue to tutor throughout your college career, each term) to see if they improve. Also, see which grades in particular are improving—are they related to the topics you are teaching to someone else? Is this consistent with what you have learned about peer tutoring? Explain.

Tutor (Name):			
Course	**Grade**	**Grade-Point Average**	**Comments**
Introductory Psychology			
Life-Span Development			

Research Project 2: The Bridge to Youth Development

After reading the Caring for Children section titled "Quantum and El Puente," consider the areas targeted for change and the methods used to achieve the targeted goals. Conduct a search (checking out your library, the Internet, local government, etc.) to assess other similar programs and to determine if your community has any programs like these to help disadvantaged youth reduce problem behaviors while developing the skills that will help them succeed in life.

1. Describe the programs that you believe are most useful in achieving their goals, explaining the specific goals and outcomes.
2. Discuss the specific outcome measures that demonstrate how effective these programs are (e.g., in numbers, state reduced levels of school dropouts, homicides, suicides, teen pregnancies; increased success rate for college graduation, etc.).
3. How are these programs funded?
4. What can you do to establish a similar program in your community?

Personal Application 1: Reflecting on What You Learned

Consider what you read in Chapter 17, then answer the following questions:
1. What information in this chapter did you already know?
2. How can/do you use that information in your own life?
3. What information in this chapter was totally new to you?
4. How can you use that new information in your own life?
5. What information in this chapter was different from what you previously believed?
6. How was this information different?
7. How do you account for the differences between what you believed and what you learned in the chapter?
8. What is the most important thing you learned from reading this chapter?

Personal Application 2: Exploring Your Identity

Note that in this chapter the author lists 10 "pieces" of our identity self-portrait. Consider the experiences you have had that stimulated you to think about your identity. Have your classmates, friends, or instructors challenged your view of yourself? Have you read or seen anything that has caused you to reevaluate the way you view the world? Have there been events in your life that have caused you to change your attitudes and behaviors, or that have affected your relationships with others? Consider your identity in the many domains of your life indicated on the charts and consider your identity status (achieved, moratorium, foreclosed, or diffused) in each of these different areas. If you are identity diffused or foreclosed, take some time to think about how you might move into a moratorium or achieved status—or consider if that is exactly where you want to be at this time.

Using the following chart (or, if you prefer, make a chart of your own), explore your identity status in each of the areas mentioned, explaining how you determined that you are in that status; then state how you might move to moratorium or achieved status if you are not there.

Identity	Status	Explanation	Plans for Changing Status
Career/Vocational			
Political			
Religious			
Relationship			
Achievement/Intellectual			
Sexual			
Ethnic/Cultural			
Interests			
Personality			
Physical			

1. As you look over the chart, are you in different statuses for different areas of your life? What does this tell you about yourself? What does it tell you about how Erikson's and Marcia's theories fit into adolescent development?
2. Santrock suggests that adolescents progress from diffused or foreclosed toward moratorium or identity achieved. Do you believe this is appropriate for you? Is there some reason why it may be more appropriate for you to be in any particular status at this point in your life? Explain your reasons.
3. The MAMA cycles are also discussed—have you noticed in your own life that you cycle from moratorium to achievement and back and forth again? Is this an ongoing process for you? Are there

certain areas where you cycle and other areas where your identity status has remained stable over time?

Internet Projects

Check out the McGraw-Hill Web site for this text (www.mhhe.com/santrockc9). You'll find numerous activities there, in particular, information that will help you research the answers and complete the exercises in the "Taking It to the Net" section at the end of the textbook chapter. Please note that all Web site addresses in this Study Guide have been checked and were correct at the time of publication; however, Web sites may be discontinued or addresses may change, so when you search a given site it may no longer be viable. If that occurs, I apologize for the inconvenience and would appreciate you notifying me so I can make appropriate revisions in future editions of this Study Guide.

Internet Project 1: Being Proactive in Your Own Socioemotional Development

An interesting Web site that offers a wide range of socioemotional topics is http://www.psybersquare.com. Check out this site, including the topics covered, the advisory board, and the services offered, feeling free to go to "Ask an Expert" or any other link you might find interesting or helpful. Once you are at the site, go to the link for depression, then check out the articles on suicide, particularly one titled "Suicide: What If Someone You Care About Is Suicidal?" Have you ever had to deal with such an experience? If so, what did you do? How might you handle such a situation now? How can you use the information to help the people close to you (including yourself)?

Internet Project 2: Rites of Passage

The text discusses rites of passage, ceremonies or rituals that mark an individual's transition from one status to another, noting how in some cultures they are the avenue through which adolescents gain access to adulthood, whereas they seem to be much more nebulous for American adolescents. A fascinating site, "The Sacred Site," presented by the Australian Broadcasting Corporations, can be found at: http://www.abc.net.au/compass/explore/rites.htm. The site offers information about rites of passage around the world, for different cultures and religions, and related to different life events. Note that there are links to specific religions and other related topics (social issues, ethics, etc.) at the bottom of the page. After exploring this site, consider what our author says about rites of passage generally, and more specifically what he says about rites of passage in the United States.

1. Do you agree that rites of passage in the United States are more subtle than those in nonindustrialized cultures? Explain your response.
2. What ceremonies are common in the United States that would be considered rites of passage?
3. What purpose do these ceremonies serve?
4. What informal events do you think might serve as rites of passage for American youth? Explain.
5. Have you personally experienced a rite of passage (e.g., bar or bat mitzvah, quinceañera, communion)? How does that compare with what you have learned from the chapter and from this Web site?
6. Before reading this chapter, had you ever thought about any of your experiences as rites of passage?
7. After reading this chapter and viewing the Web site, do you now consider any of your experiences as rites of passage? Explain.

Additional Internet Resources

AllPsych Online: The Virtual Psychology Classroom (Personality Synopsis): http://allpsych.com/personalitysynopsis/contents.html—Of particular interest for this chapter is "Chapter 5-Psychodynamic and Neo-Freudian Theories, sections 4 and 6 on Erik Erikson and Harry Stack Sullivan, respectively.

American Psychological Association: http://www.apa.org—Check out the "Public Publications."

American Psychological Society: http://www.psychologicalscience.org

Adolescence: Change and Continuity: http://inside.bard.edu/academic/specialproj/darling/adolesce.htm —This Web site addresses changes that young people go through from puberty through the end of college; it also has a special section for parents.
Centre for Suicide Prevention: http://www.suicideinfo.ca—Canada's suicide information/prevention Web site.

Children Now: http://www.childrennow.org—Uses research and mass communications to provide information about children's issues; provides many links.

Gay & Lesbian Alliance Against Discrimination (GLAAD): http://www.glaad.org/—The primary source of information about and resources for issues concerning homosexuality. In the words of GLAAD, the site is "dedicated to promoting and ensuring fair, accurate and inclusive representation of people and events in the media as a means of eliminating homophobia and discrimination based on gender identity and sexual orientation."

The Henry Kaiser Family Foundation (*Talking with Kids About Tough Issues*): http://www.talkingwithkids.org—This awesome site provides a wealth of information and tips for helping keep young people out of trouble and prepare them for the challenges they face as they mature; it also offers free publications that are extremely helpful.

Metanoia: http://www.metanoia.org/suicide—A knowledgeable site reaching down to the emotional level for suicide prevention.

National Association of Self-Esteem: http://www.self-esteem-nase.org —Offers a wide range of information about self-esteem including a self-esteem survey, ways to boost your own self-esteem, other relevant links, and educational programs.

The National Institute of Child Health: http://www.nichd.nih.gov—One of the many information sites of the National Institutes of Health. This one is devoted to all aspects of children's and adolescents' health.

NLDLine: www.nldline.com/dr.htm—"Playing with Self-Esteem: The Importance of Social Skills" is an interesting article by Dr. Stephen Rothenberg presenting some case studies of children who have problems with social skills and different therapeutic strategies that could be useful.

PFLAG (Parents, Families and Friends of Lesbians and Gays): http://www.pflag.org—Look especially at the drop-down menus for support, education, advocacy, and about PFLAG.

Personality Theories: Erik Erikson: http://www.ship.edu/~cgboeree/erikson.html—An interesting discussion of the eight stages of Erikson's psychosocial theory of development and a critique of his theory.

Psyber Square: http://psybersquare.com—Devoted to "strength and health through community and self-help" by offering guidance and assistance for such problems as anxiety, depression, work, addiction, and how to get what you want; at the "Depression" link, you can find lots of information about suicide as well.